DATE DUE			

WEST CAMPUS

GAYLORD

DEFINING MOMENTS
AMERICAN INDIAN REMOVAL AND THE TRAIL TO
WOUNDED KNEE

DEFINING MOMENTS
AMERICAN INDIAN REMOVAL
AND THE TRAIL TO
WOUNDED KNEE

Kevin Hillstrom and Laurie Collier Hillstrom

P.O. Box 31-1640
Detroit, MI 48231

Omnigraphics, Inc.

Kevin Hillstrom, *Series Editor*
Cherie D. Abbey, *Managing Editor*

Peter E. Ruffner, *Publisher*
Matthew P. Barbour, *Senior Vice President*

Elizabeth Collins, *Research and Permissions Coordinator*
Kevin M. Hayes, *Operations Manager*

Allison A. Beckett and Mary Butler, *Research Staff*
Cherry Stockdale, *Permissions Assistant*
Shirley Amore, Martha Johns, and Kirk Kauffmann, *Administrative Staff*

Library of Congress Cataloging-in-Publication Data

HHillstrom, Kevin, 1963-
  American Indian removal and the trail to Wounded Knee / by Kevin Hillstrom and Laurie Collier Hillstrom.
      p. cm. -- (Defining moments)
  Includes bibliographical references and index.
    ISBN 978-0-7808-1129-4 (acid-free paper) 1. Indians of North America--Relocation--Great Plains. 2. Indians of North America--Great Plains--Government relations--History--19th century. 3. Indians, Treatment of--United States--History--19th century. 4. Wounded Knee Massacre, S.D., 1890. I. Hillstrom, Laurie Collier, 1965- II. Title.
  E98.R4H55 2010
    973.8'6--dc22
                                                                           2010004676

The information in this publication was compiled from sources cited and from sources considered reliable. While every possible effort has been made to ensure reliability, the publisher will not assume liability for damages caused by inaccuracies in the data, and makes no warranty, express or implied, on the accuracy of the information contained herein.

This book is printed on acid-free paper meeting the ANSI Z39.48 Standard. The infinity symbol that appears above indicates that the paper in this book meets that standard.

Printed in the United States of America

TABLE OF CONTENTS

NARRATIVE OVERVIEW

BIOGRAPHIES

PRIMARY SOURCES

PREFACE

Throughout the course of America's existence, its people, culture, and institutions have been periodically challenged—and in many cases transformed—by profound historical events. Some of these momentous events, such as women's suffrage, the civil rights movement, and U.S. involvement in World War II, invigorated the nation and strengthened American confidence and capabilities. Others, such as the McCarthy era, the Vietnam War, and Watergate, have prompted troubled assessments and heated debates about the country's core beliefs and character.

Some of these defining moments in American history were years or even decades in the making. The Harlem Renaissance and the New Deal, for example, unfurled over the span of several years, while the American labor movement and the Cold War evolved over the course of decades. Other defining moments, such as the Cuban missile crisis and the terrorist attacks of September 11, 2001, transpired over a matter of days or weeks.

But although significant differences exist among these events in terms of their duration and their place in the timeline of American history, all share the same basic characteristic: they transformed the United States' political, cultural, and social landscape for future generations of Americans.

Taking heed of this fundamental reality, American citizens, schools, and other institutions are increasingly emphasizing the importance of understanding our nation's history. Omnigraphics' *Defining Moments* series was created for the express purpose of meeting this growing appetite for authoritative, useful historical resources. This series will be of enduring value to anyone interested in learning more about America's past-and in understanding how those historical events continue to reverberate in the twenty-first century.

Each individual volume of *Defining Moments* provides a valuable resource for readers interested in learning about the most profound events in our nation's history. Each volume is organized into three distinct sections—Narrative Overview, Biographies, and Primary Sources.

- The **Narrative Overview** provides readers with a detailed, factual account of the origins and progression of the "defining moment" being examined. It also explores the event's lasting impact on America's political and cultural landscape.

- The **Biographies** section provides valuable biographical background on leading figures associated with the event in question. Each biography concludes with a list of sources for further information on the profiled individual.

- The **Primary Sources** section collects a wide variety of pertinent primary source materials from the era under discussion, including official documents, papers and resolutions, letters, oral histories, memoirs, editorials, and other important works.

Individually, each of these sections is a rich resource for users. Together, they comprise an authoritative, balanced, and absorbing examination of some of the most significant events in U.S. history.

Other notable features contained within each volume in the series include a glossary of important individuals, places, and terms; a detailed chronology featuring page references to relevant sections of the narrative; an annotated bibliography of sources for further study; an extensive general bibliography that reflects the wide range of historical sources consulted by the author; and a subject index.

New Feature: Research Topics for Student Reports

Each volume in the **Defining Moments** series now includes a list of research topics, detailing some of the important topics that recur throughout the volume and providing a valuable starting point for research. Students using *Defining Moments: American Indian Removal and the Trail to Wounded Knee* will find information on a wide range of topics suitable for conducting historical research. This feature will prove especially useful for students working on essays and reports as they try to narrow down their research interests.

These research topics are covered throughout the different sections of the book: the narrative overview, the biographies, the primary sources, the chronology, and the glossary of important people, places, and terms. This wide coverage allows readers to view the topic through a variety of different approaches.

Special Note about *Defining Moments: American Indian Removal and the Trail to Wounded Knee*

Throughout the text, we have primarily used the terms "American Indian" and "Indian" to refer to the indigenous peoples of the United States. Since both these terms and the alternative term "Native American" are widely accepted by most indigenous peoples today, we based our choice of terminology on the fact that "American Indian" and "Indian" were most prevalent during the historical periods covered in this volume, whereas "Native American" originated in the late twentieth century.

Acknowledgements

This series was developed in consultation with a distinguished Advisory Board comprised of public librarians, school librarians, and educators. They evaluated the series as it developed, and their comments and suggestions were invaluable throughout the production process. Any errors in this and other volumes in the series are ours alone. Following is a list of board members who contributed to the *Defining Moments* series:

Gail Beaver, M.A., M.A.L.S.
Adjunct Lecturer, University of Michigan
Ann Arbor, MI

Melissa C. Bergin, L.M.S., NBCT
Library Media Specialist
Niskayuna High School
Niskayuna, NY

Rose Davenport, M.S.L.S., Ed.Specialist
Library Media Specialist
Pershing High School Library
Detroit, MI

Karen Imarisio, A.M.L.S.
Assistant Head of Adult Services
Bloomfield Twp. Public Library
Bloomfield Hills, MI

Nancy Larsen, M.L.S., M.S. Ed.
Library Media Specialist
Clarkston High School
Clarkston, MI

Marilyn Mast, M.I.L.S.
Kingswood Campus Librarian
Cranbrook Kingswood Upper School
Bloomfield Hills, MI

Rosemary Orlando, M.L.I.S.
Library Director
St. Clair Shores Public Library
St. Clair Shores, MI

Comments and Suggestions

We welcome your comments on *Defining Moments: American Indian Removal and the Trail to Wounded Knee* and suggestions for other events in U.S. history that warrant treatment in the *Defining Moments* series. Correspondence should be addressed to:

Editor, *Defining Moments*
Omnigraphics, Inc.
P.O. Box 31-1640
Detroit, MI 48231

E-mail: editorial@omnigraphics.com

HOW TO USE THIS BOOK

*D*efining Moments: American Indian Removal and the Trail to Wounded *Knee* provides users with a detailed and authoritative overview of the December 1890 massacre of more than 250 Native American men, women, and children by U.S. Cavalry troops at Wounded Knee Creek in South Dakota, as well as background on the principal figures involved in this pivotal episode in U.S. history. The preparation and arrangement of this volume—and all other books in the *Defining Moments* series—reflect an emphasis on providing a thorough and objective account of events that shaped our nation, presented in an easy-to-use reference work.

Defining Moments: American Indian Removal and the Trail to Wounded Knee is divided into three primary sections. The first of these sections, the **Narrative Overview**, provides a detailed, factual account of the development of Indian removal policies and the tragedy at Wounded Knee, all within the wider context of Indian-white relations in America. Special areas of coverage include European colonization, westward expansion of the United States and related government efforts to relocate American Indian nations to federal reservations, and the Indian Wars for control of the Great Plains, including the famous 1876 Battle of Little Bighorn. The narrative overview also chronicles the history of reservation life and federal Indian policies in the twentieth century, details the emergence of the radical American Indian protest movement of the 1960s and 1970s, and explains economic and social conditions in American Indian communities in the twenty-first century.

The second section, **Biographies**, provides valuable biographical background on leading figures involved in Indian removal and the incident at Wounded Knee, including Andrew Jackson, the U.S. president who signed the Indian Removal Act of 1830; John Ross, the Cherokee chief who mounted a furious legal battle to ward off removal; Red Cloud, the Lakota chief whose successful military campaign against the United States led to the historic Fort Laramie Treaty of 1868; George Armstrong Custer, the flamboyant U.S. Cavalry leader who was killed at Little Bighorn; Wovoka, the Paiute prophet whose vision launched the Ghost Dance movement; and Sitting Bull, the influential Lakota chief who fought to preserve his people's land and dignity. Each biography concludes with a list of sources for further information on the profiled individual.

The third section, **Primary Sources**, collects essential and illuminating documents related to Wounded Knee and Indian removal. This diverse collection includes an 1830 speech in which Andrew Jackson attempts to justify Indian removal; eyewitness accounts of the Battle of Little Bighorn and the Wounded Knee Massacre; white and Indian descriptions of the impact of western expansion on the health and vitality of Indian nations; the memoir of a Native American child wrenched from her family to attend a white boarding school; and a manifesto of the radical American Indian Movement.

Other valuable features in *Defining Moments: American Indian Removal and the Trail to Wounded Knee* include the following:

- A list of Research Topics that provides students with a starting point for research.
- Attribution and referencing of primary sources and other quoted material to help guide users to other valuable historical research resources.
- Photographs of the leading figures and major events associated with the massacre at Wounded Knee and Indian removal policies.
- Glossary of Important People, Places, and Terms.
- Detailed Chronology of events with a *see reference* feature. Under this arrangement, events listed in the chronology include a reference to page numbers within the Narrative Overview wherein users can find additional information on the event in question.
- Sources for Further Study, an annotated list of noteworthy works about the event.
- Extensive bibliography of works consulted in the creation of this book, including books, periodicals, and Internet sites.
- A Subject Index.

RESEARCH TOPICS FOR
AMERICAN INDIAN REMOVAL AND THE TRAIL TO WOUNDED KNEE

Starting a research paper can be a challenge, as students struggle to decide what area to study. Now, each book in the **Defining Moments** series includes a list of research topics, detailing some of the important topics that recur throughout the volume and providing a valuable starting point for research. Students working on essays and reports will find this feature especially useful as they try to narrow down their research interests.

These research topics are covered throughout the different sections of the book: the narrative overview, the biographies, the primary sources, the chronology, and the important people, places, and terms section. This wide coverage allows readers to view the topic through a variety of different approaches.

Students using *Defining Moments: American Indian Removal and the Trail to Wounded Knee* will find information on a wide range of topics suitable for conducting historical research and writing reports:

- Factors behind the Wounded Knee Massacre, including white desires for Indian land, living conditions on reservations, and the Ghost Dance movement

- Federal Indian removal policies and their impact on Indian tribes, with special focus on the Trail of Tears

- Relations between American Indians and settlers in colonial America, from the development of the fur trade to the transmission of European diseases into Native communities

- Westward expansion and its impact on the Indian nations of the west

- Tecumseh's Rebellion, Red Cloud's War, and other major conflicts in the "Indian Wars"

- The Battle of Little Bighorn, including coverage of the disastrous tactics of Custer and the motivations of his Indian foes

- The Dawes Act and the devastating impact of "allotment" on tribal fortunes
- Indian boarding schools and their impact on families and tribal communities
- The Indian Reorganization Act and its impact on Indian families and communities
- Native activism during the 1960s and 1970s, including the rise of the American Indian Movement
- American Indian life in the twenty-first century, from pressing social problems on reservation communities to the growth of Indian-owned gambling casinos

NARRATIVE OVERVIEW

PROLOGUE

On the cold winter morning of December 29, 1890, some 350 tired, hungry, demoralized American Indians emerged from makeshift shelters in a windswept river valley. Looking around, they saw that they were surrounded by more than 500 well-armed U.S. soldiers. Officers separated out the men and marched them forward, leaving around 230 women and children huddled in the camp. As the Indian men lined up to face the commander of the troops, they noticed four large cannons perched on the hillside above them, poised to fire on a moment's notice. Their chief, desperately ill with pneumonia, quietly urged them to cooperate.

The commander ordered his troops to search the prisoners and confiscate their weapons. As the soldiers moved to disarm them, though, some of the Indians grew upset. They needed their rifles, knives, and bows to hunt for food and to protect their families. Without their weapons, they would be helpless as they traveled across the desolate plains. The Indians had already lost their land, their cherished traditions, and their hope for the future. They did not have much left to lose.

Determined to keep his precious rifle, one of the men struggled with the soldiers. The gun went off, setting a terrible tragedy in motion. An Indian witness recalled what happened next:

> When the firing began, of course the people who were standing immediately around the young man who fired the first shot were killed right together, and then they turned their [Hotchkiss cannons] upon the women who were in the lodges standing there under a flag of truce, and of course as soon as they were fired upon they fled, the men fleeing in one direction

3

and the women running in two different directions. So that there were three general directions in which they took flight.

There was a woman with an infant in her arms who was killed as she almost touched the flag of truce, and the women and children of course were strewn all along the circular village until they were dispatched. Right near the flag of truce a mother was shot down with her infant; the child not knowing that its mother was dead was still nursing, and that especially was a very sad sight. The women as they were fleeing with their babes were killed together, shot right through, and the women who were very heavy with child were also killed.... After most all of them had been killed a cry was made that all those who were not killed or wounded should come forth and they would be safe. Little boys who were not wounded came out of their places of refuge, and as soon as they came in sight a number of soldiers surrounded them and butchered them there.[1]

By the time the shooting ended, between 250 and 300 Indian men, women, and children lay dead in the hills along Wounded Knee Creek in South Dakota. The victims came from the Lakota or Teton Sioux tribe, and they died at the hands of the U.S. Army's Seventh Cavalry. This tragic incident, known to history as the Wounded Knee Massacre, marked the end of four centuries of armed conflict between Indians and whites in North America. But the memory of the shameful events at Wounded Knee continues to resonate across America more than a century later.

Notes

[1] American Horse, "The Indian Story of Wounded Knee." *Report of the Commissioner of Indian Affairs,* February 11, 1891. In Mooney, James. *The Ghost Dance Religion and the Sioux Outbreak of 1890.* Washington, D.C.: U.S. Government Printing Office, 1896, p. 885. Available online at http://www.pbs.org/weta/thewest/resources/archives/eight/wklakota.htm.

Chapter One

EUROPEAN COLONIZATION
OF THE "NEW WORLD"

We know our Lands are now become more valuable. The
white People think we do not know their Value; but we are
sensible that the Land is everlasting, and the few Goods we
receive for it are soon worn out and gone.

—Canassateego, Onondaga Chief, 1742

When the first European explorers and colonists arrived on the shores of North America in the late fifteenth and early sixteenth centuries, they found a continent already teeming with an estimated two to ten million people. These Native Americans were the distant descendents of people who had migrated to the Americas from northern Asia via a land "bridge" that once connected Siberia to Alaska. By the time English, French, Dutch, Spanish, and other western Europeans landed in North America, these early nomads had evolved into hundreds of tribes scattered across every region of the continent.

The Native American societies that existed in North America at the time of European discovery were distinct from one another in numerous ways. These tribes spoke more than two hundred different languages, and their everyday activities—from their methods of gathering food to their expressions of religious belief—were influenced greatly by their physical surroundings. Tribes that lived near fish-filled rivers and coastal areas, for example, developed permanent communities that made salmon and water the center of their cultural, spiritual, and economic lives. Other tribes developed nomadic hunting cultures that followed game throughout their seasonal migrations. Still others nurtured farming societies that tended fields in the same region for years at a time. Wherever they lived, though, Native Americans learned to shape their lives in accordance with the natural resources available to them. Those tribes that failed to do so either perished or were absorbed by other, healthier groups.

The white people who established the earliest European colonies in North America were a similarly diverse lot. The European traders, explorers, soldiers, and settlers who set out for the "New World" hailed from England, France, Spain, Denmark, Portugal, Sweden, and Holland. All of these nations possessed unique languages, histories, religious beliefs, and cultural traditions and values. But Native Americans—or "Indians," as Christopher Columbus reputedly called them out of a mistaken belief that he had landed in India—quickly learned that whatever the differences in customs, dress, and language among these white "tribes," the newcomers all had one thing in common: They viewed the New World as a place where they could enrich themselves, build a fresh start, or otherwise improve their lives. And most of them did not have any qualms about doing so at the expense of the continent's indigenous (native) peoples, whom they viewed as inferior "savages."

The Spanish and French Empires in the New World

Visitors from numerous European states made pilgrimages to the North American continent during the sixteenth and seventeenth centuries. The biggest impact on the New World, however, was made by England, Spain, and France, the three great European empires of that historical era. These nations employed different strategies and pursued different priorities as they established a presence in America. The Spanish, for example, came as conquerors, whereas the French became known primarily as traders, and the English made their most enduring mark as settlers. But despite these differences, all three empires had a huge impact on the American Indians of North America.

Spain's arrival in the New World was grim from the outset for the Indian tribes unfortunate enough to cross the paths of its countrymen. The Spanish conquistadors who sailed for the New World were armed with superior weapons, a war culture that did not flinch from bloodshed, and a deep conviction that their Christian God wanted Spain to rule over all the earth. Most important of all, the Spaniards brought infectious diseases like smallpox and measles that killed vast numbers of Indians without any immunity. All of these factors enabled the Spaniards to cut a wide and deadly swath across the Americas.

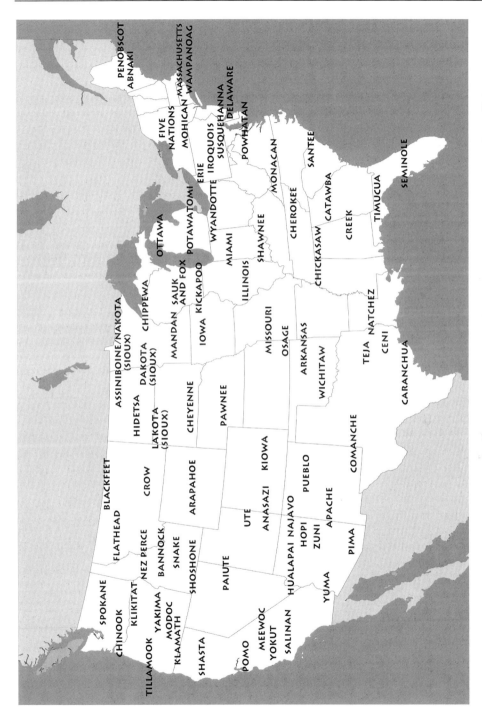

This map shows the distribution of major American Indian nations before white incursions pushed tribes off their traditional lands.

Most Spanish activity in the Americas was concentrated in the Caribbean, Mexico, Central America, the American Southwest, and modern-day California (Spain also claimed Florida in the early sixteenth century, but it exerted only a very tenuous hold on the peninsula through 1819, when it sold the land to the United States). The Spanish referred to its captured territories in the west as "New Spain," and they treated the indigenous peoples of those regions with cruelty and contempt. Proud civilizations like the Aztecs of Mexico and the various Pueblo tribes of the American Southwest were destroyed or enslaved to meet Spanish appetites for silver, crops, and other riches discovered in the New World. By the close of the sixteenth century, stories of Spanish atrocities were commonplace among the Indian peoples living in New Spain.

Yet Spain never really made a sustained effort to attract Spanish colonists to America. By the opening of the seventeenth century, it had established only scattered missions in Mexico, the Southwest, and California. These outposts remained dependent on native tribespeople for most of their labor needs, from harvesting crops and mining silver to tending to the sheep, cattle, horses, and other livestock that the Spanish introduced to New Spain. In 1680 the Pueblo tribes staged a stunning revolt against their persecutors, and for the next twelve years they were free of Spain's hard rule. In 1692 the Spaniards managed to regain control of their territories in the Southwest. But from this point forward their reign over the Pueblos—and all of New Spain—began to crumble. This slow fade reflected the gradual decline of Spain's power and prestige on the wider world stage. By the 1820s Spain had lost all of its American territories to the English crown or indigenous independence movements.

France, by contrast, adopted a much more cooperative approach in its dealings with the Indian tribes its traders encountered in North America. Like the Spanish, the French saw the New World as an opportunity to expand and strengthen their empire. And like their Spanish counterparts, early French explorers laid claim to a huge swath of the continent on behalf of their masters back in Europe. The territory of "New France" stretched all the way from eastern Canada and the Great Lakes region down to the Gulf of Mexico, with the Mississippi River serving as its western border and its eastern flanks marked by the Appalachian Mountains. But unlike the Spaniards, who regularly mistreated and took advantage of Indians, the early French fur traders, known as *voyageurs,* who came to North America cultivated mutually rewarding partnerships with area tribes. In fact, historian Peter Nabokov observed that many of

French traders or *voyageurs* who came to the New World used massive birchbark canoes to carry furs they obtained from friendly Indian nations.

the French voyageurs who "paddled their canoes up and down the rivers of the New World … became absorbed in Indian life, adopting Indian customs and dress, learning native languages, and intermarrying."[1]

During the course of the seventeenth and eighteenth centuries, France established several significant towns in the New World, like Quebec and Montreal. But for much of this time, the French showed more interest in trading with Indians for commercially valuable beaver pelts and other furs than they did in establishing permanent settlements in the New World. This emphasis on trade over land acquisition helped ensure continued good relations with Algonquin, Huron, and other tribes who delighted in the muskets, blankets, jewelry, axe heads, and other goods they received in return for pelts.

France's occasional efforts to actively encourage colonization of New France were severely hampered by rules that restricted the number of people who could go. In 1627, for example, French King Louis XIII and his closest advisor, the Roman Catholic Cardinal Richelieu, announced plans to encourage the agricultural and commercial development of New France by releasing crown lands in Canada. But they limited eligibility for ownership of these parcels to Roman Catholics, a decision that reflected long years of anti-

Protestant feelings in France. This discriminatory measure convinced many French Protestant families, known as Huguenots, to settle in *England's* North American colonies instead.

Jamestown and Plymouth

From the very beginning, the English settlements that were carved out of the New World wilderness were of a much different character than those established by Spain and France. These early communities were composed of families seeking religious freedom, economic opportunity, and a better way of life than they could claim back in England. They came to North America with the intention of staying forever, so they built homes, barns, and churches, cleared forests to create crop fields, and introduced English concepts of religion, law, and social customs to the New World.

These early efforts to build a new civilization on the eastern rim of North America might well have failed without the assistance of area tribes. Setting aside their anxieties about the sudden arrival of these strange white men and women, Indians helped the colonists survive early struggles with cold, hunger, and disease. But gratitude for this assistance was short-lived. By the mid-seventeenth century rapidly expanding English colonies up and down the Atlantic seaboard threatened to overwhelm regional tribes.

The first permanent English settlement was Jamestown, which was founded in 1607 in modern-day Virginia. Led by John Smith, this colony was in its earliest days at the mercy of Powhatan (also known as Wahunsonacock), the leader of a powerful confederacy of Algonquin tribes. This alliance, known to historians as the Powhatan Confederacy, included 14,000-20,000 Indians. Jamestown, by contrast, housed only about 100 colonists when it was first established. White-Indian relations were strained from the start, but Powhatan let the colonists live in the belief that they could be an ally—and a source of weapons—in fights against other Indian tribes. This hope faded, however, as waves of new colonists poured into the Virginia colony to raise tobacco and other crops suitable for export to Europe.

White demands for traditional Indian lands became so aggressive that the Algonquins launched a major assault on settlements and tobacco plantations in 1622. By some estimates, these attacks claimed the lives of more than a quarter of the colonial population. But new colonists quickly took their place, and British retaliation against the Algonquins was swift and fierce.

This 1932 painting provides a depiction of the first "Thanksgiving" meal that brought together Wampanoag Indians and Plymouth colonists.

These military actions, combined with the ravages of European diseases, destroyed the last remnants of the once-grand Powhatan Confederacy by the close of the 1640s. And as the Indians dwindled in numbers, colonists continued to rush in to fill the spaces they once occupied. By the close of the seventeenth century more than 100,000 European settlers lived in the Virginia, Maryland, and South and North Carolina colonies.[2]

The second permanent English colony in North America was founded further north, in Plymouth, Massachusetts, by English pilgrims. Established in 1620, this settlement sought out friendlier relations with area Indians than did Jamestown. In fact, the region's Wampanoag Indians, led by their chieftain Massasoit, saved these colonists from starvation during their first months in the New World by showing them how to cultivate corn, squash, and other crops and catch fish and shellfish from area waterways. After a successful harvest in the fall of 1621, the pilgrims and Wampanoag even joined together in the first Thanksgiving celebration.

But the Indians of southern New England soon found themselves in the same situation as the Virginia Algonquins. New colonial settlements sprouted along the northern Atlantic coastline with each passing year. By the 1640s the Indians were under intense pressure from colonists to formally surrender ownership of valuable tracts of land that they had used for hunting, fishing, and farming for generations. This steady loss of territory, combined with alarming declines in wild game populations, left New England tribes feeling trapped and desperate. These fears were further intensified by the mysterious plagues—smallpox, measles, diphtheria, and other European diseases—that virtually destroyed some tribes. "The Indians affirm," wrote one Dutch settler in 1650, "that before the arrival of the Christians, and before the small pox broke out amongst them, they were ten times as numerous as they now are."[3]

> *"The Indians affirm," wrote one Dutch settler in 1650, "that before the arrival of the Christians, and before the small pox broke out amongst them, they were ten times as numerous as they now are."*

In the summer of 1675 this tense environment exploded into King Philip's War. This bloody clash pitted white New Englanders against area tribes. Whites even fought with the Wampanoag, the same Indian nation that had shared the first Thanksgiving meal with the pilgrims a half-century earlier. In the early stages of King Philip's War—named after the English name for Metacom, the leading war chief of the Wampanoag—widespread Indian attacks put New England's white settlers on the defensive. More than 50 English frontier settlements were burned or damaged by Indian war parties, and frightened colonists reported that Indian warriors lurked on the fringes of settlements "like the lightning on the edge of clouds."[4]

But English muskets and cannons were too much for the Indians to overcome. British forces launched ruthless attacks on Indian villages that claimed dozens of lives at a time. The white colonists also successfully enlisted the help of longtime Indian allies such as the Mohegan to hunt down "hostiles." By the summer of 1676 the Wampanoag, Nipmuck and Narragansett warriors that had led the revolt were fleeing for their lives from relentless bands of well-armed pursuers. On August 12, 1676, King Philip himself was killed by an Indian mercenary. His head was cut off and mounted on a pole in Plymouth, where it remained on display for the next two decades. By the time of Philip's death, however, the war had already been lost. In fact, King Philip's War reduced the populations of the once-plentiful Wampanoag and Narragansett nations to a few hundred members. Smaller tribes were eliminated from New England entirely by the war. Members of these tribes died in the violence, fled to the wilds of Canada, or were captured and shipped off to serve as slaves to white masters in the Caribbean, Spain, Portugal, and the southern tobacco-growing colonies.[5]

White and Indian Concepts of Property Ownership

The rising level of conflict between whites and Indians in the seventeenth century stemmed in large part from the colonists' understandable desires to improve their economic standing and quality of life. The early European colonists recognized that by making use of America's amazing bounty of timber, wildlife, water, and farmable land, they could enrich themselves and provide food, shelter, warmth, and a sense of community for their families. But these resources had also been used by generations of Indians. The various tribal nations that had once had the woods, streams, and meadows to themselves felt growing alarm at the rate at which those places became filled with forts, homes, barns, fences, and other signs of European "civilization."

In the first decades of European colonization, Indian concerns about these incursions were relieved somewhat by the benefits of trade with English, French, and Dutch colonists. In addition, the vast lands extending from the coastal plains to the Appalachian Mountains (which stood as the primary barrier to western expansion of the British colonies for more than a century) initially seemed great enough to accommodate everyone, white and Indian. But as the number and size of colonial settlements grew, various Indian nations were crowded to the edges of their territories—and in some cases pushed entirely into the traditional territories of other tribes. This sequence of events, which played out time and time again during the course of the seventeenth and eighteenth centuries, reflected major differences in the way that Native Americans and Europeans viewed land ownership.

Among the Indian nations of North America, land and resources were shared in common. Individuals, families, clans, and tribes all took what they needed for nourishment, shelter, and comfort, but they did not hoard resources or claim tribal lands for their own exclusive use and benefit (nations did, however, stake out hunting grounds and other territories that were off-limits to other tribes). "Individuals did not own parcels of real estate, so status and power had nothing to do with the acquisition of acreage, as it did in Europe,"[6] wrote historian Peter Iverson.

13

White colonizers of the New World used treaties and other European-style land transfer agreements to claim ancestral territories and resources from Indian nations.

English and other European colonists who came from societies based on private ownership and the acquisition of personal riches were amazed by this attitude, and they wasted little time in taking advantage of it. First, the white settlers convinced themselves that the Indians had only a limited right to the land since they left so much of it in an "undeveloped" or "unimproved" state. Next, the colonists crafted land deeds and other legal documents that exploited the Indians' ignorance of European-style property rights.

When Indians signed these land deeds—essentially statements of ownership of land—over to British colonists in exchange for blankets, tools, jewelry, and other trade goods, they viewed the transaction as one that guaranteed all parties, white and Indian, the right to hunt, fish, and raise crops on the land in question. And some land transfers were worded so that Indians had the continued right to hunt, travel, or live on the land. But many of these deals featured language that explicitly forbade Indians from setting foot on the land in question without the permission of the new "owner." Since wild game and other natural resources on these lands were viewed by the English as important economic assets, they frequently refused to give such permission.

Many Indian nations ignored or did not understand these new restrictions. They tried to hunt and fish and pick nuts and berries in the newly private woodlands and meadows just as they had always done before. When the English colonists responded by arresting these Indian "trespassers," area tribes began to realize that signing land over to the whites was fraught with peril. At the same time, however, the steadily growing population and power of the colonies gave the Indians little choice but to agree to many of these land deals. They came to realize from experience that if they refused to sign over ownership of the land, the whites would just move in anyway and gradually squeeze them out.

Giving Way to the Whites

By the late seventeenth century, colonies that had once been limited to the Atlantic coastal region were penetrating deep into the North American interior. Great Lakes tribes such as the Ojibwa (Chippewa), Ottawa, Potawatomi, and Huron that had once received only occasional visits from French fur traders watched anxiously as colonial settlements sprouted across their lands. Further south, tribes of the interior like the Cherokee, Chickasaw, and Choctaw, which had long been shielded from the Europeans by the Appalachian mountains, also found that they were no longer alone. They confronted a steady stream of white settlers looking to establish farms on the frontier, which was retreating further west with each passing year.

For these Indian nations, the growing white threat was further complicated by the fact that the steady westward expansion of colonists pushed displaced eastern tribes into their midst. In many cases, the arrival of these uprooted tribes from the east triggered explosive, violent conflicts with established tribes determined to protect their territory. Sometimes the established tribes fended off the new arrivals, forcing them to continue their desperate search for a new place to call home. On other occasions tribes settled into an uneasy coexistence based on the knowledge that whites posed the greater threat. And sometimes the tribes from the east acted as conquerors themselves, most notably in the Great Lakes and Ohio Valley. In the second half of the seventeenth century, for example, the Iroquois—a confederacy of six east-

Introducing Firearms to the New World

Samuel de Champlain was a French soldier, explorer, and author who played a major role in advancing French relations with Indian tribes in the New World. In 1609, during one of his many forays deep into the heart of the North American wilderness, Champlain's small party of fellow French traders and Huron, Algonquin, and Montagnais hunters encountered a larger war party of as many as 200 Iroquois. During this violent clash, Champlain and his French comrades fired their arquebuses (an early type of musket) on the Iroquois with deadly results. This display of firepower, which stunned both the Iroquois and Champlain's Indian allies, is regarded as one of the first instances in which European weaponry was used in a native conflict in North America. The following is an excerpt from Champlain's account of the battle:

> As soon as we landed, our Indians began to run some two hundred yards towards their enemies, who stood firm and had not yet noticed my white companions who went off into the woods with some Indians. Our Indians began to call to me with loud cries; and to make way for me they divided into two groups, and put me ahead some twenty yards, and I marched on until I was within some thirty yards of the enemy, who as

ern tribes (the Onondaga, Oneida, Mohawk, Seneca, Cayuga, and Tuscarora) that had become heavily dependent on the fur trade with the British colonies—moved into the northern Great Lakes region after depleting their own lands of beaver and other valuable fur-bearing game. Using violence and intimidation, the Iroquois seized large swaths of territory from the Hurons and other regional tribes that had traditionally traded with the French.

While most Indian tribes retreated before the crashing waves of white settlement, not all of them fled. Some groups tried to cling to their ancestral lands by adopting white farming practices, political systems, religious beliefs, and other aspects of European culture. These "accommodationists," as some historians call them, were aided to a degree by colonial authorities who sometimes set aside land for friendly Indians willing to embrace the Christian faith soon as they caught sight of me halted and gazed at me and I at them. When I saw them make a move to draw their bows upon us, I took aim with my arquebus and shot straight at one of the three chiefs, and with this shot two fell to the ground and one of their companions was wounded who died thereof a little later. I had put four bullets into my arquebus. As soon as our people saw this shot so favourable for them, they began to shout so loudly that one could not have heard it thunder, and meanwhile the arrows flew thick on both sides. The Iroquois were much astonished that two men should have been killed so quickly, although they were provided with shields made of cotton thread woven together and wood, which were proof against their arrows. This frightened them greatly. As I was reloading my arquebus, one of my companions fired a shot from within the woods, which astonished them again so much that, seeing their chiefs dead, they lost courage and took to flight, abandoning the field and their fort, and fleeing into the depth of the forest, whither I pursued them and laid low still more of them.

Source: Samuel de Champlain, *The Works of Samuel de Champlain.* Vol. 2. Toronto: Champlain Society, p. 101.

and other aspects of English society. These land parcels, the forerunners of later Indian reservations, gave some tribal members a measure of temporary peace and stability.

The other Indian response was to strike back against their white enemies with violence. Deadly white-Indian clashes had flashed across the continent ever since Europeans landed in the New World. But this bloodshed became heavier following the French and Indian War, which began in 1754 and ended nine years later.

The French and Indian War

The French and Indian War brought the long-simmering conflict between France and England over control of the eastern half of the modern-day United

States to a boil. Ever since they had arrived on the continent more than a century earlier, the two European powers had been jockeying for possession of its rich array of forests, rivers, and tillable lands. The French strategy in this empire-building contest was to cultivate strong relations with their Indian trading partners as a way of keeping the much more numerous British from taking over. On several occasions, bloody wars nonetheless broke out between Indian peoples and French settlers and traders over unfair land deals and broken trade agreements. The Natchez people of the Southeast and Fox tribe of the Great Lakes region, for example, both entered into bitter conflicts with the French during the eighteenth century. But on the whole, the French recognized the importance of maintaining good relations with America's indigenous peoples.

Despite French-Indian alliances, though, the British colonies continued to expand ever deeper into the western frontier. Using their greater numbers and military superiority to great advantage, the English repeatedly pressured Indian tribes to sign land transfer agreements like the 1744 Treaty of Lancaster. Colonial leaders seized on the vague language of this treaty with leaders of the Iroquois Confederacy to send the first settlers into the "Ohio Country." These vast lands stretched north to south from the Great Lakes down to the Ohio River, and east to west from the Allegheny Mountains to the Mississippi River.

The Ohio Country, however, had already been formally designated as part of New France, so the French and their Indian allies were angered and alarmed by this development. Determined to defend their ownership of the region, the French launched construction of several forts in the upper Ohio River Valley. Diplomatic negotiations failed to settle the crisis, and in early 1754 the rising tensions finally exploded into all-out war.

Most of the Indian nations in the Ohio Country sided with the French. Tribes like the Shawnee and Delaware believed that a British victory would be disastrous for their peoples, and so they willingly took up arms. The powerful Six Nations of the Iroquois maintained an official stance of neutrality in the conflict because of their longstanding ties to the English, but some bands of Iroquois warriors fought on the side of the French as well. In the opening years of the conflict, the combined French and Indian forces delivered a series of stinging defeats to the British. But a big infusion of British soldiers from Europe helped the English colonies turn the tide, and by the early 1760s it was clear that France would not be able to hold onto its claims in the Ohio Country. In February 1763 the two powers signed the Treaty of Paris, in

An artist's rendition of Indian warriors, who primarily sided with France during the so-called French and Indian War, engaged in a fierce woodlands skirmish against British forces.

which France relinquished virtually all of its land in North America east of the Mississippi River to England.

The British victory was very bad news for the Indians. When France gave up its territorial claims, tribes that had long reaped benefits from playing the two European powers against one another became much more vulnerable. The increased presence of the British in forts and outposts around the Great Lakes quickly led to Pontiac's Rebellion, a 1763 bid by several allied tribes to drive the British out of their territories. Named for Chief Pontiac, an Ottawa chieftain who was one of the main architects of the uprising, this bloody war resulted in the burning of several forts and the loss of hundreds of white and Indian lives—many of them the victims of horrible atrocities committed by both sides.

British authorities tried to quiet the unrest in the west in October 1763 by issuing a "royal proclamation" establishing the lands between the

19

Appalachians and the Mississippi River as a permanent Indian Territory. But colonists eager to claim frontier lands ignored the proclamation and pressed westward. In fact, this decree's unpopularity among the colonists has been cited by some historians as one of the factors that contributed to the American colonies' decision to declare their independence from Britain in 1776.

The sheer numbers and military superiority of the colonists soon overwhelmed the rebellious tribes, which faded away one by one as bloody skirmishes, epidemics of smallpox, and exhaustion all took their toll. Many of the disillusioned tribes made individual treaties with the colonies, and by 1765 Pontiac's Rebellion was no more. Pontiac himself eluded capture for the next several years, but in 1769 the fugitive was murdered by another Indian in the Ohio Country wilderness.

American Independence and Its Impact on the Indians

When the Revolutionary War flared to life in 1775, many tribes cast their lot with the British crown. They believed—or at least hoped—that they had a better chance of preserving their lands and way of life by dealing with the British rather than the rebellious American colonists who were moving onto their lands with such swiftness. But this war did not go in the favor of the Indians, either. In fact, both during and after the Revolutionary War, American troops repeatedly took revenge on various Indian tribes for allying themselves with Britain. In August 1779, for example, American forces under the command of future president George Washington burned 40 Iroquois towns to the ground. From that point forward, Washington was known to members of the Onondaga, Seneca, and Mohawk nations as "the Town Destroyer."[7]

"In times past our forefathers lived in peace, love and great harmony, and had every thing in great plenty," summarized two Mohegan Indian leaders from Connecticut in 1789. *"But alas! It is not so now."*

After the United States gained its independence in 1783 with the end of the Revolutionary War, Indian tribes in the Ohio Country periodically tried to resist the oncoming Americans. In 1785 this resistance once again took the form of a loose confederation of tribes that united to fight off their common enemy. But this so-called Northwest Indian War (1785-1795) ended in a decisive victory for the United States. After suffering a crushing defeat in 1794 at the Battle of Fallen Timbers, tribal leaders had little choice but to sign an agreement—the Treaty of Greenville—in which they formally relinquished their claims on the Ohio Country to the U.S. government.

In the wake of these events, Indian tribes from the Great Lakes to the Gulf Coast openly wondered about their ability to survive in the frightening, white-dominated world they now confronted. "In times past our forefathers lived in peace, love and great harmony, and had every thing in great plenty," summarized two Mohegan Indian leaders from Connecticut in 1789. "But alas! It is not so now."[8]

Notes

[1] Nabokov, Peter. *Native American Testimony: A Chronicle of Indian-White Relations from Prophecy to the Present, 1492-2000.* 1978. Revised ed. New York: Penguin Books, 1999, p. 19.

[2] Gitlin, Jay. "Empires of Trade, Hinterlands of Settlement." In *The Oxford History of the American West.* Edited by Clyde A. Milner II, Carol A. O'Connor, and Martha A. Sandweiss. New York: Oxford University Press, 1994, p. 89.

[3] Quoted in Jennings, Francis. *The Invasion of America: Indians, Colonialism, and the Cant of Conquest.* New York: Norton, 1976, p. 24.

[4] Quoted in Josephy, Alvin M., Jr. *500 Nations: An Illustrated History of North American Indians.* New York: Knopf, 1994, p. 215.

[5] Josephy, p. 217.

[6] Iverson, Peter. "Native Peoples and Native Histories." In *The Oxford History of the American West.* Edited by Clyde A. Milner II, Carol A. O'Connor, and Martha A. Sandweiss. New York: Oxford University Press, 1994, p. 15.

[7] Nabokov, p. 92.

[8] Henry Quaquaquid and Robert Ashpo. "Petition to the Connecticut State Assembly." In De Forest, John W. *History of the Indians of Connecticut from the Earliest Known Period to 1850.* Hartford, CT: Wm. Jas. Hamersley, 1851, p. 480.

Chapter Two

A VANISHING WAY OF LIFE

———◆———

When I was a boy, I saw the white man afar off, and was told
that he was my enemy. I could not shoot him as I would a
wolf or a bear, yet he came upon me. My horse and fields he
took from me. He said he was my friend—he gave me his
hand in friendship; I took it, he had a snake in the other.

—Wild Cat, Seminole, 1841

After the United States successfully waged its war of independence and freed itself from the control of the British crown, the new nation sought to reassure Indian tribes that a new era of peaceful coexistence was at hand. Representatives of the U.S. government made these claims even when they engaged in activities that posed a clear threat to indigenous peoples. The 1787 Northwest Ordinance, for example, formally opened the entire Northwest Territory/Ohio Country to white settlement and specified how various parts of the region could become states (modern-day Ohio, Illinois, Indiana, Michigan, and Wisconsin were all created out of these lands).

In crafting this ordinance, the U.S. Congress declared that "the utmost good faith shall always be observed towards the Indians: their lands and property shall never be taken from them without their consent; and, in their property, rights, and liberty, they shall never be invaded or disturbed, unless in just and lawful wars authorized by Congress; but laws founded in justice and humanity, shall from time to time be made for preventing wrongs being done to them, and for preserving peace and friendship with them."[1] As land speculators, settlers, and surveyors poured into the region, however, the government failed to honor its commitment to the Indians. Instead, authorities

"[Once] there was no white man on this continent," Tecumseh declared. "It then all belonged to red men, children of the same parents, placed on it by the Great Spirit that made them, to keep it, to traverse it, to enjoy its production, and to fill it with the same race. Once a happy race. Since made miserable by the white people, who are never contented, but always encroaching."

pressured tribes into handing over their traditional grounds piece by piece. Some Indians managed to hang on to fragments of their once-vast territories despite the white flood. Others, though, were swept entirely away from the lands of their ancestors.

This grim drama played out in similar fashion again and again. Over the next half-century, the United States absorbed vast areas of western land. It acquired some of this territory through treaties with European powers, such as the 1803 Louisiana Purchase from France, the 1819 purchase of Florida from Spain, and the 1846 acquisition of the Oregon Country from England. At other times it used brute force to take the land, as in the 1846-1848 Mexican-American War that brought California and the Southwest under U.S. control. U.S. officials and lawmakers then turned their attention to tribes that made their homes in these regions—and who were completely oblivious that the land beneath them was being bought and sold by white men thousands of miles away.

With each territorial acquisition, new waves of white settlers moved onto the land. And just as they had done during the colonial era, American Indians responded to the white incursions in different ways. Some bands reluctantly fled further west or up into Canada, searching for lands far from white settlements and migration routes. Other northern tribes, faced with a choice between "exodus and life on individual allotments surrounded by whites,"[2] managed to keep a grip on small sections of their ancient homelands. Finally, some Indians took up weapons in desperate bids to stop the white invasion.

The most famous advocates of armed resistance to white settlement in the early nineteenth century were Tenskwatawa and Tecumseh. These brothers from the Shawnee nation led a military campaign that unified thousands of warriors from different Midwestern tribes against the white invaders. This formidable movement began around 1805 and aroused widespread anxiety in white frontier communities by 1808. Undeterred by U.S. military efforts to crush the rebellion, Tecumseh recruited warriors from nations throughout the upper Midwest from 1809 through 1812. "Once … there was no white man on this continent," he declared. "It then all belonged to red men, children of the same parents, placed on it by the Great Spirit that made them, to keep it, to traverse it, to enjoy its production, and to fill it with the same race. Once a happy race. Since made miserable by the white people, who are never contented, but always encroaching."[3]

The resistance eventually became known as Tecumseh's War and Tecumseh's Rebellion in recognition of the Shawnee warrior's gradual emergence as its leading figure (see "Tecumseh Calls for Indian Unity against the White Invaders," p. 159). Charismatic and smart, Tecumseh became known not only for his battle-field heroics, but also for his refusal to allow the slaughter of captured Americans. But although he gained a measure of British military support after the War of 1812 erupted between Britain and the United States, Tecumseh's grand alliance fell apart after his death in battle in October 1813. "The tragedy of Tecumseh was twofold," wrote historian Jake Page. "In urging Indian people to put aside their age-old differences, he was … ahead of

TECUMSEH.

The famed Shawnee warrior Tecumseh led a formidable Indian uprising in the Ohio River Valley in the early nineteenth century.

his time; in trying to carve out a separate Indian country in the Ohio Valley in the face of a rapidly growing white presence, he was too late."[4]

Other tribes fought against the white invaders as well. Despite occasional successful raids against settlements and victories in skirmishes against white soldiers, all of these campaigns ended in defeats that left Indian nations in bloody tatters. The Black Hawk War of 1832 in the upper Midwest, for example, claimed the lives of hundreds of women, children, and elderly members of the Sauk and Fox tribes after warriors from those nations fought back against white incursions onto their lands.

Ralph Waldo Emerson Condemns Indian Removal

Indian removal policies were not universally popular with white Americans. Some prominent Southerners, including Tennessee Congressman Davy Crockett, condemned such acts as immoral and unfair. Efforts to push the Cherokee and other nations from their ancestral lands were even less popular in the North. In the following excerpt from an 1836 letter to President Martin Van Buren, the famous Massachusetts writer Ralph Waldo Emerson explains the strong opposition to Cherokee removal that existed in some parts of white America:

> The newspapers now inform us that, in December, 1835, a treaty contracting for the exchange of all the Cherokee territory was pretended to be made by an agent on the part of the United States with some persons appearing on the part of the Cherokees; that the fact afterwards transpired that these deputies did by no means represent the will of the nation; and that, out of eighteen thousand souls composing the nation, fifteen thousand six hundred and sixty-eight have protested against the so-called treaty. It now appears that the government of the United States chooses to hold the Cherokees to this sham treaty, and are proceeding to execute the same. Almost the entire Cherokee Nation stand up and say, "This is not our act. Behold us. Here are we. Do not mistake that handful of deserters for us;" and the American President and the

Indian Dislocation in the South

There were fewer major American Indian uprisings in the South than in the North during the early 1800s. The larger Indian nations in this part of the country recognized that whites, who had already moved into the South in large numbers during the second half of the eighteenth century, had the power to wipe them out if war broke out. As a result, they tried to find a path that would allow them to stay on their ancestral lands without arousing white hostility and violence. Leading tribes like the Cherokee, Choctaw, and Creek (also known as Muskogee) turned to strategies of "assimilation"—the adop-

Cabinet, the Senate and the House of Representatives, neither hear these men nor see them, and are contracting to put this active nation into carts and boats, and to drag them over mountains and rivers to a wilderness at a vast distance beyond the Mississippi....

We only state the fact that a crime is projected that confounds our understanding by its magnitude, a crime that really deprives us as well as the Cherokees of a country for how could we call the conspiracy that should crush these poor Indians our government, or the land that was cursed by their parting and dying imprecations our country, any more? ... Will the American government steal? Will it lie? Will it kill? — We ask triumphantly. Our counselors and old statesmen here say that ten years ago they would have staked their lives on the affirmation that the proposed Indian measures could not be executed; that the unanimous country would put them down. And now the steps of this crime follow each other so fast, at such fatally quick time, that the millions of virtuous citizens, whose agents the government are, have no place to interpose, and must shut their eyes until the last howl and wailing of these tormented villages and tribes shall afflict the ear of the world....

Source: Emerson, Ralph Waldo. Letter to Martin Van Buren, April 23, 1838. In *The Works of Ralph Waldo Emerson*. Vol. 3. New York: Hearst's International Library, 1914, p. 501.

tion of European-style religious, cultural, and political practices. Members of these nations accepted Christianity, turned to European farming practices, opened mission schools for instruction in the English language, and drafted tribal laws and constitutions closely patterned after those of the whites.

Most of these efforts to ward off the seizure of their lands failed, however. Citizens of newly created states like Tennessee (1796), Mississippi (1817), Alabama (1819), Florida (1821), and Arkansas (1836) joined with the white people of the original Southern states in demanding the removal of tribes that stood in the way of gold mining, tobacco and cotton growing, and other forms of economic development. White Southerners rationalized these demands by dismissing Indians as "savages" unworthy of the land upon which they lived (similar racist sentiments were also used to excuse the enslavement of Africans in the South).

Indian removal proposals also became popular in the Northern states and territories, especially in the wake of Tecumseh's Rebellion. As the white outcry grew for a solution to the "Indian problem," politicians responded by instituting sweeping new Indian removal policies. "The hunter state [of the Indian] can exist only in the vast uncultivated desert," declared President James Monroe in his 1817 State of the Union address. "It yields to the more dense and compact form and greater force of civilized population; and of right it ought to yield, for the earth was given to mankind to support the greatest number of which it is capable, and no tribe or people have a right to withhold from the wants of others more than is necessary for their own support and comfort."[5]

These sentiments angered and frustrated American Indians who had labored mightily to find a path of peaceful coexistence with whites. Some Indians gloomily concluded that the whites who had invaded their lands would simply never be satisfied until all tribespeople had been removed from their sight. "Brothers! I have listened to many talks from our great white father," lamented the Creek Chief Speckled Snake in 1829:

> When he first came over the wide waters, he was but a little man … very little. His legs were cramped by sitting in his big boat, and he begged for a little land to light his fire on…. But when the white man had warmed himself before the Indians' fire and filled himself with their hominy [dried corn], he became very large. With a step he bestrode the mountains, and his feet covered the plains and the valleys. His hand grasped the eastern and the western sea, and his head rested on the moon. Then he became our Great Father. He loved his red children, and he said, "You must move a little farther, lest by accident I tread on thee." … Now he says, "The land you live upon is not yours. Go beyond the Mississippi; there is game; there you may remain while the grass grows and the rivers run."
>
> Brothers! I have listened to a great many talks from our Great Father. But they always began and ended in this—"Get a little farther; you are too near me."[6]

28

From 1816 to 1850 more than 100,000 American Indians from 28 tribes were deported from their ancestral homelands to territories west of the Mississippi River.[7] These deportations were carried out according to language contained in dozens of treaties that native leaders signed with heavy hearts. In cases where chieftains refused to sign despite the overwhelming pressure on them, U.S. officials simply forged their names or expelled the bands at gunpoint. White negotiators also secured the cooperation of some tribal leaders through outright bribery.

America's relentless campaign of officially sanctioned robbery opened great expanses of new land for white development. But it also ripped apart Indian cultures that had prospered for hundreds of years. "Generation after generation of Native American families

President Andrew Jackson viewed American Indians as troublesome obstacles to U.S. empire building.

came to know only the sorrows and terrors of exile," wrote historian Peter Nabokov. "All their worldly goods on their backs, the Indian refugees suffered harassment from unfriendly whites along the way. Starvation and disease were their constant companions as they walked along unfamiliar roads to country they had never seen. Sometimes friendly Indians gave them shelter; sometimes enemy tribes took the opportunity to attack them."[8]

Andrew Jackson Targets Southern Indians

Many tribes suffered greatly during this period, but the Cherokee nation almost certainly ranks as the best-known victim of U.S. Indian removal policies. Cherokee culture had thrived in the southeast for thousands of years prior to European contact. When whites swept into their territories, the Cherokee agreed to cede large tracts of land to the U.S. government. Members also took up all sorts of "civilized" ways, including European-style forms of farming, government, law, and religious practice, to stay in the good graces of the whites that surrounded them. In the end, though, all of their desperate efforts were not enough to stem white demands for their remaining lands.

The single greatest blow to the Cherokee nation was the election of Andrew Jackson, a southern planter, slave owner, and war hero, to the presidency in 1828 (see Jackson biography, p. 134). Jackson possessed a deep well of hostility toward all Indians, and he was eager to help his fellow southern planters gain access to the so-called "cotton frontier"—Indian lands suitable for growing the valuable crop.

From the very beginning of his presidency, Jackson made Indian removal a top priority of his administration (see "Andrew Jackson Praises Indian Removal," p. 162). His declarations on this subject aroused criticism from lawmakers and newspapers in the North, but his stance enjoyed broad support in the South. By February 1830 both the Senate and the House of Representatives (which were led by Southerners at the time) passed bills calling for the removal of all Indians from lands east of the Mississippi River. Three months later Jackson signed the Indian Removal Act. This ruthless piece of legislation opened up all remaining Indian territories in the South to white settlement—and it formally authorized the president to relocate all eastern tribes to reservations west of the Mississippi.

Cherokee Chief John Ross waged a valiant—but ultimately unsuccessful—legal and political campaign to keep the Cherokee nation on their ancestral lands.

Cherokee Removal

Over the next several years the Cherokee nation made a valiant stand against removal under the leadership of Chief John Ross (see Ross biography, p. 143). Despite several clear victories in U.S. courts, however, the tribe suffered a fatal legal blow in December 1835, when several Cherokee representatives signed the Treaty of New Echota. Under the terms of this treaty, the Cherokee accepted U.S. government terms for removal of the entire nation from its long-held lands in the East to a reservation in the Oklahoma Territory.

Ross and other Cherokee leaders charged that the treaty was invalid. They noted that the Cherokees who signed the

Treaty of New Echota had no legal authority to do so, and they pointed out that the same U.S. government proposal had already been rejected by the Cherokee National Council.

The Jackson administration ignored these protests. The Treaty of New Echota paved the way for the removal of the Cherokee, so U.S. authorities treated it as a completely legitimate agreement. Ross responded to these developments with a mixture of outrage and mourning, but the federal government ignored his entreaties (see "Cherokee Chief John Ross Denounces Indian Removal Policies," p. 166).

On May 26, 1838, federal troops moved to enforce the Treaty of New Echota. They evicted thousands of Cherokee from their homes and forced them to travel a thousand miles to official reservation land in eastern Oklahoma. An estimated 4,000 tribal members died on the journey from disease and starvation. The ordeal became known among the Cherokee as the "Trail of Tears" and "The Trail Where They Cried," and it ranks today as one of the most shameful episodes in American history.

The Trail of Tears

Jackson's successor, President Martin Van Buren, assigned General Winfield Scott to oversee the forced removal of the Cherokee. Although Scott ordered the 7,000 U.S. troops and state militia members under his command to show the Indians "every possible kindness, compatible with the necessity of removal,"[9] many soldiers disobeyed his orders and treated the Cherokee brutally. Troops often arrived at Cherokee homes without advance warning and rounded up the residents at gunpoint. In many cases, families did not even have time to pack their belongings. White looters sometimes followed the soldiers to Cherokee homesteads, collected all the valuables, and then destroyed the property. The removal process swept across the Cherokee Nation quickly, and by early June the troops had rounded up an estimated 15,000 Indians. "I fought through the Civil War and have seen men shot to pieces and slaughtered by thousands, but the Cherokee Removal was the cruelest work I ever knew,"[10] declared a Georgia soldier who participated in the removal action.

Three groups of Cherokee, totaling around 3,000 people, left immediately for Oklahoma Territory. They traveled by barge and steamship on what came to be known as the "water route": northwest on the Tennessee River from Ross's Landing (present-day Chattanooga) to the Mississippi River, south to the Arkansas River, and west to Fort Smith, Arkansas. River levels were low during the height of summer, making navigation slow and difficult. Once they arrived at Fort Smith, the Cherokee had to travel over land in extreme heat with little food or water. Between three and five people died each day from exhaustion, dehydration, and illness.

Meanwhile, federal troops herded more than 12,000 Cherokee to 31 forts in Georgia, Tennessee, North Carolina, and Alabama. After several weeks, most Cherokee were transferred to 11 internment camps in Tennessee to await removal to Oklahoma. Conditions at these facilities were crowded and unsanitary, and the Cherokee prisoners suffered terribly. Families were often separated, their meager possessions were stolen, they suffered from hunger and illness, and they were mistreated by guards. Some Cherokee were forced to live in these conditions for up to five months, and more than 1,000 people died from disease or starvation in the camps.

In the midst of these struggles, Chief John Ross approached General Scott and requested that the Cherokee be allowed to postpone removal until fall and lead their own groups on the journey. Scott granted his request but required the Cherokee to remain in the internment camps until travel resumed. The first of 12 wagon trains left the Cherokee Agency near Rattlesnake Springs, Tennessee, in October 1838. Although the land routes varied, many groups traveled northwest past Nashville, crossed the Ohio and Mississippi Rivers, then proceeded southwest across Missouri and Arkansas to Oklahoma.

The 800-mile journey was an arduous one for the poorly equipped Cherokee. Heavy rains and hundreds of wagons left the roads muddy and rutted, food was scarce, and the weather grew bitterly cold with the onset of winter. Thousands of Cherokee found themselves trapped between the icy Ohio and Mississippi Rivers during a harsh January freeze. Most did not have enough warm clothing, and some did not even have shoes or moccasins. Many people succumbed to disease or died of exposure. One survivor remembered the harrowing ordeal: "Long time we travel on way to new land. People feel bad when they leave Old Nation. Women cry and make sad wails. Children cry and many men cry....But they say nothing and just put heads down and keep on go towards West. Many days pass and people die very much."[11]

By March 1839 the last Cherokee survivors of the Trail of Tears had straggled into Oklahoma. Ross immediately went to work to reunite the

An artist's rendering of the 1838 Trail of Tears, in which the Cherokee Nation was forced by the U.S. government to leave their home in the American Southeast and relocate in Oklahoma Territory.

demoralized and divided tribe. The various factions came together to draw up a new constitution and form the United Cherokee Nation. In 1841 a new capital was established in Tahlequah. By the 1850s the Cherokee Nation once again had its own roads, businesses, newspaper, and public school system. Meanwhile, around 1,000 Cherokee in Tennessee and North Carolina escaped removal. Some lived on land owned by whites or protected by treaty, while others simply managed to hide. They gained federal recognition in 1866 as the Eastern Band of Cherokee Indians and established a tribal government in Cherokee, North Carolina.

Although the Cherokee managed to move forward following the Trail of Tears, they continued to feel the impact of this tragic episode for generations. "I know what it is to hate," explained Cherokee survivor Samuel Cloud, who was nine years old when he accompanied his family on the journey to Oklahoma. "I hate those white soldiers who took us from our home. I hate the soldiers who make us keep walking through the snow and ice toward this new home that none of us ever wanted. I hate the people who killed my father and mother. I hate the white people who lined the roads in their woolen clothes that kept them warm, watching us pass. None of those white people are here to say they are sorry that I am alone. None of them care about me or my people. All they ever saw was the colour of our skin. All I see is the colour of theirs and I hate them."[12]

Notes

[1] "Northwest Ordinance." Transcript. *Ohio History Central: An Online Encyclopedia of Ohio History.* Available online at http://www.ohiohistorycentral.org/entry.php?rec=1462&nm=Northwest-Ordinance-Transcript.

[2] White, Richard. "Expansion and Exodus." In *The Native Americans: An Illustrated History.* Edited by Betty Ballantine and Ian Ballantine. Atlanta: Turner Publishing, 1993, p. 298.

[3] Quoted in Drake, Samuel Gardner. *Biography and History of the Indians of North America: From Its First Discovery to the Present Time.* Boston: Antiquarian Institute, 1837. Book V, p. 121.

[4] Page, Jake. *In the Hands of the Great Spirit: The 20,000 Year History of American Indians.* New York: Free Press, 2003, p. 249.

[5] Monroe, James. First Annual Message to Congress, Dec. 12, 1817. *The American Presidency Project* [online]. Available at http://www.presidency.ucsb.edu/ws/?pid=29459.

[6] Quoted in O'Brien, Sharon. *American Indian Tribal Governments.* Norman: University of Oklahoma Press, 1993, p. 124.

[7] Nabokov, Peter. *Native American Testimony: A Chronicle of Indian-White Relations from Prophecy to the Present, 1492-2000.* 1978. Revised ed. New York: Penguin Books, 1999, p. 148.

[8] Nabokov, p. 145.

[9] "General Winfield Scott's Order to U.S. Troops Assigned to Cherokee Removal," May 17, 1838. Available online at http://georgiainfo.galileo.usg.edu/scottord.htm.

[10] Quoted in Mooney, James. *Myths of the Cherokee and Sacred Formulas of the Cherokee.* New York: Kessinger, 2006, p. 130.

[11] National Park Service. "Stories," Trail of Tears National Historic Trail, n.d. Available online at http://www.nps.gov/trte/historyculture/stories.htm.

[12] Quoted in Rutledge, Michael. "Forgiveness in the Age of Forgetfulness." Available online at http://www.cherokeehistory.com/law.html.

Chapter Three

STANDING IN THE WAY OF WESTWARD EXPANSION

⟨⟨⟨ ⟩⟩⟩

The greatest object of their lives seems to be to acquire possessions—to be rich. They desire to possess the whole world.

—Mysterious Medicine, Lakota, 1860s

For much of the first half of the nineteenth century, white settlers and politicians saw the Great Plains of North America as unattractive "Indian Country" unsuitable for farming or other development. They regarded the region as more of an obstacle than anything else—a hurdle that had to be crossed to reach booming mining and agricultural regions in California, Oregon, and the Rocky Mountains. As a result, they were perfectly content to leave this flat, dry, and mostly treeless midsection of the continent to the Indians that had long resided there. By the 1830s, in fact, white authorities treated the Great Plains as a convenient dumping ground for the eastern tribes that it was uprooting.

In the 1840s and 1850s, however, white perspectives on the Great Plains began to change. Growing numbers of Americans became believers in "manifest destiny," a belief that God specially favored the United States and wanted it to have dominion over the entire continent, from the Atlantic to the Pacific. This conviction was fed by dawning recognition that the oceans of grass covering the plains could be plowed up and turned into fertile farmland. It was also spurred by the growing prominence of steam-powered railroads and boats, which gave farmers and ranchers in even the most remote pockets of the country the capacity to deliver their goods to distant markets.

The Western Indian Wars Begin

As white settlers, surveyors, miners, railroad workers, buffalo hunters, and shop owners poured across the Mississippi River into the West, they quickly ran into trouble with Indian nations that had thrived there for centuries. So-called "Indian Wars" flared up all across the West in the 1850s and 1860s, and in some cases these conflicts lasted for decades. In modern-day Arizona and New Mexico, U.S. Army troops and settlers battled fierce Navajo and Apache warriors. In present-day Oklahoma, Texas, Kansas, and Colorado, whites fought the Kiowa, Comanche, southern Cheyenne, and Arapaho nations for control of the southern Plains. California and the Pacific Northwest became the site of violent clashes between whites and the Nez Perce and Modoc tribes. The Rocky Mountain region, meanwhile, was wracked by bloodshed between whites and members of the Shoshone, Ute, Bannock, and Paiute nations.

All of these wars ultimately ended in the same way: the Indian tribes were vanquished and herded onto reservations, and white Americans moved onto their old hunting grounds to seek gold and silver, cut timber, plant crops, and build railroads and towns. "[The white man's] numbers were greater than blades of grass," summarized one American Indian elder. "They took away the buffalo and shot down our best warriors. They took away our lands and surrounded us by fences....They forced our children to forsake the ways of their fathers. When I turn to the east I see no dawn. When I turn to the west the approaching night hides all."[1]

The most famous Indian War of all took place on the northern Great Plains from the 1850s through 1890. This war was waged primarily between the U.S. Army and the powerful Lakota nation—known to white people as the Sioux. It ended the same way as the other conflicts. But the events that took place during this long and bitter struggle occupy a special place in American history. Today, in fact, the names of the chieftains, military leaders, and battles that shaped this conflict remain familiar to white Americans and Native Americans alike. And the triumphs and tragedies experienced by the Lakota serve as powerful symbols of the wider Indian experience in America during the centuries following European contact.

Lords of the High Plains

The Indian people that whites called Sioux—after a French word for snake—were actually comprised of three main groups that spoke different

A small group of Lakota men on horseback on the northern Great Plains, where the Lakota nation became renowned for their skills as horsemen and warriors.

dialects (versions) of the same language. The Dakota group, known to whites as the Santee Sioux, made their homes in modern-day Minnesota. The Nakota group, also known as the Yankton Sioux, occupied a region that is now eastern South Dakota. The third group was the Lakota, also known as the Teton Sioux. The Lakota group, which became concentrated in the region west of the Missouri River, was the one that became dominant across the northern Great Plains in the eighteenth and nineteenth centuries. The Lakota were themselves organized into seven distinct subgroups or bands: Hunkpapa, Miniconjou, Oglala, Sihi Sapa (also known as Blackfeet—but not affiliated with the Blackfoot nation of Montana and western Canada), Brulé (Sicangu), Sans Arc (Itazipco), and Two Kettle (Oohenopa).

The Lakota Indians arrived on the northern Great Plains in the early 1700s. They migrated there from the western Great Lakes region after warriors of the Chippewa nation, a traditional enemy from that same area, became armed with firearms obtained from French fur traders. The infusion of guns to the Chippewa altered the balance of power between the two nations to such a great degree that relocation became necessary for the Lakota.

"[The white man's] numbers were greater than blades of grass," summarized one American Indian elder. "They took away the buffalo and shot down our best warriors. They took away our lands and surrounded us by fences."

When they first moved onto the plains, the Lakota struggled in their new surroundings. Over time, however, they obtained their own rifles from trade. Even more importantly, they acquired horses, which had been reintroduced to North America by Spanish colonizers in the 1600s. By the close of the eighteenth century, the Lakota had turned themselves into accomplished horsemen. Their skill at riding made it easier for them to find and kill buffalo, also known as bison. The meat of the buffalo, which roamed the Plains in astounding numbers in the seventeenth and eighteenth century, served as the tribal bands' leading source of food. Buffalo skins, bones, and other body parts, meanwhile, became the Lakota's principal material for clothing, tools, and shelter. "After decades of retreat, pushed hither and yon by other tribes, the Lakota were now fierce and demanding warriors who roamed the Great Plains from the Missouri River to the Bighorn Mountains, from the Canadian prairies to the Platte River and down into the Kansas plains," summarized historian Roger L. Di Silvestro. "Taken together, the Lakota were not just a force to be reckoned with in the northern plains; they were *the* force."[2]

Growing Tensions with White Settlers and Soldiers

At first, the intrusions of whites onto the hunting grounds of the Lakota and other Plains Indians were brief and infrequent. The white presence on the Great Plains was mostly limited to the Oregon Trail, the great pathway that pioneers used to get to the Rockies and points further west. The Indians were disturbed by the wagon trains that passed down this corridor, which some whites called the Holy Road, as well as by the sprinkling of forts that were established along the trail by the U.S. Army. This uneasiness was relieved somewhat by the Indians' enthusiasm for various white goods that they acquired in trade. But as time passed and the white population steadily increased, their tools, beads, whiskey, and blankets were not enough to

The arrival of the railroad in the West made it much easier for market hunters to harvest huge numbers of buffalo.

soothe the Lakota and other smaller nations in the region. "By 1850 all the Plains Indians had to reckon with the fact that though the whites were going through, they weren't going away," stated Western writer Larry McMurtry. "Friction steadily increased along the Holy Road; immigrant trains were attacked, the occasional immigrant killed. There was no full-scale warfare yet, just an ominous, continuous rumbling."[3]

During this same period, the U.S. government decided that the nation's westward expansion would be much easier to accomplish if the Lakota and other northern Plains tribes were moved onto reservations far from the Oregon Trail and other pioneer highways. In 1849 government officials approached the leaders of Great Plains nations with a proposal for a great conference to discuss white-Indian relations. This meeting was held in September 1851 at Fort Laramie in present-day Wyoming, and it attracted an estimated 10,000 Indians from across the plains.

On September 17 the U.S. negotiators announced the signing of a major new treaty with leaders not only of the Lakota, but also of the Arapaho, Assiniboine, northern Cheyenne, Mandan, Shoshone, and other northern Plains tribes. Under this arrangement, the Indians agreed to stay away from the main settlers' routes and accept new forts and other outposts in Indian territory. In return, the government would keep settlers out of large sections of the Great Plains and provide goods and equipment worth $50,000 a year for a fifty-year period (Congress reduced the terms of the contract to ten years when it approved the treaty).

This treaty was hailed by some whites as the foundation for improved relations with the Indians of the Great Plains. But the Indian nations became disillusioned when the U.S. government failed to fulfill many of the promises contained in the Fort Laramie treaty. Several tribes never received the promised payments, and gold and silver strikes like the Colorado Gold Rush of 1858 kept whites streaming into Indian Territory. In addition, white "market hunters" became an increasing problem, especially with the arrival of regular rail service. These hunters mowed down entire herds of bison—the cornerstone of the Great Plains Indian societies—for their valuable pelts, then left the skinned carcasses to rot on the plains. Lakota and other tribes also continued to suffer from "white man diseases" like smallpox, typhus, and cholera (see "A Cheyenne Recalls the Deadly Impact of Cholera on His Tribe," p. 170).

Some Indians responded to these pressures by abandoning their old ways of life. They went to live by the forts, where they became completely dependent on government rations. But many other Lakota, Cheyenne, and other Plains Indians decided to ignore the terms of the treaty themselves. As they resumed their harassment of miners and settlers, U.S. officials demanded that the tribal chiefs restore order. But these demands reflected a fundamental misunderstanding of the Indian societies of the Great Plains, and especially of the Lakota, which ranked as the most powerful of those tribes. The nations accorded great respect to influential elders within their ranks. But they did not have single chieftains whose word was law—let alone an individual who ruled over the entire nation. "The Indians had no political mechanism for selecting such a leader, and no intention of obeying him should he appear," explained McMurtry. "There was no chief of all the Sioux—never had been, never would be....The Sioux were highly individualistic people; though they often acted in concert on hunts and raids, at other times each man simply went his own way."[4]

Rising Bloodshed and Failed Diplomacy

As populations of buffalo and other important game dropped and Indian access to traditional hunting grounds declined, many tribes became more dependent on U.S. government rations than ever before. Too often, however, federal authorities failed to follow through on treaty promises of food supplies and other benefits for cooperative Indians. Hungry and disillusioned, some Indians lashed out with violence. In 1861, for example, the Treaty of Fort Wise promised the Cheyenne and Arapaho tribes ample food supplies as part of an agreement that placed them on a Colorado reservation. But when food deliveries failed to materialize, bands of warriors launched raids on mining camps, homesteads, and wagon trains. White Coloradans saw these raids as evidence that the Indians were untrustworthy savages. But even a government agent charged with overseeing the Colorado reservation admitted that "most of the depredations committed by [the Indians] are from starvation."[5]

One year later, a far more deadly revolt took place in Minnesota. That year, Dakota (also known as Santee Sioux) Indians under the direction of a chief named Little Crow went to war against Minnesota settlers. Several years earlier, the Dakota had peacefully moved onto reservation lands in return for promises of food and other benefits. But when U.S. authorities failed to honor their end of the agreement, rising levels of hunger and anger led the Indians to take up arms. The desperate Dakota killed hundreds of settlers (including women and children) and U.S. Army soldiers in the second half of 1862 in an all-out campaign to drive the whites out of their territory. But white counterattacks smashed the rebellion by the end of the year, and Little Crow was killed by a white settler in July 1863.

Dakota leader Little Crow was a leading force behind the great 1862 Indian uprising against white settlers in Minnesota.

In 1863 the administration of President Abraham Lincoln tried to defuse rising tensions with the Plains Indians by transporting a delegation of Indian chieftains to Washington, D.C. Lincoln himself met with Kiowa, Cheyenne, Arapaho, and Comanche leaders during their visit to the nation's capital. This diplomatic effort infuriated some white Americans. "Instead of taking delegations of savages to Washington, at enormous expense," wrote the editors of the *Rocky Mountain News*, "would it not be better to ... wipe the treacherous vagabonds from the face of the earth? The experiences of the past year, in Minnesota and elsewhere, afford the most positive evidence of the brutal and treacherous character of the Indian tribes. They seem to feel no gratitude for the liberal manner in which the Government has provided them with the necessities and comforts of life, and do not hesitate to violate the most solemn treaties."[6]

As it turned out, these visits did not really improve white-Indian relations—though they did convince some of the participating Indian chieftains that the United States was far too large and powerful to oppose. In fact, relations rapidly worsened in some parts of the West. In Colorado, for instance, the territory's leading lawmakers and military officers adopted ever more ruthless measures to deal with the "savages" in their midst. The most notorious of these actions was the November 29, 1864, Sand Creek Massacre. In this tragic event, a civilian cavalry regiment under the command of John M. Chivington—a former minister who harbored a deep hatred of all Indians—launched a deadly dawn attack on a peaceful encampment of Cheyenne and Arapaho. An estimated 200 Indian men, women, and children were killed in the onslaught. Many of these victims were grotesquely mutilated by the troops: "I saw the bodies of those lying there cut all to pieces, worse mutilated than any I ever saw before; the women cut all to pieces," said one white eyewitness, translator John S. Smith, in later testimony. "[They were cut] with knives; scalped; their brains knocked out; children two or three months old; all ages lying there, from sucking infants up to warriors."[7]

The Indian Peace Commission

As news of the Sand Creek Massacre spread across the Great Plains, tensions between whites and Indians spiraled to new heights. Nowhere were these tensions higher than among the Lakota who lived in present-day Wyoming. They became even more upset when the U.S. Army began construction of several forts along the Bozeman Trail, a route to the west that was becoming increasingly popular with gold miners and pioneer families—and which ran through the heart of their traditional territory. Convinced that the future of the Lakota nation hinged on beating back these growing incursions, an Oglala

A portrait of the Indian delegation that met with President Abraham Lincoln in 1863. The woman standing at far right is often identified as Mary Todd Lincoln, the president's wife. The identities of the Indians in the second row are unknown. The four Indian chiefs in the front row are Yellow Wolf, War Bonnet, Standing in the Water, and Lean Bear—all of whom were dead less than two years after this photograph was taken.

Lakota chieftain named Red Cloud organized war parties to attack the military garrisons along the Bozeman Trail (see Red Cloud biography, p. 138).

The most deadly of these attacks, which became collectively known as Red Cloud's War, was a December 1866 ambush that took the lives of eighty U.S. Army soldiers stationed at Fort Phil Kearny. This clash came to be known to the Plains Indians as the Battle of the One Hundred Slain and to whites as the Fetterman Massacre in recognition of William J. Fetterman, the

This illustration from an 1867 newspaper provides a white viewpoint of the "Fetterman Massacre" of U.S. troops from Fort Phil Kearny at the hands of Lakota and Cheyenne Indians.

officer who commanded the slain troops. One of the key Indian leaders in this battle—the worst defeat suffered by the U.S. Army to that point in the Indian Wars—was a young Lakota warrior named Crazy Horse, who would eventually become one of the most famous American Indians in history.

Many white soldiers, settlers, and lawmakers reacted to the Fetterman Massacre with expressions of fear or fury. Union Civil War hero William T. Sherman, who was given charge over all U.S. Army troops on the Great Plains after the 1865 conclusion of the war between the states, expressed a widespread sentiment among whites when he wrote that "we must act with vindictive earnestness against the Sioux, even to their extermination—men, women, and children."[8]

Lawmakers in Washington, however, were reluctant to approve a massive military campaign against the Plains Indians. They knew that they could win such a conflict eventually, but they were wary of the great financial expense of outfitting the Army for an all-out war with the Lakota and other regional tribes. In addition, they worried that the war would disrupt western railroads, mining operations, and farming efforts that were lifting the United States to new heights of economic power. With these factors in mind, Congress instead approved the creation of an Indian Peace Commission in 1867. This collection of white officials from the Bureau of Indian Affairs and other federal agencies spent the next several months touring the forts and reservations of the Great Plains. During this time they talked with a variety of fort commanders, Indian agents, and tribal leaders, including several "hostiles."

In January 1868 the Indian Peace Commission submitted its report to President Andrew Johnson. According to the commission, instances of white treaty breaking and other misbehavior were responsible for most of the incidents of Indian violence in the West over the previous few decades. The authors also condemned the living conditions on many reservations and the performances of some of the Indian agents responsible for the welfare of reservation residents. "It is our duty to remark that the condition of these tribes demands prompt and serious attention," stated the Commission report. "The treaty stipulations with many of them are altogether inappropriate. They seem to have been made in total ignorance of their numbers and disposition, and in utter disregard of their wants. Some of the agents now among them should be removed, and men appointed who will, by honesty, fair dealing, and unselfish devotion to duty, secure their respect and confidence."[9]

The centerpiece of the Indian Peace Commission report, however, was a recommendation that the United States solve the region's "Indian problem" by placing all the Plains tribes in two massive Indian reserves—one for the Lakota and other northern nations, and one for the southern nations. In between these two reservations, the railroads and wagon trains would be able to pass from one end of the continent to the other without any Indian interference.

The 1868 Fort Laramie Treaty

The Johnson administration moved quickly to make the Commission's reservation proposal a reality. Negotiators returned once again to the West. In late 1867 U.S. officials and representatives of the Comanche, Kiowa, Cheyenne, Arapaho and other southern Plains tribes signed the Medicine Lodge Treaty (actually a set of three treaties with individual tribes), which moved all the signatories onto reservation lands in present-day Oklahoma. In

The Disappearance of the Buffalo

The American buffalo occupied a central place in the culture of the Lakota and other Great Plains Indians. Buffalo meat was the main staple of the Plains Indian diet, and the tough hides of the beasts were treated to make robes, blankets, shirts, ropes, bags, moccasin bottoms, and tipi covers. Internal organs like the stomach and bladder were sometimes used as containers for water, and buffalo sinew was used as sewing thread. Horns, hooves, and bones, meanwhile, were used to make everything from arrowheads to game dice to rattles. This all-around importance of the buffalo to the existence of the Plains inhabitants also made the animal a key element in the religious life of the tribes.

Before large-scale white migration to the West, there were plenty of buffalo for all of the Indian nations who lived there. At the beginning of the nineteenth century, in fact, up to thirty million buffalo covered the continent. But over the course of the next one hundred years, the creature was virtually wiped off the face of the earth by the white invasion. Diseases introduced by domestic cattle played a role in the population decline, as did habitat loss from the white conversion of grazing lands to farms and towns. The single greatest destroyer of the buffalo, though, was the market hunter. These professional hunters laid waste to the great herds in order to ship their skins and tongues to the big cities of the East. As white demand for buffalo robes and blankets and smoked buffalo

return, the Indians were promised schools, agricultural help, and generous allowances of food, clothing, equipment, and ammunition for hunting.

Securing an agreement with the powerful Lakota tribes of the northern Plains, however, was more difficult. White negotiators knew that they would have to give much more generous terms to this nation, which had already proven on a number of occasions that it possessed the warriors, rifles, and horses to create big problems. With this in mind, U.S. military officials took a two-pronged approach when they met with Lakota chieftains at Fort Laramie in 1868. They issued dark warnings about their capacity to destroy tongue remained high—and the railroads snaked ever deeper into the West, opening remote lands to the rifles of the hunters—the great herds vanished, leaving only tattered remnants behind. "Up and down the plains those men ranged, shooting sometimes as many as a hundred buffalo a day," recalled Kiowa Indian Old Lady Horse. "Behind them came the skinners with their wagons....[They] took their loads to the new railroad stations that were being built, to be shipped east to the market. Sometimes there would be a pile of bones as high as a man, stretching a mile across the railroad track."

Some whites mourned the loss of the great buffalo herds as well. But others saw their falling numbers as a crucial blow to the Indian tribes that stood in the way of American progress. In 1875, in fact, U.S. Army General Philip Sheridan described the market hunters as heroes. "These men have done more in the last two years, and will do more in the next year, to settle the vexed Indian question than the entire regular army has done in the last thirty years," he proclaimed. "For the sake of a lasting peace, let them kill, skin, and sell until the buffaloes are exterminated. Then your prairies will be covered with speckled cattle and the festive cowboy."

Sources: Geist, Valerius. *Buffalo Nation: History and Legend of the North American Bison.* Stillwater, MN: Voyageur Press, 1998.
Nabokov, Peter. *Native American Testimony: A Chronicle of Indian-White Relations from Prophecy to the Present 1492-2000.* Rev. ed. New York: Penguin, 1999.

uncooperative tribes, but they also pledged to honor tribal wishes on several important matters. The United States offered the Lakota permanent possession of a reservation that spanned the western half of South Dakota—including the sacred Black Hills area—and large expanses of present-day Montana and Wyoming. The government also agreed to build schools, sawmills, and other facilities on this "Great Sioux Reservation," as it was called, and to make regular deliveries of food and clothing to tribal members. It even agreed to abandon all of its forts located on the Bozeman Trail. Finally, a large area adjacent to the reservation known as the Powder River Country would be declared "unceded Indian territory" available to Lakota for hunting—and off-limits to white settlers and miners (see "Negotiating the Fort Laramie Treaty of 1868," p. 172).

Leaders of several Lakota bands signed the Fort Laramie Treaty on April 29, 1868. But chieftains of Lakota tribes that lived far from the Bozeman Trail, like Black Moon and a young but influential chief named Sitting Bull, refused repeated invitations to attend the negotiations. Red Cloud also refused to sign, and white negotiators knew that the treaty would be worthless in the minds of area Lakota without his signature. "We are on the mountains looking down on the soldiers and the forts," Red Cloud reputedly said in a message to U.S. officials at the fort. "When we see the soldiers moving away and the forts abandoned, then I will come down and talk."[10] A few months later, the forts along the Bozeman Trail were abandoned by the U.S. Army. The desertion of these forts finally convinced Red Cloud to join with Sherman in signing the treaty in November 1868.

Notes

[1] Quoted in Wissler, Clark. *Indian Cavalcade.* New York: Sheridan House, 1938, p. 351.
[2] Di Silvestro, Roger L. *In the Shadow of Wounded Knee: The Untold Final Story of the Indian Wars.* New York: Walker, 2005, p. 21.
[3] McMurtry, Larry. *Crazy Horse: A Life.* New York: Lipper/Penguin, 1992, p. 19.
[4] McMurtry, p. 24.
[5] Quoted in Viola, Herman J. *Trail to Wounded Knee: Last Stand of the Plains Indians, 1860-1890.* Washington, DC: National Geographic Society, 2003, p. 43.
[6] Quoted in Viola, p. 28.
[7] Smith, John S. Congressional testimony, March 14, 1865. *New Perspectives on the West: Archives of the West, 1856-1868.* Available online at http://www.pbs.org/weta/thewest/resources/archives /four/sandcrk.htm#smith.
[8] Quoted in Lewis, Lloyd. *Sherman: Fighting Prophet.* Lincoln: University of Nebraska Press, 1993, p. 597.
[9] Report to the President by the Indian Peace Commission, January 7, 1868. *Annual Report of the Commissioner of Indian Affairs for the Year 1868.* Washington, DC: Government Printing Office, 1868. Available online at http://facweb.furman.edu/~benson/docs/peace.htm.
[10] Utley, Robert M. *The Indian Frontier of the American West, 1846-1890.* Albuquerque: University of New Mexico Press, 1984, p. 118.

Chapter Four

SITTING BULL
AND THE SIOUX WARS

⟿⟍⟍⟨ ⟩⟋⟋⟿

I am a red man. If the Great Spirit had desired me to be a
white man he would have made me so in the first place. He
put in your heart certain wishes and plans, in my heart he put
other and different desires.... Now we are poor, but we are
free. No white man controls our footsteps. If we must die ...
we die defending our rights.

—Sitting Bull, Lakota, 1876

Under the terms of the Fort Laramie Treaty of 1868, the Lakota people received a permanent reservation of 60 million acres—or about 93,000 square miles—west of the Missouri River in South Dakota. They were also granted hunting access to a large area of unceded Indian territory outside of the reservation. In addition, the U.S. government agreed to build an agency for each tribal subgroup on the Great Sioux Reservation to distribute food rations, make annuity payments for lands given up in the treaty, and provide education and other services. In exchange, the Lakota promised to stop harassing white settlers and disrupting road and railroad construction outside of reservation lands.

Despite the seemingly generous terms of the Fort Laramie Treaty, however, many Lakota viewed the agreement with emotions ranging from disappointment to outrage. They resented giving up lands their ancestors had occupied for generations and submitting to the authority of a white government. "Millions of buffalo to furnish unlimited food supply, thousands of horses, and hundreds of miles of free range made the Sioux, up to the year 1868, the richest and most prosperous, the proudest, and ... the wildest of all the tribes of the plains," ethnologist James Mooney explained. "At one stroke they were reduced from a free nation to dependent wards of the government."[1]

Concerned about the erosion of tribal independence, culture, and pride, several prominent Lakota chiefs refused to sign the Fort Laramie Treaty. These "non-treaty Lakota," led by Hunkpapa spiritual leader Sitting Bull (see Sitting Bull biography, p. 147) and Oglala war chief Crazy Horse (see Crazy Horse biography, p. 125), also refused to settle on the Great Sioux Reservation. Instead, they remained in unceded Indian territory along the Powder River in Wyoming, where they continued to hunt buffalo, follow traditional customs, and clash with white settlers and railroad builders. These bands of Lakota did not accept any government food rations or annuity payments.

Over the next decade, however, thousands of white settlers, hunters, traders, and miners flocked to the Dakota Territory by railroad and steamboat. The idea of "wild" Indians roaming the plains proved upsetting to them, as well as to the powerful eastern business interests that stood to benefit from unobstructed development of the western frontier. In support of these interests, the U.S. government sent military expeditions into Indian country in violation of the Fort Laramie Treaty. They hoped that a show of military force might convince the non-treaty Lakota to give up their nomadic lifestyle and move onto the reservations.

Gold Is Discovered in the Black Hills

The largest of these expeditions set out for the Black Hills of South Dakota on July 2, 1874. Its leader was Lieutenant Colonel George Armstrong Custer, an ambitious man who had earned a reputation as a fierce and determined fighter in the Indian Wars (see Custer biography, p. 130). Custer's massive wagon train included 700 soldiers of the Seventh Cavalry and 300 civilian surveyors, miners, geologists, and newspaper reporters. Soon after reaching its destination, the expedition turned up evidence of significant deposits of gold in the Black Hills. "Gold has been found at several places," Custer wrote in a letter to the expedition's sponsors, "and it is the belief of those who are giving their attention to this subject that it will be found in paying quantities."[2]

The discovery of gold in the Black Hills brought a rush of miners and speculators to the region. Seeking to stake claims, many white prospectors entered the Great Sioux Reservation illegally. The encroachment of whites on

This cover illustration from an 1876 issue of *Harper's Weekly* portrays gold prospectors looking to "strike it rich" in the Black Hills of the Dakota Territory.

reservation lands angered the Lakota and increased the potential for conflict. President Ulysses S. Grant was aware that the gold rush violated the terms of the Fort Laramie Treaty, but he made only a halfhearted effort to prevent miners from invading Indian territory. The U.S. economy had entered a recession, and Grant felt that the discovery of gold might provide a boost. In addition, he and many other white citizens believed that "the American continent should be given over to the progress of enlightenment and the temporal advancement of those who are willing to make use of God's best gifts,"[3] as an editorial writer of the period put it.

In 1875 a U.S. government commission, headed by Senator William Boyd Allison of Iowa, approached Lakota leaders with the goal of purchasing or leasing the Black Hills in order to exploit the gold deposits legally. They offered to pay $400,000 per year to lease the land, or $6 million to purchase it outright. But the Black Hills held great spiritual significance for the Lakota people. The area also served as a protective sanctuary against summer heat and winter cold, as well as an important source of game and lodgepole pine. Tribal leaders, who attended the meeting dressed in full war regalia, insisted that the land could not be sold. "I think that the Black Hills are worth more than all the wild beasts and all the tame beasts in the possession of the white people," Oglala chief Red Cloud told the commission. "God Almighty placed these Hills here for my wealth, but now you want to take them from me and make me poor."[4]

> *"I think that the Black Hills are worth more than all the wild beasts and all the tame beasts in possession of the white people," Oglala Chief Red Cloud declared. "God Almighty placed these Hills here for my wealth, but now you want to take them from me and make me poor."*

Unable to convince the Lakota to sell the Black Hills, the U.S. government decided that the best way to prevent further conflict was to force the non-treaty Indians onto reservations. In December 1875 the Bureau of Indian Affairs ordered the Lakota to abandon all unceded hunting grounds and report to the Great Sioux Reservation by January 31, 1876. Several bands spread across the countryside, including those led by Sitting Bull and Crazy Horse, did not obey the order. They were reluctant to submit to the government's authority, and they also knew that it was impossible for their people to travel all that distance in the dead of winter. When the non-treaty Lakota failed to show up as ordered, however, the U.S. military planned a campaign to crush the Indian resistance and take control of the plains.

The Battle of Little Bighorn

As the spring of 1876 approached, the Lakota prepared to make a stand in defense of the Black Hills. Thousands of tribal members slipped away from the Great Sioux Reservation and joined Sitting Bull's band near the Little Bighorn River in present-day Montana. A number of Northern Cheyenne and Arapaho also traveled to the area, eager to aid in the fight. By June an estimated 10,000 Indians, including 1,800 warriors, had gathered there in huge camps that stretched for three miles.

On the morning of June 25, 1876, Custer led an estimated 700 soldiers of the U.S. Army's Seventh Cavalry toward the Little Bighorn. His forces were accompanied by about 50 Crow and Arikara scouts. Longtime rivals of the Lakota, they had agreed to assist the government in hopes of gaining more favorable treatment for their own people. Custer's scouts brought him to a high bluff where he could look down over the Lakota camp from a distance. Seeing little activity and few signs of military preparedness, he decided to launch an immediate attack.

Custer divided his troops into three groups. He assigned one column of cavalry, under the command of Major Marcus Reno, to attack the camp from the south. Meanwhile, he planned to circle around the camp with a second column of cavalry and attack from the north. He stationed the third group, under Captain Frederick Benteen, in the valley of the Little Bighorn to block off the Indians' best escape route. In devising his strategy, however, Custer severely underestimated the number of warriors in the camp. He also assumed that the Indians would choose to run away rather than stand and fight.

Pte-San-Waste-Win was with a group of young Lakota women digging turnips when Reno's column of cavalry launched its attack on the camp. "Like that, the soldiers were upon us," she recalled. "Through the tepee poles their bullets rattled."[5] Although the sudden attack took Lakota leaders by surprise, they quickly recovered and prepared for battle. Sitting Bull was asleep when he realized that the camp was under attack. "I jumped up and stepped out of my lodge," he remembered. "The old men, the women, and the children were hurried away. There was great confusion." Sitting Bull rallied his warriors around him and announced, "Warriors, we have everything to fight for, and if we are defeated we shall have nothing to live for; therefore, let us fight like brave men."[6]

The Indians turned back the initial attack by Reno's troops and chased the first wave of cavalry toward the river, where they were pinned down on a bluff. When Custer's forces arrived from the opposite direction, they were met by a large group of warriors led by Crazy Horse. The Oglala chief had studied the U.S. Army's tactics in a number of battles, and he had taught his warriors how to identify the enemy's weaknesses. They trapped Custer's troops in an indefensible position and swarmed in to annihilate them. "Some soldiers became panic stricken, throwing down their guns and raising up their hands, saying, 'Sioux, pity us; take us prisoners,'" Miniconjou chief Red Horse recalled. "The Sioux did not take a single soldier prisoner. They killed all of them. None were left alive even for a few minutes."[7]

By the time the clash ended, Custer and more than 260 of his men were dead, including his brothers Tom and Boston (see "Eyewitness Recollections of the Battle of Little Bighorn," p. 177). The Battle of Little Bighorn went down in history as one of the worst defeats the U.S. Army ever suffered in the Indian Wars. It had a tremendous impact on public opinion across the country. Many people had followed the exploits of the handsome and flamboyant Custer with great interest. Some supporters even predicted that the popular military leader would be elected president of the United States someday. Custer's disastrous defeat was widely interpreted as a massacre of heroic American soldiers by hostile savages, and it created a thirst for revenge that indiscriminately targeted all Native Americans.

Breakup of the Great Sioux Reservation

Following the Battle of Little Bighorn, the victorious tribal forces scattered. Some bands returned to the reservations, while others retreated into the wilderness to live off the land. But those Indians who refused to go on the reservations were harassed relentlessly by large U.S. Army forces seeking revenge. "The Lakota were on the anvil of civilization, and the hammer of American destructive power fell full force upon them,"[8] wrote one historian. Within a year, most tribal members gave up the fight and gathered around the federal agencies.

Crazy Horse surrendered in the spring of 1877 at Fort Robinson in Nebraska. He lived on a reservation for a few months, but white authorities continued to view him with fear and suspicion. When rumors circulated that Crazy Horse planned to leave the reservation without permission, a military force was sent to arrest him. On September 5 the great war chief died of a stab wound that was inflicted under mysterious circumstances while he was being taken into custody. Sitting Bull thus became the last holdout among the Lako-

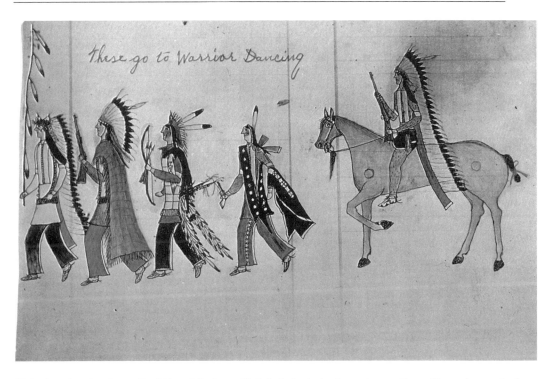

These go to Warrior Dancing

This drawing by Amos Bad Heart Bull, an Oglala Lakota Indian, shows Crazy Horse (mounted) and other warriors going to a celebratory dance after the Battle of Little Bighorn.

ta leaders. He avoided capture by taking 2,000 of his followers across the border into Canada.

Meanwhile, the U.S. Congress took advantage of public outrage over the Battle of Little Bighorn to grab more Lakota land. Even though Custer had attacked first, lawmakers claimed that the Indians had broken the Fort Laramie Treaty by going to war against the United States. They used this line of reasoning to circumvent the treaty and take control of the Black Hills. With the Indian Appropriation Act of 1876, Congress threatened to cut off all federal funding for food rations and annuities unless the Lakota handed over the Black Hills. "Your words are like a man knocking me in the head with a club," said Brulé Chief Standing Elk. "By your speech you have put great fear upon us."[9] This policy, described by critics as "sell or starve," left Lakota leaders no choice but to give up the Black Hills. This loss reduced the size of the Great Sioux Reservation from 60 million to 21.7 million acres.

The Lakota Reservations

The Lakota people, sometimes known as the Teton Sioux, can be divided into seven subgroups or bands: Oglala, Hunkpapa, Miniconjou, Brulé (Sicangu), Sans Arc (Itazipco), Blackfoot (Sihasapa), and Two Kettles (Oohenumpa). Toward the end of the nineteenth century, all of these bands were placed on reservations created by the U.S. government. The Oglala were placed on the Pine Ridge Reservation in southwestern South Dakota. The Hunkpapa received the Standing Rock Reservation, which straddles the border of North Dakota and South Dakota. The Miniconjou lived on the Cheyenne River Reservation in north-central South Dakota, adjacent to Standing Rock. The Brulé lived on both the Rosebud Reservation in south-central South Dakota and the Lower Brulé Reservation in central South Dakota. The Blackfoot were divided between the Standing Rock and Cheyenne River Reservations, and the Sans Arc and Two Kettle also lived on the Cheyenne River Reservation. Although thousands of tribal members continued to live on the reservations in the twenty-first century, many others chose to live elsewhere.

Unfortunately for the Lakota, white demand for reservation lands did not end there. Although the Lakota lost the entire western section of their territory in 1876, they kept a tract of land stretching from the Standing Rock Agency at the northern edge of South Dakota to the Pine Ridge Agency at the southern edge. Before long, it became clear that the reservation blocked the most direct east-west route to the gold deposits in the Black Hills. Miners, speculators, settlers, railroad builders, and politicians all demanded better access for industrial mining operations. They sought a corridor from Rapid City, at the foot of the Black Hills, east to the Missouri River. Of course, the proposed corridor passed right through the middle of the remaining Great Sioux Reservation.

Under the Fort Laramie Treaty, three-quarters of all adult male Lakota tribal members had to approve any sale of reservation lands. Government officials made several attempts to acquire land to build a railroad line across South Dakota without gathering the necessary Lakota signatures, but these efforts

Lakota tribes were pried off their lands in the Black Hills to make way for white mining towns such as Lead City, seen here around 1890.

were blocked by non-Indian reformers. Then the officials came up with a new scheme to take control of reservation lands. Under the General Allotment Act of 1887, also known as the Dawes Act, they proposed distributing a plot of reservation land to the head of each Lakota family. Anyone who claimed an allotment of land and lived there for twenty-five years would be granted U.S. citizenship. Once all of the eligible Lakota tribal members had claimed their allotments, the government planned to sell off any "surplus" reservation land to white homesteaders. The money from the sale of the land would be used to fund Indian education and employment programs. The Dawes Act gained the approval of non-Indian reformers, who believed that "the law would replace tribal ownership with individual ownership, get the Indians to farm, and solve the problem of what to do with them,"[10] as one historian explained.

In 1889 a commission headed by General George Crook met with Lakota leaders on the Great Sioux Reservation. An experienced Indian fighter and negotiator, Crook recommended that the Lakota accept the allotment deal or risk losing their land without compensation. "It is certain that you will never get any better terms than are offered in this bill," he declared, "and the chances are that you will not get so good."[11] Through a combination of

General George Crook was a tenacious Indian fighter, but unlike most of his fellow officers in the U.S. Army, he treated Indians as tough adversaries worthy of respect.

threats, promises, and bribes, Crook gathered the signatures of 4,463 of the 5,678 eligible Lakota voters, giving the allotment plan the three-quarters majority needed for approval.

Afterward, each Lakota family received 320 acres of land and basic farming equipment. The government moved quickly to sell off the surplus reservation lands, which amounted to 9 million acres. The overall size of the Great Sioux Reservation thus shrunk again, from 21.7 million to 12.7 million acres—or about 20 percent of its original size. Instead of possessing one continuous tract of land, the Lakota people were relegated to six small reservations centered around the federal agencies at Pine Ridge, Rosebud, Cheyenne River, Standing Rock, Crow Creek, and Lower Brulé.

Despair of the Reservation Indians

The land allotment program was merely the latest in a long series of government initiatives designed to force the Lakota to abandon their traditional lifestyle and become more "civilized." It encouraged Lakota families to settle on separate tracts of land rather than live in communal villages. It also attempted to turn them into farmers and ranchers rather than nomadic hunters. Other government efforts, instituted throughout the 1880s, had discouraged the Lakota from practicing their traditional religion and medicine and required Lakota children to be educated in government schools, where they were taught to speak English and assimilate into white society.

These programs destroyed Lakota culture and tribal identity and left the people completely dependent upon the government for survival. Educator Elaine Goodale Eastman remarked that the Lakota's last buffalo hunt on the northern plains in 1883 marked "the end of their independence as a nation.

There remained a confused, depressed, and humiliated dark folk ... subsisting literally from hand to mouth upon a monthly or fortnightly dole of beef, pork, flour, and coffee."[12] Although many Lakota leaders resented the government's interference in their lives, they found themselves powerless to resist. With few weapons and no access to their old hunting grounds, they required government assistance to feed and clothe themselves. The agents in charge of the reservation used their control over food rations to reward "progressive" Indians who cooperated with them and punish tribal members who resisted.

Even Sitting Bull eventually gave up his steadfast resistance and agreed to live on the reservation. After returning from Canada in 1881, he was held at a military prison for two years before being transferred to the Hunkpapa agency at Standing Rock. James McLaughlin, the federal agent sent to Standing Rock to keep Sitting Bull under control, worked to isolate him from his followers and reduce his power.

The Lakota who submitted peacefully to U.S. government authority did not fare much better. Although the government insisted that the Lakota become farmers, they lacked the tools, training, and desire to work the land. To make matters worse, the reservation land was poorly suited to growing crops. "Dakota is an arid country with thin soil and short seasons. Although well adapted to grazing it is not suited to agriculture," one historian explained. "Thousands of white settlers after years of successive failures had given up the struggle and left the country, but the Indians, confined to reservations, were unable to emigrate, and were also as a rule unable to find employment, as the whites might, by which they could earn a subsistence."[13]

Stuck on hardscrabble farms, with the buffalo wiped out and other food sources scarce, the Lakota became completely dependent on government food rations for their survival. As part of the allotment deal the Lakota signed in 1889, Crook promised that the U.S. government would maintain the current level of food rations. But this turned out to be yet another in a long string of broken promises. When the results of a federal census showed a smaller population of Lakota living on the reservation than expected, the U.S. Congress used the data to justify reducing the amount of money budgeted for Lakota rations by $1 million per year. Federal agents and non-Indian reformers argued that the count was wrong. They pointed out that many Lakota viewed the census with suspicion and avoided the census takers. But the U.S. government refused to listen to these arguments, and Congress let the budget cuts stand.

Lakota women and children wait outside the agency office at the Pine Ridge Reservation for government rations.

The reduction in rations took effect during the hard winter of 1889-90, shortly after the Lakota signed the allotment deal. At the Pine Ridge Agency alone, the beef ration was cut by one million pounds. Frederic Remington, a famous artist of the West, complained about the unfairness of the situation. "We are year after year oppressing a conquered people, until it is now assuming the magnitude of a crime," he wrote. "The short ration which is issued to them keeps them in dire hunger, and if starving savages kill ranchmen's cattle I do not blame them. I would do the same under similar circumstances."[14]

Within the space of two decades, then, the Lakota had been transformed from a proud, independent people following the buffalo herds on the Great Plains, to a broken, desperate people forced to depend on the U.S. government for their survival. During these years, they endured the loss of their traditional territory and way of life, the destruction of their tribal identity and culture, and a steady deterioration in their living conditions. By 1890 they were even facing starvation. It is hardly surprising, therefore, that when a spiritual movement promising a return to glory swept through the reservations in 1890, thousands of Lakota seized on it as an antidote to their pain and misery.

Notes

[1] Mooney, James. *The Ghost Dance Religion and the Sioux Outbreak of 1890.* Lincoln: University of Nebraska Press, 1991, p. 824.

[2] Quoted in Clowser, Don C. *Dakota Indian Treaties: From Nomad to Reservation.* Deadwood, SD: Don C. Clowser, 1974, p. 169.

[3] Quoted in Di Silvestro, Roger L. *In the Shadow of Wounded Knee.* New York: Walker, 2007, p. 55.

[4] Quoted in Lazarus, Edward. *Black Hills, White Justice: The Sioux Nation versus the United States.* New York: HarperCollins, 1991, p. 82.

[5] Quoted in McLaughlin, James. *My Friend the Indian.* Boston: Houghton Mifflin, 1910, p. 168.

[6] Quoted in Viola, Herman J. *Trail to Wounded Knee: The Last Stand of the Plains Indians 1860-1890.* New York: National Geographic, 2006, p. 118.

[7] Quoted in Viola, p. 119.

[8] Di Silvestro, p. 56.

[9] Quoted in Hyde, George E. *Spotted Tail's Folk: A History of the Brulé Sioux.* Norman: University of Oklahoma Press, 1974, p. 255.

[10] Di Silvestro, p. 59.

[11] Quoted in Utley, Robert M. *Last Days of the Sioux Nation.* New Haven, CT: Yale University Press, 1963, p. 50.

[12] Eastman, Elaine Goodale. "The Ghost Dance War and Wounded Knee Massacre of 1890-91." *Nebraska History* 26, 1945, p. 26.

[13] Mooney, p. 826.

[14] Remington, Frederic. *The Collected Writings of Frederic Remington.* Peggy Samuels and Harold Samuels, eds. Seacaucus, NJ: Castle, 1986, p. 62.

Chapter Five

THE MASSACRE AT WOUNDED KNEE

⊸⫘⫘ ⌠ ⫘⫘⊷

There was no hope on earth, and God seemed to have forgotten us. Some said they saw the Son of God; others did not
see Him.... The people did not know; they did not care. They
snatched at the hope. They screamed like crazy men to Him
for mercy. They caught at the promise they heard He had
made. The white men were frightened and called for soldiers. We had begged for life, and the white men thought
we wanted theirs.

—Red Cloud, Lakota, 1890

In 1890 a new religious movement called the Ghost Dance swept through
the Indian tribes of the western United States. It promised followers that
everything on earth would be restored to the way it was before the white
men came, with abundant land and game, if the people performed a ritual
dance. The Ghost Dance originated with a Paiute prophet named Wovoka
who lived on the Walker Lake Reservation in Nevada. Also known as Jack
Wilson, Wovoka had lived with a white family during his youth and learned
the principles of Christianity (see Wovoka biography, p. 152).

On New Year's Day 1889, a total eclipse of the sun occurred in the western United States. As this unusual and startling event unfolded, Wovoka suddenly became terribly ill with a high fever. Delirious, he returned to his home
and fell unconscious. During this period, Wovoka said that he experienced a
powerful dream or vision. "When the sun died, I went up to heaven and saw
God and all the people who had died a long time ago," he related. "God told
me to come back and tell my people they must be good and love one another,
and not fight, or steal, or lie. He gave me this dance to give to my people."[1]

The Paiute prophet Wovoka, also known as Jack Wilson, introduced the Ghost Dance movement to the long-suffering tribes of the Great Plains.

According to Wovoka's vision, which he interpreted as a spiritual prophecy, God wanted the Indians to live peacefully together and perform a ritual dance. If they did so, God would reward them in the spring of 1891 by restoring everything in the world to the way it was before the white man arrived. Wovoka said that God planned to cover the land with 30 feet of rich soil. All the white people would be buried underneath, and only the Indians would survive. The fresh earth would be planted with trees and grasses, and vast herds of buffalo and horses would thrive there once again. All of the Indians' ancestors would then come back to life, and the people would be free to ride, hunt, practice their traditional religion, and follow their ancient customs. As word of Wovoka's vision spread, it generated a great deal of excitement among the Plains Indians, who had lost so much since the arrival of white people (see "A Lakota Indian Recalls the Ghost Dance," p. 187).

In the fall of 1889 Lakota leaders in South Dakota sent a delegation to Nevada to see Wovoka and learn more about the new religion. When the delegates returned in early 1890, they were filled with excitement. "My brothers, I bring you the promise of a day in which there will be no white man to lay his hand on the bridle of the Indian's horse, when the red men of the prairie will rule the world and not be turned from the hunting-grounds by any man,"[2] the Miniconjou delegate Kicking Bear announced to Sitting Bull's followers. Some Lakota were skeptical about the Ghost Dance and chose not to adopt it. But many others embraced the new religion enthusiastically. Already hungry and desperate, they decided that the glimmer of hope it provided was worth defying the reservation's ban on traditional dancing.

Near the Oglala agency at Pine Ridge, tribal members gathered in large camps during the summer of 1890 to perform the Ghost Dance. A typical ceremony started around noon and lasted well into the night. Participants wore white shirts made of cotton or buckskin with feathers on the sleeves and bright symbols painted on the front. The dancers joined hands in a circle and shuffled to the right, and then to the left, while chanting the Ghost Dance song:

> The whole world is coming,
> A nation is coming, a nation is coming,
> The eagle has brought the message to the tribe,
> The father says so, the father says so.
> Over the whole earth they are coming,
> The buffalo are coming, the buffalo are coming,
> The crow has brought the message to the tribe,
> The father says so, the father says so.[3]

As the dance went on into the evening, the participants gradually increased the speed of their dancing and the volume of their singing. The pace eventually became frenzied, until participants finally grew dizzy and fell down in exhaustion. Some people lost consciousness and experienced visions of the spirit world and their dead ancestors. When they woke up, they discussed the visions and incorporated them into the group's future dances.

White Agents and Settlers Panic

As it was originally taught by Wovoka, the Ghost Dance was a peaceful religious movement that focused on restoring hope and bringing happiness to the Indians. Although it foresaw a future without white people, it was not overtly hostile. In fact, it told followers to refrain from fighting and rely instead on supernatural means to achieve that goal. But each tribe that adopted the Ghost Dance changed Wovoka's original teaching in some way. The Lakota adopted a more militant version of the religious movement than some other groups. For instance, Lakota followers believed that the white "ghost shirts" they wore while dancing had the power to protect them from harm, including bullets. This conviction inspired some Lakota dancers to stand up to federal agents and Indian police officers.

White agents on the reservations watched with interest as the Ghost Dance took hold. Some experienced agents reacted calmly to the religious movement. They interpreted the Ghost Dance as an outlet that Indians were using to cope

This work by the famous Western painter Frederic Remington shows Oglala Lakota Indians engaged in the Ghost Dance ceremony at the Pine Ridge Reservation.

with the many blows that they had suffered over the previous few decades (see "A BIA Assessment of the Causes of Lakota Discontent," p. 189). They found the dancing relatively harmless, and they figured that it would die out on its own when the events Wovoka predicted failed to occur. But other agents viewed Wovoka's apocalyptic vision as a threat to their authority. They felt that practicing a mystical religion and performing traditional dances were incompatible with government efforts to civilize the Lakota and help them assimilate into white society. Many agents used reservation police officers to arrest followers and suppress the Ghost Dance. A few agents grew so alarmed by the Indians' strange behavior that they requested military troops to protect them.

Daniel F. Royer took charge of the Pine Ridge Agency in October 1890. A pharmacist and leading citizen from the town of Alpena, Royer received the appointment because of his political connections to newly elected South

Dakota Senator Richard Pettigrew. Royer had no experience dealing with Indians, no knowledge of conditions on the reservation, and no understanding of the Ghost Dance movement. A journalist of the time described him as "destitute of any of those qualities by which he could justly lay claim to the position—experience, force of character, courage, and sound judgment."[4] In fact, he appeared so nervous around the Lakota when he assumed his post at Pine Ridge that he earned the nickname Young Man Afraid of Indians.

Shortly after Royer arrived at Pine Ridge, the Bureau of Indian Affairs took some action to address the Ghost Dance phenomenon. It asked all of its agents to compile lists of Indian "troublemakers" who might need to be removed from their reservations in order to maintain order and security. Royer sent a list of sixty-four names, while the agents at the other five Lakota reservations sent a combined total of fifteen. Royer also sent a stream of panicky telegrams to Washington, D.C., demanding military intervention. "Indians are dancing in the snow and are wild and crazy," he wrote in November 1890. "I have fully informed you that the employees and the government property at this agency have no protection and are at the mercy of the Ghost Dancers.... We need protection and we need it now. The leaders should be arrested and confined at some military post until the matter is quieted, and this should be done at once."[5]

> *"Indians are dancing in the snow and are wild and crazy," Indian Agent Daniel F. Royer wrote in November 1890. "We need protection and we need it now."*

Rumors of strange dances, mystical visions, and potentially hostile Indians soon attracted widespread attention. Reporters flocked to South Dakota to see what all the fuss was about. Many newspapers published sensational stories about the Indians' behavior that served to increase fears. "Settlers on the farms and ranches south of Mandan are fleeing their homes, believing that an Indian uprising is at hand," the *Chicago Tribune* reported on November 16, 1890. "They urgently demand protection and many a farmhouse in North Dakota will soon be deserted unless the settlers receive some assurance that they will not be left to the mercy of the murderous redskins, who are now whetting their knives in anticipation of the moment when they begin their bloody work."[6]

A few writers protested against such irresponsible journalism. One local reporter who actually visited the Pine Ridge Agency found the Oglala going about their business in a peaceful and orderly fashion. Nevertheless, concerns about the Ghost Dance escalated into full-fledged terror among white settlers on the plains. "The panic among the frontier settlers of both Dakotas, Nebraska, and Iowa was something ludicrous," noted ethnologist James Mooney. "The inhabitants worked themselves into such a high panic that ranches and even whole villages were temporarily abandoned and the people flocked into the railroad cities with vivid stories of murder, scalping, and desolation that had no foundation whatever in fact."[7]

On November 17 the U.S. government finally responded to the growing tension surrounding the Ghost Dance movement by sending military troops to South Dakota. The authorities decided that a display of overwhelming force was necessary to prevent an all-out Indian uprising and reassure white communities. They dedicated one-third of the U.S. Army—the largest muster of military force since the Civil War (1861-65)—to occupying reservations where the Ghost Dance religion had taken hold. Although the arrival of troops convinced some frightened Lakota to stop dancing and report to the nearest agency, many others decided to stay as far away from the soldiers as possible. Thousands of Lakota fled to the Badlands, a rugged, rocky region north of Pine Ridge, to hide out until the Ghost Dance prophecy came true.

The Death of Sitting Bull

Sitting Bull had arrived at the Hunkpapa agency at Standing Rock in 1883, after returning from Canada and spending two years in a military prison. In the fall of 1890 he remained one of the most influential Lakota leaders. He and about 250 followers lived in cabins along the Grand River and maintained a degree of independence. Although Sitting Bull kept livestock and did some farming, he also refused to give up many of his people's traditions and customs. His defiant attitude kept him at odds with Major James McLaughlin, the longtime agent in charge of Standing Rock.

When Kicking Bear first brought the Ghost Dance to Standing Rock, Sitting Bull harbored some doubts about Wovoka's prophecy. He set his personal feelings aside, though, and allowed his followers to learn the Ghost Dance. When McLaughlin ordered the dancing to stop, Sitting Bull grew determined to protect his people's right to practice the new religion. The situation soon escalated into a tense standoff between the two strong-willed men.

On October 16, 1890, McLaughlin sent tribal police officers to escort Kicking Bear off of the Standing Rock reservation. Even after Kicking Bear left, however, the Ghost Dance continued to be practiced among the Hunkpapa. McLaughlin eventually decided that the only way to stop the Ghost Dance was to arrest Sitting Bull and send him back to prison. "Sitting Bull is high priest and leading apostle of this latest Indian absurdity," the agent wrote in a letter to the commissioner of Indian Affairs. "In a word he is the chief mischief-maker at this agency, and if he were not here, this craze, so general among the Sioux, would never have gotten a foothold."[8]

General Nelson Miles, the man in charge of the U.S. military forces sent to keep order on the Lakota reservations, came up with a plan to convince Sitting Bull to surrender peacefully. Miles suggested sending in William F. "Buffalo Bill" Cody—a legendary cowboy who had become close friends with Sitting Bull when they toured the country together in 1885 as part of Cody's famous Wild West Show—as a negotiator. Miles

The 1890 death of Sitting Bull, seen here in an 1885 portrait, further deepened white-Indian tensions across the Dakota territory.

arranged for Cody to travel to Standing Rock for a meeting with the Hunkpapa leader. But McLaughlin viewed the scheme as a dangerous publicity stunt that might cause unrest on the reservation. He arranged to keep Cody and Sitting Bull apart and went ahead with his own plans to arrest the chief.

Early on the morning of December 15, McLaughlin sent a 43-member tribal police force under the command of Captain Henry Bull Head to Sitting Bull's cabin on the Grand River. The officers arrived while Sitting Bull was still asleep. When the influential chief first woke up, he agreed to surrender and accompany the police to the Standing Rock agency. By the time Sitting Bull was dressed and ready to go, however, his followers had been alerted to the situation. When the police brought Sitting Bull out of his cabin, they were surrounded by an angry crowd. People shouted insults, brandished weapons, and encouraged Sitting Bull to resist arrest. In the midst of the confusion, shots rang out. The resulting clash took the lives of Sitting Bull and eight of his followers, including his teenage son Crowfoot, as well as six reservation police officers.

People across the country mourned the shocking death of Sitting Bull, who was widely known as the last of the great Indian chiefs to refuse to abandon his traditional ways. "The proud spirit of the original owners of these vast prairies inherited through centuries of fierce and bloody wars for their possession, lingered last in the bosom of Sitting Bull,"[9] South Dakota newspaper owner L. Frank Baum wrote in the *Aberdeen Saturday Pioneer.*

McLaughlin had hoped that taking Sitting Bull into custody would help put an end to the Ghost Dance and prevent a violent uprising on the reservation. Instead, the death of Sitting Bull and the arrival of federal troops in South Dakota created a panic among the Lakota. Afraid for their lives, thousands of tribal members fled the reservations. Many of Sitting Bull's followers headed for Pine Ridge, where they sought the protection of the Oglala chief Red Cloud. Many others headed for the Stronghold, a large plateau in the Badlands that could be easily defended in case of attack. Within a week, about 3,000 Lakota gathered there.

The Wounded Knee Massacre

Among the groups of Lakota on the move at this time was a band of Miniconjou led by Chief Sitanka, also known as Big Foot (see Big Foot biography, p. 121). After hearing about the death of Sitting Bull, Big Foot decided to make the 150-mile journey from the Cheyenne River agency to Pine Ridge. Although some of his followers still performed the Ghost Dance, Big Foot no longer believed that it was the answer for his people. He wanted to assist Red Cloud in his efforts to resolve the dispute between the Lakota and the government without further bloodshed.

Big Foot's band consisted of about 350 people, including 230 women and children. As they made their way toward Pine Ridge, they suffered from shortages of food and inadequate clothing for the winter weather. Big Foot became so ill with pneumonia that he was forced to ride in the back of a wagon. Nevertheless, government authorities viewed him as a threat. The Miniconjou chief's name appeared on the list of potential troublemakers maintained by the Bureau of Indian Affairs. General Miles worried that Big Foot's band might join the hostile Lakota at the Stronghold, or might start an uprising when they reached Pine Ridge. He decided that they could not be allowed to reach their destination. Miles dispatched U.S. Army troops with orders to disarm the Miniconjou and transport them by train to a military prison in Omaha, Nebraska.

On December 28 about 500 troops of the Seventh Cavalry—the same unit that had been crushed in the Battle of Little Bighorn—caught up with Big Foot's band at Wounded Knee Creek, about 20 miles away from the Pine Ridge agency. Big Foot tied a white flag to his wagon and told the army's advance scouts that he intended to surrender. The Miniconjou set up camp near the creek, and the cavalry took up positions nearby.

Colonel James W. Forsyth was the commanding U.S. Army officer at the massacre at Wounded Knee.

The next morning, December 29, Colonel James W. Forsyth took charge of disarming and arresting the Indians. He ordered all of the Miniconjou to assemble in an open area near the creek. He stationed his troops in a circle surrounding the area and placed two powerful Hotchkiss guns on the hillside above to discourage any resistance during the council. Then Forsyth asked Big Foot to hand over all of his weapons. Reluctant to leave his people completely defenseless, the chief told his warriors to give up a few older guns. Since he had already offered to surrender peacefully, Big Foot hoped that a token gesture of disarmament would satisfy Forsyth's demand.

The colonel had little experience dealing with Indians, however, and did not trust Big Foot. When the chief only offered a few guns, Forsyth ordered his men to search the Miniconjou individually as well as their camp. The soldiers found additional guns hidden under blankets, in wagons, behind the flaps of tipis, and beneath people's clothing. Forsyth confiscated those weapons as well as the Miniconjou's knives, bows, and arrows. As the search progressed, the Indians felt humiliated and grew increasingly restless.

At one point a medicine man named Yellow Bird began performing the Ghost Dance in protest. He encouraged the Miniconjou to stand up to the soldiers, reminding them that their Ghost Shirts would protect them from harm. "Do not be afraid," he declared. "I have assurance that the soldier bul-

An undated photograph of Chief Big Foot of the Miniconjou band of Lakota.

lets cannot penetrate us; the prairie is large and the bullets will not go toward you; they will not penetrate us."[10] Yellow Bird's actions put Forsyth and his soldiers on edge. Since they could not understand the medicine man's words, they worried that he was calling for the band's warriors to attack.

The tense situation exploded into violence a few moments later, when a deaf Indian named Black Coyote responded defiantly to the soldiers' efforts to disarm him by holding his rifle over his head. During a scuffle over the gun, it went off. The troops immediately opened fire on the assembled Indians. Big Foot was among the first to be killed. Some Miniconjou warriors tried to fight back, but most had already surrendered their guns and were soon cut down by the soldiers surrounding the area.

As soon as the shooting began, the Miniconjou women and children ran for their lives. Many took cover in a dry ravine, where they desperately tried to dig protective holes in the frozen earth. But they were targeted by the Hotchkiss rapid-fire cannons perched on the hillside, which rained down two-pound explosive shells at a rate of fifty per minute. Many other Miniconjou kept on running, but the cavalry set off in pursuit and shot everyone they caught, including women and children. "We tried to run," recalled Louise Weasel Bear, "but they shot us like we were buffalo."[11] In fact, the soldiers chased down fleeing survivors for the next couple of hours (see "Black Elk Recounts the Massacre at Wounded Knee," p. 192). Some bodies were later found up to three miles away from the site of the original fight. "There can be no question that the pursuit was simply a massacre," wrote ethnologist James Mooney, "where fleeing women, with infants in their arms, were shot down after resistance had ceased and when almost every warrior was stretched dead or dying on the ground."[12]

Counting the Dead

When the shooting finally ended, Forsyth ordered his soldiers to load the wounded into wagons and take them to the Pine Ridge agency. A blizzard blew into the area in the late afternoon, which made it difficult for the cavalry

Lost Bird Survives the Wounded Knee Massacre

When a group of Lakota returned to the site of the Wounded Knee Massacre following a three-day blizzard, they were shocked to hear a baby crying. They found a healthy infant girl who had been sheltered from the elements by her mother's dead body. She wore a tiny cap decorated with beads in the shape of an American flag. One woman named the baby Zintkala Nuni, meaning "Lost Bird." The remarkable story of her survival appeared in newspapers across the country.

Lost Bird was soon adopted by Brigadier General Leonard Colby, whose army regiment had been called to South Dakota following Wounded Knee, and his wife Clara, a leading activist in the women's suffrage movement. Clara Colby frequently published cheerful updates about her young daughter in suffragist newspapers. Although her adoptive parents gave her a privileged upbringing, Lost Bird struggled to adapt to white society and was often the victim of racism. She developed emotional and behavioral problems that resulted in her being expelled from several schools. Clara Colby eventually realized that the child should have been allowed to remain on the reservation. "She has been sinned against in being taken from her proper surroundings," she wrote of Lost Bird.

At sixteen Lost Bird ran away from home and found work in a Wild West Show. Longing to connect with her Indian roots, she often visited reservations. With no understanding of the Lakota language, culture, or manners, however, she found it impossible to fit in. Over the next decade, Lost Bird married several times and gave birth to a son, whom she gave up to be raised by an Indian woman. She lived mostly in California, where she appeared as an extra in silent movie Westerns and performed in saloons and dance halls. Lost Bird eventually contracted a venereal disease that affected her eyesight. On February 14, 1920, her short, unhappy life ended after 29 years as a result of heart problems related to the venereal disease. In 1991 the Lakota Nation recovered Lost Bird's remains and brought them back to Pine Ridge. Following a traditional ceremony intended to release her spirit, they laid her to rest near the mass grave at Wounded Knee.

Sources: Flood, Renee Sansom. *Lost Bird of Wounded Knee: Spirit of the Lakota.* New York: Scribner, 1995.
Smith, Gene. "Lost Bird." *American Heritage*, April 1996. Available online at http://www.americanheritage.com/articles/magazine/ah/1996/2/1996_2_38.shtml.

to locate and transport survivors. Fifty-one wounded Lakota eventually were deposited at Pine Ridge, where the church was transformed into a makeshift hospital. "We laid the poor creatures side by side in rows, and the night was devoted to caring for them as best we could," recalled Charles Eastman, a doctor on the reservation. "Many were frightfully torn by pieces of shells, and the suffering was terrible."[13] Seven people later died of their injuries.

The Lakota at Pine Ridge, already on edge from hearing the sound of cannon fire in the distance, grew terrified when the wounded began to arrive. Hundreds of people hurriedly packed up their belongings and left the agency. Scattered raids and fighting took place throughout the reservation and surrounding areas. On December 30 a group of Lakota warriors ambushed members of the Seventh Cavalry along White Clay Creek, about seventeen miles north of Pine Ridge. General Miles quickly sent an additional 3,500 troops to South Dakota to restore order.

On January 1, 1891, when the blizzard finally subsided, Eastman accompanied a group of 100 Lakota to Wounded Knee to search for survivors (see "Looking for Survivors at Wounded Knee," p. 197). The search party found a woman named Blue Whirlwind and her two young sons. Although all three had suffered shrapnel wounds in the massacre, they had survived three days in the snow with no food or water. The search party also found a healthy infant girl who had been shielded from the elements by her mother's dead body (see "Lost Bird Survives the Wounded Knee Massacre," p. 73).

Mostly, though, the search party found dead bodies frozen in the snow. On January 3, a group of U.S. Army soldiers dug a large trench—fifty feet long and six feet wide—on the hill where the Hotchkiss guns had been placed during the massacre. The site became known as Cemetery Hill. They buried 146 Lakota bodies in it, including 44 women, 18 children, and Big Foot himself. Most of the bodies were stripped of clothing and jewelry before they were buried, and some of the soldiers posed for pictures with the corpses. "It was a thing to melt the heart of a man, if it was of stone, to see those little children, with their bodies shot to pieces, thrown naked into the pit,"[14] one member of the burial party recalled. The Lakota were not allowed to say prayers for the dead or conduct any traditional burial ceremonies. The gravesite remained unmarked until 1907, when the Lakota Nation built a fence around it and erected a monument.

The frozen body of Big Foot in the aftermath of the Wounded Knee Massacre.

At the time, official government reports claimed that 153 Lakota had been killed at Wounded Knee (146 who were buried at the site and 7 who died at Pine Ridge). The reports also noted the loss of 25 U.S. Army soldiers, most of whom were killed accidentally by bullets or explosive shells fired by their fellow soldiers. Later investigations, however, indicated that the number of Indians killed was much higher, probably between 250 and 300 people. Many of the bodies had already been removed by relatives by the time the soldiers came back to bury them.

A Massacre Disguised as a Battle

Unlike many other episodes in the decades-long conflict between the Lakota and the U.S. government, the massacre at Wounded Knee received a great deal of attention nationwide. A number of newspaper and magazine reporters were already at Pine Ridge to cover the Ghost Dance controversy, and three newsmen actually witnessed the events at Wounded Knee. The well-known Western artist Frederic Remington was on hand when the wounded began arriving at Pine

Ridge, and he published a series of sketches based on eyewitness accounts. In addition, a photographer from Chadron, Nebraska, accompanied the search party to the site of the massacre on New Year's Day. He took shocking pictures of the mangled, frozen bodies of dead Indians, including one of Big Foot. He also captured images of soldiers posing at the mass grave.

The wealth of detailed stories and images surrounding the events at Wounded Knee greatly troubled the American people. Some people insisted that Big Foot's band was uncooperative and dangerous, so the soldiers had a right to defend themselves. But many others argued that the army overreacted and committed a senseless atrocity. They pointed out that the Miniconjou were tired, hungry, outnumbered, mostly unarmed, and had already agreed to surrender when the fight broke out.

The Bureau of Indian Affairs initially described what happened at Wounded Knee as a battle. As the testimony of survivors and eyewitnesses revealed that dozens of unarmed women and children had been killed as they fled the scene, though, the incident quickly became known as a massacre. Some observers suggested that the Seventh Cavalry may have engaged in indiscriminate killing in revenge for Custer's loss in the Battle of Little Bighorn. "From the fact that so many women and children were killed, and that their bodies were found far from the scene of action, and as though they were shot down while flying, it would look as though blind rage had been at work,"[15] noted one historian.

Miles publicly condemned the Seventh Cavalry's actions at Wounded Knee. He also relieved Forsyth of command and ordered an official inquiry into the incident. The soldiers who fought under Forsyth defended the colonel's decision to disarm the Miniconjou. They also claimed that they found it difficult to distinguish between armed warriors and unarmed women and children in the confusion of battle. In the end, Forsyth was exonerated of wrongdoing and reinstated to his previous rank and command. In addition, seventeen members of the Seventh Cavalry later received the Congressional Medal of Honor for heroism in combat at Wounded Knee.

The massacre at Wounded Knee was the last major episode in four centuries of conflict between American Indians and white settlers. The high costs of defying the reservation system and resisting assimilation into white society were made clear on that bloody morning. All across the West, Indians gave up the Ghost Dance and resigned themselves to the realities of their new way of life. Even Wovoka disavowed the Ghost Dance after hearing about the

L. Frank Baum Calls for Extermination of the Indians

L. Frank Baum is best known as the author of the classic 1900 children's book *The Wonderful Wizard of Oz.* A decade before its publication, though, he lived in South Dakota and published a small newspaper called the *Aberdeen Saturday Pioneer.* Like many white people living on the western frontier at that time, Baum held racist attitudes toward American Indians. On January 3, 1891, a few days after the Wounded Knee Massacre, he wrote the following editorial calling for their total extermination:

> The peculiar policy of the government in employing so weak and vacillating a person as General [Nelson] Miles to look after the uneasy Indians, has resulted in a terrible loss of blood to our soldiers, and a battle which, at best, is a disgrace to the war department. There has been plenty of time for prompt and decisive measures, the employment of which would have prevented this disaster.
>
> The PIONEER has before declared that our only safety depends upon the total extermination of the Indians. Having wronged them for centuries we had better, in order to protect our civilization, follow it up by one more wrong and wipe these untamed and untamable creatures from the face of the earth. In this lies safety for our settlers and the soldiers who are under incompetent commands. Otherwise, we may expect future years to be as full of trouble with the redskins as those have been in the past.

> **Source:** Venables, Robert. "Looking Back at Wounded Knee 1890." *Northeast Indian Quarterly,* Spring 1990. Available online at http://www.dickshovel.com/Twisted Footnote.html.

Wounded Knee massacre. "Today, I call upon you to travel a new trail," he told his followers, "the only trail now open—the white man's road."[16]

The Oglala holy man Black Elk, who rode to the scene of the massacre from Pine Ridge, recalled years later how the tragedy had crushed the spirit of his people. "When I look back now from this high hill of my old age, I can still see the butchered women and children lying heaped and scattered along the crooked gulch as plain as when I saw them with eyes still young," he wrote. "And I can see that something else died there in the bloody mud, and was buried in the blizzard. A people's dream died there. It was a beautiful dream."[17]

Notes

[1] Quoted in Mooney, James. *The Ghost Dance Religion and the Sioux Outbreak of 1890.* Lincoln: University of Nebraska Press, 1991, p. 834.

[2] Quoted in McLaughlin, James. *My Friend the Indian.* Boston: Houghton Mifflin, 1910, p. 185.

[3] Quoted in Viola, Herman J. *Trail to Wounded Knee: The Last Stand of the Plains Indians 1860-1890.* New York: National Geographic, 2006, p. 172.

[4] Welch, Herbert. "The Meaning of the Dakota Outbreak." *Scribner's,* April 1891, p. 450.

[5] Quoted in Olson, James C. *Red Cloud and the Sioux Problem.* Lincoln: University of Nebraska Press, 1965, p. 326.

[6] Quoted in Landau, Elaine. *Cornerstones of Freedom: The Wounded Knee Massacre.* New York: Children's Press, 2004, p. 16.

[7] Mooney, p. 892.

[8] Quoted in Commissioner of Indian Affairs. *Annual Report,* 1892, p. 125.

[9] Quoted in Di Silvestro, Roger L. *In the Shadow of Wounded Knee.* New York: Walker, 2007, p. 84.

[10] Quoted in Viola, p. 189.

[11] Quoted in McGregor, James H. *The Wounded Knee Massacre from the Viewpoint of the Survivors.* Baltimore: Wirth Brothers, 1940, p. 106.

[12] Mooney, p. 869.

[13] Eastman, Charles A. *From the Deep Woods to Civilization: Chapters in the Autobiography of an Indian,* 1916, p. 110.

[14] Quoted in Mooney, p. 878.

[15] Welch, p. 452.

[16] Quoted in O'Neill, Laurie A. *Wounded Knee and the Death of a Dream.* Brookfield, CT: Millbrook Press, 1993, p. 55.

[17] Quoted in Landau, p. 39.

Chapter Six

AMERICAN INDIANS IN A WHITE WORLD

It is important to note that in our Indian language the only translation for termination is to "wipe out" or "kill off."

—Earl Old Person, Blackfoot, 1966

In the years immediately following the Wounded Knee Massacre, Indians and whites alike openly wondered whether Native Americans would survive the upcoming twentieth century. After all, tribes from the Pacific Northwest to the Deep South—and everywhere in between—had been devastated during the course of the 1800s. They had endured horrible population losses from white man's diseases and military strikes, terrible blows to their traditional cultures, and widespread seizures of sacred lands that had also served as their finest hunting grounds. By 1900 the entire population of native peoples in the United States had shrunk to 250,000, a far cry from the estimated 2 million Indians who had roamed the land three centuries earlier, when European colonists first arrived.[1]

Tribes Pushed to the Brink

For the Indian nations that managed to survive the repeated blows that rained down on them during the nineteenth century, the twentieth century offered little in the way of relief. Politically powerless and thoroughly demoralized by the loss of ancestral lands and ways of life, the fate of the Indians of the early 1900s was completely in the hands of the white man.

Some whites exercised this power to enrich themselves or advance their careers, without any regard whatsoever for the welfare of the tribes. Western politicians continued to court favor with white citizens by criticizing the Indian as an obstacle to "progress"—despite the fact that many tribal nations had long since been pried off their economically valuable lands and deposited onto remote scraps of reservation territory that whites did not even want. Reservation operations, meanwhile, were riddled with corruption. Manufacturers who received federal contracts to supply good blankets, clothing, or farming tools to the reservations quickly learned that they could get away with delivering cheaply made goods that fell apart within a season or two of use. And just as they had done two and three decades before, white reservation agents handed out lucrative beef contracts to ranchers who delivered scrawny, unhealthy animals worth a fraction of the price paid. The rancher then gave a portion of the stunning profits derived from these deals back to the agent. Similar "kickback" payments were made to agents who signed over timber or mining rights on reservation lands to white-owned corporations.

Another trend that rocked Indian tribes during this period was the removal of large numbers of children from their homes to Indian boarding schools. The first of these schools opened in Carlisle, Pennsylvania, in 1879 under the direction of Richard Pratt, a U.S. Army officer and veteran of the Indian Wars. According to Pratt's philosophy, the only hope for Native Americans was to remove young Indian "savages" from their families and tribes and "civilize" them in boarding schools that emphasized white values and standards of behavior. "A great general has said that the only good Indian is a dead one," Pratt declared. "In a sense, I agree with the sentiment, but only in this: that all the Indian there is in the race should be dead. Kill the Indian in him, and save the man."[2]

Pratt's school in Carlisle, officially known as the U.S. Training and Industrial School, became the model for other Native American boarding schools that sprouted across the country from the 1880s through the opening years of the twentieth century. By 1900, in fact, tens of thousands of Indians had been whisked away from their families to one of the more than 150 Indian boarding schools in operation (see "Life at an Indian Boarding School," p. 200). By 1910 nearly 500 boarding schools and day schools created solely for Indian children were up and running.[3] Some of these were operated by the Bureau of Indian Affairs (BIA); others were managed by private church groups.

Some boarding schools featured large numbers of children who had essentially been kidnapped by government officials. "[Authorities] very specifically targeted Native nations that were the most recently hostile,"

A group of Apache boys and girls enrolled at Richard Pratt's boarding school for Indians in Carlisle, Pennsylvania, 1886.

added scholar Tsianina Lomawaima. "There was a very conscious effort to recruit the children of leaders ... to hold those children hostage. The idea was that it would be much easier to keep those communities pacified with their children held in a school somewhere far away."[4] Reservation agents frequently secured tribal cooperation by slashing food rations to Indian families who resisted calls for them to surrender their children to the schools. Others used soldiers from nearby forts to round up students and stifle opposition. During one such event, a witness reported that "the men were sullen and muttering, the women loud in their lamentations, and the children almost out of their wits with fright."[5]

Other Indian parents willingly signed their children up for boarding schools, although they did so with heavy hearts. Since public schools were closed to American Indian children because of racism, the boarding schools often stood as the only education option available—and these parents recognized that education in the "ways of the white man" would be essential to their children's survival in the years ahead.

The main priority at most of these white-run boarding schools and day schools was to transform the identity of the Indian children. Their instructors worked systematically to wipe away all elements of native culture and instill a new set of skills and beliefs valued by the dominant white society. Students were given new "Westernized" names, told to forget their Indian names, and sometimes kept from seeing parents and other family members who tried to visit. School staff also forced them to cut their hair, punished them if they tried to speak their native language or practice their native religions, and made them dress in European-style clothing. Punishment for disobedience in any of these areas was usually swift and severe. The subjects taught at these schools, meanwhile, ranged from vocational training to basic instruction in reading, writing, mathematics, music, history, and Christian theology.

When not in the classroom, Indian students frequently spent hours engaged in manual chores around the school and in the surrounding community. Historians believe that this grim aspect of boarding school life steadily worsened during the first few decades of the twentieth century. "Both BIA and church schools ran on bare-bones budgets, and large numbers of students died from starvation and disease because of inadequate food and medical care," stated one Amnesty International study of the history of Native American schools. "School officials routinely forced children to do arduous work to raise money for staff salaries and 'leased out' students during the summers to farm or work as domestics for white families."[6]

Nonetheless, historians acknowledge that some children thrived in these schools, in part because some institutions had much more skilled teachers and administrators than others. Caring principals and teachers—even those who pursued misguided policies designed to eradicate tribal cultures—provided much safer and more secure environments than officials who despised Indians or saw the children primarily as sources of labor. As historian Roger L. Nichols wrote, "Some of the children came to terms with their alien surroundings, making lifelong friends there and creating their own 'underground' society under the noses of the school employees."[7]

The Disastrous Consequences of Allotment

During this same time, Indian nations across the country were menaced by the emergence of another sweeping government policy toward the tribes. This policy, called "allotment," essentially sliced up all the reservation lands that tribes had received into 160-acre parcels which were distributed—or "allotted"—to individual Indian families.

The allotment era had begun in February 1887, when Congress unanimously passed the General Allotment Act. This legislation was also called the Dawes Act in recognition of its chief sponsor, Republican Senator Henry L. Dawes of Massachusetts. Supporters of the law claimed that ending tribal ownership of reservation land would give individual Indian families more economic options and further encourage them to abandon tribal customs and adopt the ways of the white man (see "White Officials Call for Dismantling of the 'Tribal Organization,'" p. 183). The General Allotment Act also contained a provision that prevented Indian families from selling their 160-acre parcels for twenty-five years—a safeguard designed to keep poor Indians in need of immediate cash from selling their lands to predatory buyers for a fraction of their value. Finally, it promised to give Indians who embraced the "habits of civilized life" eventual U.S. citizenship.

President Theodore Roosevelt described the federal government's allotment policy as a "mighty pulverizing engine to break up the tribal mass."

In practice, however, the General Allotment Act had a crushing effect on American Indians. The law's dispersal of Indian lands to individuals deeply eroded tribal cultures, which had always been based on shared responsibility, communal decisionmaking, and doing what was best for the larger nation. In addition, once every family on a reservation received its 160-acre parcel, the United States opened any land left over for white settlement. This provision drastically slashed the size of numerous reservations across the country. The money earned from the sale of these "surplus" lands was supposed to be funneled into federal programs for the assistance of American Indians, but in many cases it was diverted into other programs or pocketed by officials and white business interests.

As the U.S. government moved to make the Dawes Act a reality, allotment became a slow-moving plague marching across the continent. The first victims were the Iowa Indians, who watched helplessly as 90 percent of their reserva-

An Indian Journalist Exposes Corruption

Gertrude S. Bonnin

During the 1910s and 1920s a number of Indian activists rose up to condemn the rampant exploitation of Indian tribes that was taking place across the West. One particularly notorious example of this exploitation came in the late 1910s, when valuable oil deposits were discovered on reservation lands in northern Oklahoma. In the months following this discovery, white oilmen and government agents worked together to swindle Indian owners of these lands out of the riches contained beneath the ground.

When the Indian Rights Association learned that Indian leases to these lands were being stolen or acquired for a fraction of their worth, it sent a Nakota (Yankton Sioux) writer named Gertrude S. Bonnin (1876-1938) to investigate. Bonnin had written many fictional works about reservation life under the pen name Zitkala-sa (Red Bird), but she was also a political activist dedicated to improving the lives of her fellow Indians.

tion lands—designated as "surplus" by government surveyors—was stripped away from them and opened to white settlers. Similar stories played out time and again over the next few years. The Cheyennes and Arapahoes, for example, lost more than 80 percent of the reservation land which, only twenty years earlier, the U.S. government had promised would be theirs forever.[8]

News of the program spread like wildfire from tribe to tribe. Once government surveyors marched onto their own reservations, Indian tribes had little choice but to await the outcome of their work. As one Hopi Indian noted mournfully, the sight of white surveyors moving across Hopi land sparked tremendous levels of fear and anxiety about the future: "During the last two years strangers have looked over our land with spy-glasses and made marks upon it, and we know but little of what it means."[9]

In 1924 Bonnin published her findings in *Oklahoma's Poor Rich Indians: An Orgy of Graft and Exploitation of the Five Civilized Tribes—Legalized Robbery.* The book became a formidable political weapon in later years in the hands of John Collier and other reformers seeking to improve the lives of America's Indians. As historian Tanis C. Thorne noted, Bonnin's work "included dozens of individual case studies and described horrific abuses.... [including] the heart-wrenching story of a seven-year-old Choctaw, Ledhi Stechi, who was kept in starvation while a guardian pillaged her estate.... When the child died, grafters descended upon her grieving grandmother."

In 1926 Bonnin helped found the National Council of American Indians. She also contributed to the 1928 Meriam Report, and she remained an activist for Indian causes until her death in 1938.

Sources: Bonnin, Gertrude. *Oklahoma's Poor Rich Indians: An Orgy of Graft and Exploitation of the Five Civilized Tribes—Legalized Robbery.* Indian Rights Association, 1924.
Thorne, Tanis C. *The World's Richest Indian: The Scandal over Jackson Barnett's Oil Fortune.* New York: Oxford University Press, 2003.

The so-called Five Civilized Tribes (Choctaw, Creek, Seminole, Chickasaw, and Cherokee) of the Oklahoma Territory were initially exempted from the General Allotment Act. Treaties they had signed with U.S. authorities over the years gave them sweeping powers of self-government that even land-hungry politicians were reluctant to challenge. But pressure to make the Oklahoma Territory a new state continued to build, and in 1898 Congress passed the Curtis Act, which abolished the tribal governments of the Five Tribes and extended the powers of the General Allotment Act to include them.

As the allotment process got underway, Congress passed other laws to push it along as well. In the early 1890s three different laws were passed giving individual Indian landowners the "right" to lease or rent their acreage to wealthier white ranchers and farmers. But the money they earned from these arrangements gave them barely enough to survive. Scholar Peter Nabokov noted that other Indians tried to establish their own small cattle and farming businesses on their plots of land, only to find that their parcels "were located in isolated corners of the old reservations without streams or underground water. Other Indians either lacked the capital to carry their operation over the long seasons before cattle or crops could be sold, or else could not get used to plowing and harvesting with unfamiliar equipment."[10]

By the beginning of the twentieth century, allotment policies were pushing large swaths of American Indian tribal lands (and the timber, minerals, and other natural resources located on those lands) into white hands on a yearly basis. Most white settlers, lawmakers, and officials saw this trend as a welcome indication that Indian assimilation into the dominant white society was taking place. In his first annual message to Congress in 1901, President Theodore Roosevelt even described federal allotment policy as a "mighty pulverizing engine to break up the tribal mass." The tribes themselves recognized that they were being pulled apart at the seams, but they possessed neither the economic power nor the political influence to stop the policy from going forward.

New Depths of Despair

Redistribution of Indian lands to white ranchers, farmers, and other business interests accelerated after 1902, when Congress approved a plan to let Indian heirs sell inherited parcels of land. This change blew a big hole in the Dawes Act's twenty-five-year "no-sell" prohibition. Four years later, Congress passed the Burke Act, which gave the BIA the authority to approve proposed sales of allotted land by "competent" Indians. Some of the Indians who subsequently received approval from the BIA to sell their allotments received reasonable compensation. But others were exploited by BIA employees and white business interests who worked together to take advantage of confused Indians, many of whom were convinced to sell their allotments for a fraction of their true value. And whether the allotments passed out of Indian ownership for a "fair" price or not, each transaction diminished the unity and cultural cohesion of the larger Indian nation. All told, historians estimate that American Indian tribes lost about 65 percent of their reservation lands between 1887 and 1934 as a result of allotment.[11]

As land loss and poverty stalked the reservation, so too did alcoholism and disease. Tuberculosis, measles, and trachoma—a contagious disease that can

William "Buffalo Bill" Cody poses with two Lakota chieftains, Red Cloud (left) and American Horse, who became part of his Wild West Show in the late 1890s.

cause blindness—were particularly fearsome problems. In the early twentieth century, in fact, trachoma infected an estimated 70 percent of Oklahoma's native population.[12] Death rates and infant mortality rates on Indian reservations also soared high above the national average. All of these factors deepened the widespread sense of hopelessness among tribespeople, many of whom still remembered a time when they had roamed freely across miles and miles of prairies, forests, and mountain valleys. Some whites empathized with the Indians and tried to arouse public interest in their plight. But most white Americans seemed to prefer thinking about the Indians as they appeared in Buffalo Bill Cody's popular "Wild West" exhibition show—as exotic relics of a bygone era.

The education system continued to cast a dark cloud over the Indian nations as well. Entire generations of Indian children were forced into white-run boarding schools and day schools that remained intent on stamping out all traces of native culture. By the 1920s, however, even some longstanding champions of this assimilation policy were second-guessing themselves. They had always maintained that as these children grew into adulthood, they would lift their people out of poverty and despair. But it became clear to virtually everyone that the fortunes of America's Indians were not rising, but were instead sinking with each passing year. In 1926 this realization prompted Secretary of the Interior Hubert Work to commission a major study of American Indian tribes and federal Indian policies. The findings of this investigation, which lasted for eighteen months, marked a major turning point in the history of the American Indian.

The Meriam Report

The 1928 release of the Meriam Report, officially known as *The Problem of Indian Administration,* came at a time when political activism among American Indians was on the rise. In the 1910s and 1920s reform organizations such as the Society of American Indians and the National Council of American Indians had been formed by coalitions of bright and talented young native doctors, lawyers, and journalists who were determined to improve the lives of all Indian peoples. These reform organizations promoted a wide range of causes for Indians, including citizenship rights, better educational and employment opportunities, and respect for tribal traditions and cultures.

World War I also brought new opportunities for the American Indian. Between 10,000 and 16,000 native men who had received U.S. citizenship through the Dawes Act served in the military after the United States entered World War I in 1917. Some of these men voluntarily enlisted; others were drafted into the military. But however they arrived, they impressed their superiors with their dedication, toughness, and skills as trackers and riflemen. Their collective wartime performance in service to the United States helped convince Congress to award citizenship to all Native Americans in 1924. (A handful of states, though, still resisted giving Indians full voting rights. The last holdout states—Maine, Arizona, and New Mexico—did not grant full voting rights to Indians until the 1940s).

These events created favorable conditions for the release of the massive Meriam Report, which was named after its lead author, social scientist Lewis Meriam. The survey blasted virtually every federal Indian policy as ineffective, and it characterized some policies—including allotment—as complete failures. "Several past policies adopted by the government in dealing with the Indians have been of a type which, if long continued, would tend to pauperize any race," the authors concluded. "It almost seems as if the government assumed that some magic in individual ownership of property would in itself prove an educational civilizing factor, but unfortunately this policy has for the most part operated in the opposite direction."[13]

"Several past policies adopted by the government in dealing with the Indians have been of a type which, if long continued, would tend to pauperize any race," the authors of the 1928 Meriam Report concluded.

The report also harshly criticized the Bureau of Indian Affairs, the federal agency responsible for oversight of the reservation life and Indian welfare. Meriam and his colleagues stated that health and economic development programs on the reservations were shockingly poor, and it documented widespread instances of physical and emotional abuse of Indian children in the boarding schools: "The survey staff finds itself obligated to say frankly and unequivocally that the provisions for the care of the Indian children in boarding schools are grossly inadequate."[14] Based on these findings, the members of the Meriam Commission recommended a complete overhaul of the BIA's programs and orientation.

A New Deal for Indians

The publication of the Meriam Report sent shock waves through the Bureau of Indian Affairs. Faced with clear evidence that American Indian nations were struggling for survival on a host of fronts, agency officials were forced to admit that the BIA needed to change the ways in which it worked with the tribes.

A few of the Meriam Report's reform recommendations were quickly put into place. More broadly, the U.S. government also began to shift away from its decades-long dedication to "assimilation" policies and convey greater respect for native customs and institutions. But major changes in federal Indian policy did not take place until 1933, when the Democratic administration of President Franklin D. Roosevelt took the reins of government.

Roosevelt took office at the height of the Great Depression, a period of terrible economic turmoil marked by widespread unemployment, hunger, and business closings. The Roosevelt administration had great faith that new government programs and initiatives—collectively known as the "New Deal"—could effectively combat the Depression and restore America's economic strength and vitality. Not surprisingly, Roosevelt and his fellow "New Dealers" also believed that new government policies and programs could solve—or at least relieve—many of the problems afflicting the American Indian. With this in mind, Interior Secretary Harold Ickes selected the reform-minded John Collier to head the Bureau of Indian Affairs in the spring of 1933.

Collier served as commissioner of Indian Affairs from 1933 to 1945, when Roosevelt died. During this twelve-year stint, Collier was a tireless advocate for the long-suffering American Indian nations under his charge. His crowning achievement was the Indian Reorganization Act (IRA) or Wheeler-Howard Act, which Congress passed and Roosevelt signed into law in 1934. This legislation, which Collier and other supporters described as a "New Deal for American Indians," dramatically changed the relationship between the tribes and the U.S. government. The IRA greatly increased the self-governing powers of Indian tribes, who were given the right to form tribal governments. It also authorized new funding programs to support Indian farms and businesses, overhauled education and health programs for the tribes, promoted soil conservation and other environmental initiatives on reservation lands, established an Indian court system, and restored Indian religious and cultural freedoms. Finally, the IRA ended the government's hated allotment policies once and for all, and it returned large expanses of unsold "surplus" reservation lands to the tribes.

90

Commissioner of Indian Affairs John Collier poses with Blackfoot Indian chieftains during a 1934 meeting in South Dakota.

Within a few months of passage, 181 out of 263 recognized tribes had voted to join in the provisions of the Indian Reorganization Act. The Five Civilized Tribes of Oklahoma initially voted against joining out of a combination of skepticism about white motives and anger that the bill did not grant complete self-rule. This was an important development, because the Oklahoma tribes constituted the single largest group of Indians in the country. But as the benefits of IRA acceptance for other tribes became clear, the Five Tribes reconsidered. In 1936 Congress passed a second piece of legislation, the Oklahoma Indian Welfare Act, which effectively included them in the IRA provisions as well.

Still, some nations refused to participate, usually because of controversy over the new tribal governments created by the legislation. Some critics complained that the new governments undercut the authority of traditional tribal

91

and clan leaders. Other Indians who had entered the mainstream of white religious and cultural life argued that the new governments amounted to "steps backward and away from Americanization," in the words of Nichols. "Most of this opposition caught the bureaucrats by surprise and worsened existing divisions within tribal communities," he explained. "Despite the confusion, debate, and rancor, most present-day tribal governments got their start under the IRA."[15]

Despite some tribal holdouts, by the late 1940s the Indian Reorganization Act was being touted as a milestone that revitalized the fortunes of the American Indian. It helped dozens of tribes launch successful new cattle ranches and other business enterprises and created important new health programs. It also transferred thousands of Indian children out of boarding schools and into new day schools on reservation land, which enabled them to continue living with parents and maintain strong community ties. The IRA also helped many Indian nations increase their tribal territory and gain greater control over the natural resources on their lands. Finally—and perhaps most importantly—it has been credited with nurturing a new age of ethnic and cultural pride among the various Indian nations. The Act "allowed at least a partial restoration of tribal integrity," wrote scholar Tom Holm. "It halted the allotment of tribal lands, permitted ceremonies to be held again, and generally attempted to preserve Indian arts. It thus promoted the maintenance of a tribal identity which was crucial to the continuity of American Indian values."[16]

Losing Ground Once Again

The pride and self-confidence of American Indians received another boost during World War II. From 1941 to 1945, when U.S. military forces led the successful Allied war effort to defeat Germany and Japan, an estimated 40,000 American Indian men and women supported the war effort by taking jobs in factories that provided tanks, ammunition, rifles, clothing, and other essential wartime supplies. Another 25,000 Indians served directly in the armed forces. The most famous Indian contributors to the war effort were probably the Navajo "code talkers" who helped the Marines defeat Japanese forces in the South Pacific. These Navajo soldiers developed a coded form of the Navajo language for use in transmitting vital military messages. Japanese forces that intercepted these massages were never able to decipher them, which gave U.S. forces an important strategic advantage during the war's final years.

Navajo code talkers like these two Marines provided invaluable service to the United States during World War II.

When the Navajo code talkers and other American Indian soldiers returned home after the war, they thought that the sacrifices and contributions they had made during the war might result in greater acceptance and respect from the dominant white society. Instead, Indian tribes found themselves fighting off another wave of potentially devastating policies and unfriendly bureaucrats in the late 1940s and early 1950s. The reformers that had controlled policymaking in Washington in general—and the BIA in particular—during the New Deal era no longer held office, and they had been replaced by lawmakers and officials who wanted to steer federal Indian policy in a new direction.

One factor in these proposed policy changes was the widespread post-war enthusiasm for new dams, highways, reservoirs, recreation areas, and other economic development projects. Many of these politically popular projects, though, required the sacrifice of Indian reservation lands. This was especially true in the West, where most of the major projects—and most of the Indian reservations—were concentrated. Indian nations fought off some of these proposals and preserved their lands, but others succumbed to intense state and federal pressure to sell. Possibly the most famous example came in 1948, when tribes in North Dakota reluctantly signed an agreement to sell 155,000 acres of reservation land to the U.S. government for the Garrison Dam and Reservoir project.

During this same period, reservation administrators and other officials within the Bureau of Indian Affairs signed leasing deals that gave white-owned ranching and mining operations bargain rates for using tribal lands. BIA officials frequently funneled the money that was generated from these leasing deals directly to their offices, then doled it out to the Indians as they saw fit. This was a humiliating arrangement for the tribes, which "essentially had to get permission to spend their own money," according to historian Charles Wilkinson.[17]

The most serious threat to the fragile economic, political, and cultural gains the Indians had made during the 1930s and 1940s, though, came in the form of a new governmental policy called "termination." This scheme essentially ended all federal support for the tribes, wiped out all of the government's treaty obligations to the Indians, and made all Indians subject to state and federal taxes and laws. Because of termination, wrote Wilkinson, the early 1950s became a "time of hopelessness, confusion, and fear in Indian country. Never had the age-old specter of the 'Vanishing Indian' come so close to reality."[18]

Termination and Relocation

The march toward implementation of the so-called termination policy began in 1950, when the Truman Administration named Dillon S. Myer as its commissioner of Indian affairs. During World War II Myer had directed the United States' Japanese-American internment program. Under this shameful program, more than 120,000 Japanese-Americans and Japanese living in the United States were forcibly relocated into detention camps following the December 1941 Japanese attack on the U.S. Navy Base in Pearl Harbor, Hawaii.

Tribal chairman George Gillette (left), who represented the Mandan, Hidatsa, and Arikara tribes of North Dakota's Fort Berthold Reservation, weeps during a May 20, 1948, signing ceremony in which Interior Secretary J. A. Krug (seated) signed a contract that transferred 155,000 acres of reservation land to the U.S. government for the Garrison Dam and Reservoir project.

Myer agreed with critics of the Indian-government relationship who claimed that the best way to "Americanize" Indians and lift them out of poverty was to end federal support programs for the tribes, treat the tribes as private corporations rather than sovereign nations, and entice natives off the reservations and into the mainstream of American society. They argued that if Indians were freed from well-documented BIA mismanagement and given the full slate of rights and responsibilities of U.S. citizens, they could chart productive and independent courses for their lives. In practical terms, this meant phasing out various economic, educational, and health benefits contained in the Indian Reorganization Act, turning responsibility for the reservations over to the states in which they were located, and implementing "relocation" programs that would coax Indians off their reservations and into big cities that were in need of labor.

Some proponents of termination sincerely believed that these policy changes would help native tribes. Other supporters, though, were motivated by bigoted beliefs that American Indians were a bunch of freeloaders who did not deserve "special" support from the government or taxpayers. This perspective completely ignored the history of white-Indian relations in the United States, as well as the terrible economic and political disadvantages under which most Indians existed, but it was a definite factor in Congressional deliberations.

The U.S. Congress began implementing the termination policy in late 1953 with a series of bills that dealt with individual tribes. The earliest tribes targeted for termination were the Menominee and Klamath tribes of Wisconsin and Oregon, respectively. These nations were selected because they were in relatively good economic shape and possessed significant natural resources that could be developed. Other termination bills quickly followed, and by 1964 Congress had imposed termination upon 12,000 American Indians in 109 tribes and bands.[19]

The termination policy, though, was a disaster for most tribes—including the Menominee and Klamath nations—from the outset. The loss of education, health, and economic assistance programs devastated the tribes, which did not possess the resources to fund their own hospitals, fire departments, schools, and other services. The imposition of state and federal taxes on their businesses and lands worsened the financial pinch, making it even harder for Indian communities to address rising rates of poverty, crime, and sickness. In the end, most tribes were simply not prepared to be treated as corporations rather than sovereign nations.

The "relocation" aspect of termination did not work as intended, either. Termination policies did succeed in pushing Indians off reservations. From 1960 to 1970, the percentage of American Indians living off reservations jumped from 30 percent to 44 percent.[20] Many Indians built rewarding lives for themselves off the reservation, but many others struggled. Some "urbanized" Indians floundered because they possessed limited education and work skills, others were victimized by racial discrimination, and still others found it difficult to adapt to city environments that were so unlike the social and geographic surroundings in which they had grown up. "Unfortunately," summarized scholar Philip J. Deloria, "relocation frequently involved nothing more than a trade of rural for urban poverty. Many relocated Indians soon made their way back to the reservations where poverty could be ameliorated to some extent by extended family relationships."[21]

Within a few years, termination was being attacked from all sides. Former supporters admitted that it was not working as they had hoped, education and health experts reported that it was worsening conditions in Indian communities, and social justice activists declared that termination was nothing more than a fancy disguise for government abandonment of a poverty-stricken people. As these groups urged the U.S. government to "terminate the termination policy," they were joined by Indian organizations like the National Congress of American Indians (NCAI).

Founded in 1944, the NCAI had quickly emerged as the most influential native voice on Indian policy issues in Washington. As momentum turned against termination, the NCAI leadership seized the moment. It argued that termination should only be applied to tribes that explicitly asked for such a change of status, and it further urged the United States to recognize Indians as *both* American citizens and members of sovereign tribes. In 1958 the U.S. Congress formally agreed that no tribe should be terminated against its will. Over the next few decades many terminated tribes, including the Menominee and Klamath tribes, were officially restored to their "pre-termination" status as sovereign nations. But by the time of restoration, these and other Indian groups had suffered heavy damage to their economies, land holdings, and cultures.

The abandonment of termination was a victory for the American Indian. But the entire experience left many tribes feeling angry, weary, and frustrated as they entered the 1960s. Around this same time, explosive social protests over African-American civil rights, the Vietnam War, and women's rights rocked the United States. These militant protests caused great disruptions

"Relocation frequently involved nothing more than a trade of rural for urban poverty," explained historian Philip J. Deloria. "Many relocated Indians soon made their way back to the reservations where poverty could be ameliorated to some extent by extended family relationships."

within American society, but they also forced the government and the public to take note of—and respond to—the protestors' grievances. Indian activists took note of this phenomenon, and in the mid-1960s they launched their own angry, confrontational campaign of social protest. This crusade, which documented centuries of abuse and mistreatment at the hands of white society and government, eventually returned to the streets of a small South Dakota village called Wounded Knee—the site of the most infamous massacre of Native Americans in U.S. history.

Notes

[1] Nabokov, Peter. *Native American Testimony: A Chronicle of Indian-White Relations from Prophecy to the Present, 1492-2000.* 1978. Revised ed. New York: Penguin Books, 1999, p. 259.

[2] Pratt, Richard H. "The Advantages of Mingling Indians with Whites." *Americanizing the American Indians: Writings by the "Friends of the Indian" 1880–1900.* Cambridge, MA: Harvard University Press, 1973, p. 260.

[3] Smith, Andrew. "Soul Wound: The Legacy of Native American Schools." *Amnesty Magazine,* Summer 2003, p. 14. Available online at http://www.amnestyusa.org/amnestynow/soulwound.html.

[4] Quoted in Bear, Charla. "American Indian Boarding Schools Haunt Many." *NPR,* May 12, 2008. Available online at http://www.npr.org/templates/story/story.php?storyId=16516865.

[5] Quoted in Nichols, Roger L. *American Indians in U.S. History.* Norman: University of Oklahoma Press, 2003, p. 155.

[6] Smith, "Soul Wound."

[7] Nichols, p. 157.

[8] Nabokov, p. 258.

[9] Nabokov, p. 249.

[10] Nabokov, p. 258.

[11] Weaver, Jace. "The Pendulum Swings of Indian Policy." *America.gov,* June 1, 2009. Available online at http://www.america.gov/st/peopleplace-english/2009/June/20090612143011mlenuhret0.8493159.html.

[12] Nabokov, p. 259.

[13] Brookings Institution. *The Problem of Indian Administration: Report of a Survey Made at the Request of the Honorable Hubert Work, Secretary of the Interior, and Submitted to Him, February 21, 1928.* Baltimore: Johns Hopkins University Press, 1928, p. 7.

[14] Brookings Institution, p. 11.

[15] Nichols, p. 184.

[16] Holm, Tom. "The Crisis in Tribal Government." In Deloria, Vine, Jr., ed. *American Indian Policy in the Twentieth Century.* Norman: University of Oklahoma Press, 1985, p. 140.

[17] Quoted in Wilkinson, Charles F. *Blood Struggle: The Rise of Modern Indian Nations.* New York: W.W. Norton, 2005, p. 9.

[18] Wilkinson, p. xiii.

[19] Wilkins, David E. *American Indian Politics and the American Political System.* Lanham, MD: Rowman and Littlefield, 2006.

[20] Nichols, p. 193.

[21] Deloria, Philip J. "The Twentieth Century and Beyond." In *The Native Americans: An Illustrated History.* Edited by Betty Ballantine and Ian Ballantine. Atlanta: Turner Publishing, 1993, p. 427.

Chapter Seven

THE LEGACY OF WOUNDED KNEE

Our languages are still strong, ceremonies that we have been conducting since the beginning of time are still being held, our governments are surviving and most importantly, we continue to exist as a distinct cultural group in the midst of the most powerful country in the world.

—Wilma Mankiller, Principal Chief, Cherokee Nation, 1992

The American Indian protest movement of the 1960s and early 1970s arose out of native anger over historical injustices, as well as dissatisfaction with termination and other federal Indian policies of the 1940s and 1950s. Like other social protest movements that shook American society during the 1960s, Indian activism was militant, confrontational, and—at times—simmered with the potential for violence. "As I look around at the Indian situation," Cherokee scholar and activist Robert K. Thomas stated in 1964, "it looks like one big seething cauldron about ready to explode."[1]

Important activist organizations founded during this period included the National Indian Youth Council (NIYC), which was established in 1961 by a group of young, urbanized, and college-educated Indians. Leaders of the NIYC included Clyde Warrior (a member of the Ponca Indians), Mel Thom (Paiute), and Shirley Hill Witt (Mohawk). Another major organization was the American Indian Movement (AIM), a radical group that was founded in 1968 on the streets of Minneapolis, Minnesota, then quickly established chapters in Los Angeles, Denver, Chicago, Cleveland, San Francisco, and elsewhere. AIM founders included Clyde and Vernon Bellecourt, Dennis Banks, Mary Jane Wilson, and George Mitchell, all of whom hailed from the Ojibwa (Chippewa) nation.

During this same period, hard-hitting literary works like Nakota (Yankton Sioux) author Vine Deloria Jr.'s *Custer Died for Your Sins: An Indian Manifesto* (1969) and white writer Dee Brown's *Bury My Heart at Wounded Knee* (1970) appeared in bookstores across America. Both of these powerful works reminded white and Native Americans alike about the historical record of U.S. subjugation of Indians. Deloria's essay collection also explained the demands and aspirations of a new generation of Indians to the rest of America.

A Pan-Indian Movement

This rise in activism was a response to continued terrible social and economic conditions on the reservations and in American Indian communities in U.S. cities. During the 1960s, for example, nearly 40 percent of the American Indian population lived below the federal poverty level—three times the poverty rate for the overall population. Infant mortality rates, teen suicide rates, homelessness rates, and crime rates were all far higher in Indian communities than the national average. In addition, many Indian nations felt that the few rights and resources they did possess were under constant attack from the federal government or white business owners.

Some of the protests that erupted out of these conditions were local in nature. Indians in the upper Great Lakes and the Pacific Northwest waged demonstrations to defend or expand their hunting and fishing rights. Tribes in the Southwest protested against new energy projects that they viewed as environmentally damaging or sacrilegious because of their location on lands that held religious significance for them. Mohawk activists in New York State demonstrated against longstanding and widespread discrimination against Indian students in the state's public school system.

During the course of the 1960s, though, many Indian activists came to see these local battles as part of a wider struggle that concerned *all* American Indians. This shift in perspective was due in large part to the fact that Indians who had left reservation life for the big city typically flocked to neighborhoods with large populations of Indians from other bands and tribes. This heightened exposure to Indians from other tribes convinced many urban Indians that their similarities were much more important than their differences. Before long, their longstanding emphasis on tribal self-identification was matched by a more general Indian unity.

100

Vine Deloria Jr. and His "Indian Manifesto"

When militant Indian activism soared across the United States in the 1960s and 1970s, Nakota author and activist Vine Deloria Jr. stood as one of its most important pillars. Deloria was born on March 26, 1933, in Martin, South Dakota, a small town near the Pine Ridge Reservation. His ancestors included both a French fur trader and a Nakota (Yankton Sioux) chieftain. After spending two years in the U.S. Marine Corps, Deloria studied theology at Iowa State University. In 1964, though, he decided to accept the executive directorship of the National Congress of American Indians (NCAI) rather than pursue a career in the ministry. During the next four years at the helm of NCAI, Deloria's work exposed him to all sorts of injustices and problems facing his fellow Indians.

In 1969 Deloria published his impressions of Indian life in America in *Custer Died for Your Sins: An Indian Manifesto.* The book instantly became a sort of Bible for the American Indian Movement (AIM) and other native activists of that time period. Writing in a simultaneously angry and entertaining fashion, Deloria spelled out all the ways in which Indian nations had been mistreated over the years. Yet he also painted American Indians as a proud and resilient people. As scholar Charles Wilkinson wrote, *Custer Died for Your Sins* not only "humanized" Indians in the eyes of whites, it also portrayed Indians as "survivors who endured wave upon wave of tragedy yet somehow never lost either their lightheartedness or the grit to preserve their ways of life. For Indians, *Custer* inspired empowerment and pride. It offered hope in a time when hope seemed the province of all in America save Natives. It allowed Indians to dream their own real dreams. There had never been anything like it."

In the three decades following the publication of *Custer Died for Your Sins,* Deloria became the nation's leading scholar on American Indian history, religion, and culture. As a lawyer, professor, and author he worked tirelessly to advance the cause of American Indians, both in the public sphere and in the halls of Washington, D.C. Deloria died on November 13, 2005.

Source: Deloria, Vine, Jr. *Custer Died for Your Sins: An Indian Manifesto.* New York: Macmillan, 1969.

Before long, tribal lines that had long posed an obstacle to Indian unity were being dissolved. Activists increasingly saw their crusade as a "pan-Indian" movement intent on working to lift the fortunes of every Indian in America. These protestors still treasured their distinctive tribal identities, but they also recognized that all native tribes benefited when they worked together to demand better treatment and policies from the dominant society.

Alcatraz and the Trail of Broken Treaties

The first American Indian protest event to attract sustained national attention was the 1969 occupation of Alcatraz prison, an abandoned federal facility located on Alcatraz Island in San Francisco Bay. The occupation was led by Mohawk activist Richard Oakes, who argued that an old treaty that granted "surplus" unused federal land to America's native peoples made Indians the rightful owners of the island. The occupation of Alcatraz attracted hundreds of activists, a wide range of celebrity supporters, numerous reporters from across the country—and a federal blockade of the island by the U.S. Coast Guard.

The seizure of the island initially attracted broad support from an American public that sympathized with the activists' complaints about historical injustices and impoverished reservations (see "Indian Activists Issue the Alcatraz Proclamation," p. 206). Living conditions on the island plummeted during the nineteen-month duration of the occupation, however. The island's electric power was cut off, and food and fresh water supplies became scarce. Two months into the siege, Oakes and his family left the island after his thirteen-year-old stepdaughter died in an accidental fall. Reports of escalating drug use and violence on Alcatraz also generated negative news coverage. Most of the occupiers left the island over time. On June 11, 1971, FBI agents, federal marshals, and other forces took over the island and removed the last holdouts.

Despite the problems associated with the Alcatraz occupation, many participants felt that the takeover had its desired effect: it publicized mistreatment of indigenous peoples by the U.S. government and inspired other Indians to join what some were calling the "Red Power" movement. Wilma Mankiller, who became the first female chief of the Cherokee Nation in 1985, agrees with this analysis. "The incredible publicity generated by the occupation served all of us well by dramatizing the injustices that the modern Native Americans have endured at the hands of white America," she wrote. "The Alcatraz experience nurtured a sense among us that anything was possible—even, perhaps, justice for native people."[2]

Image Courtesy IlkaHartmann.com © Ilka Hartmann 2010

American Indian activists demonstrating on Alcatraz Island, which protestors occupied in November 1969 to dramatize their anger over federal Indian policies.

Over the next few years, Indian activists staged more than seventy occupations of other federal offices and facilities across the country. Many of these political actions were organized and led by activists who had participated in the seizure of Alcatraz. The most famous of these events was the 1972 Trail of Broken Treaties, in which members of AIM, NIYC, and several other Indian activist groups traveled in a caravan from the West Coast to Washington, D.C., to demand new programs to help distressed Indian communities and fulfillment of various treaty rights. The cross-country journey ended with a six-day occupation of Bureau of Indian Affairs (BIA) headquarters by radical AIM members who vandalized the offices before leaving.

The impact of these various protest events and publicity campaigns on the U.S. government became plain for all to see during the early 1970s. Lawmakers in Congress passed dozens of bills that granted increased self-rule to individual tribes and increased funding for Indian education, economic development, housing, and other social programs. President Richard M.

Nixon expressed support for many of these steps, and his administration dramatically increased its own funding for college scholarships, health care initiatives, school construction, and other needs in native communities.

Return to Wounded Knee

These policy changes and funding increases pleased Indian activists, but they viewed these victories as only the first steps in a long quest for equality and essential quality-of-life improvements. In February 1973 these goals led American Indian Movement leaders to turn their attention to the Oglala Lakota Pine Ridge Reservation in South Dakota, where descendants of the victims of the 1890 Wounded Knee Massacre still lived.

AIM activists journeyed to Pine Ridge in response to two events. The first was a legal case in Buffalo Gap, a small ranch town near the reservation. The case involved a white man who had killed a Lakota man outside a bar. The man was charged not with murder, but with a lesser charge of second-degree manslaughter. Local Indians were outraged by this news, even though the slain Lakota man had apparently instigated the fight.

A much greater factor in AIM's decision to go to Pine Ridge, however, was a request for help from members of the reservation community who were engaged in a bitter battle with Richard Wilson, the Pine Ridge tribal chairman. After winning the chairmanship in 1972 in a BIA-managed election, Wilson had governed in ways that deeply angered and offended reservation traditionalists. He handed out jobs to friends and family, pursued schemes to sell off Lakota land for cash payments, and built up a tribal security force that terrorized and beat up his political opponents.

All of these actions by Wilson infuriated AIM leaders, but their decision to confront him also stemmed from the activists' longstanding belief that his position—tribal chairman—was not legitimate to begin with. According to this perspective, elections and the majority rule concept were instruments of government that the white man had unilaterally imposed on tribes with the Indian Reorganization Act of 1934. Traditionalists within AIM and the Pine Ridge community argued that this type of rule ignored tribal traditions of governance that emphasized group consensus and inherited authority. As one Lakota activist explained, the Indian Reorganization Act "tried to say they were giving us self-government. But as you know, self-government by permission is no self-government at all.... [The Act] placed us under a situation

A U.S. flag flies upside down on March 3, 1973, outside a Pine Ridge Reservation church occupied by members of the American Indian Movement (AIM) during their protest.

where we were ruled by a minority of Indian people under the guidance and direction of the Bureau of Indian Affairs."[3]

Critics also charged that politicians who won these elections were typically more concerned with acquiring money and power, and punishing political opponents, than with preserving tribal culture and independence. As historians Raymond Wilson and James S. Olson observed, militant Indians believed that "most tribal leaders were assimilated mixed-bloods [people of mixed white and Indian ancestry]" who were "willing pawns of the BIA.... Militants found [elected tribal leaders] to be conservative and subservient, representative only of rural mixed-bloods and not full-bloods and urban Native Americans."[4]

Showdown at Pine Ridge

The AIM activists arrived on the Pine Ridge Reservation on the evening of February 27, 1973. Led by Dennis Banks and Russell Means, an Oglala Lakota AIM member who lived on the reservation, a combined force of about 200 AIM members and local Lakota seized control of the small hamlet of Wounded Knee. They occupied the village's modest Catholic Church and several other buildings to publicize their demand that Wilson be removed from his position as tribal chairman. Federal authorities responded to this event by surrounding the entire village with a fearsome military force that included everything from U.S. troops equipped with armored personnel carriers, machine guns, and gas grenade launchers to members of Wilson's own security squad.

In its opening stages the siege at Wounded Knee generated huge amounts of sympathetic media coverage for the Indian protestors. The occupation remained front page news for the next few weeks, in part because heavy gunfire erupted on several occasions between the two sides during this time (two Indians were killed in the violence). As the standoff deepened, AIM leaders demanded federal fulfillment of longstanding treaty rights and a thorough investigation of political corruption in Wilson's administration at Pine Ridge. Federal negotiators reacted with vague assurances that the government would look into the protestors' complaints, but they did not commit to anything. The government recognized that as supplies in Wounded Knee became scarce and media coverage of the standoff faded, the negotiating position of the protestors would decline.

The tense confrontation at Wounded Knee ended quietly on May 8, 1973, when the U.S. government and AIM leaders reached a settlement after

71 days. Federal forces agreed to remove the blockade of Wounded Knee, and the Indians relinquished their grip on the village and departed. After the end of the siege, though, Pine Ridge remained a focus of Indian anger and discontent. The government did not review AIM claims of treaty violations, and it failed to undertake a serious investigation of grievances against Wilson. In addition, the U.S. Department of Justice filed criminal charges against Means, Banks, and hundreds of other activists who participated in the Wounded Knee occupation. Few people were convicted—and the charges against Banks and Means were eventually dismissed because of government misconduct— but the legal battle occupied AIM's time, energy, and limited financial resources for months on end.

In the meantime, many AIM members and supporters who lived on the Pine Ridge reservation died under mysterious but violent circumstances. These deaths were blamed on Wilson and his security forces. Before long a virtual "civil war" of arson attacks and drive-by shootings had erupted between armed supporters of AIM and Wilson's tribal police. All told, 69 AIM-affiliated residents were reportedly killed at Pine Ridge—which only had a population of about 15,000 people—and another 350 assaulted in a three-year period beginning with the February 1973 occupation of Wounded Knee.[5]

> *"Addressing what might be called our social and economic crisis on this reservation could be real difficult,"* acknowledged an Oglala Lakota resident of Pine Ridge. *"These things cannot be changed with the flick of a wand."*

The escalating violence at Pine Ridge prompted FBI agents to return to the reservation. Almost immediately, they became engaged in a gun battle with American Indian activists that claimed the lives of two agents. AIM member Leonard Peltier was arrested and ultimately convicted of murder in the deaths of the two FBI men. Many Indians and some white observers charged that Peltier was convicted on trumped-up charges and false evidence. The best-known argument for Peltier's innocence was penned by the well-known white author Peter Matthiessen in his 1991 book *In the Spirit of Crazy Horse*. Despite ongoing "Free Leonard Peltier" campaigns, however, Peltier remained in prison as of 2009—which is where FBI officials, South Dakota state officials, some Indians, and other investigative journalists believe he belongs.[6]

The American Indian Movement never fully recovered from the legal battles and public controversies that followed the Trail of Broken Treaties and the

The U.S. Government Settles Debts with Indians

In December 2009 President Barack Obama announced that the U.S. government had reached a settlement to conclude a longstanding lawsuit over royalty payments owed to American Indians. The dispute concerned land trusts first created in 1887 with the passage of the General Allotment Act or Dawes Act. This legislation divided tribal land into small parcels that were allotted to individuals and heads of families. The government held millions of acres of the remaining "surplus" land in trusts and leased it to private individuals or companies for livestock grazing, timber harvesting, oil and gas drilling, and other commercial activities. The Department of the Interior was placed in charge of managing the land trusts and paying the Indians royalties from the leases.

Over the years, the allotment program came under intense criticism. Many people complained that the Interior Department mismanaged the land trusts and failed to pay the Indians the royalties owed. In 1996 Elouise Cobell, a banker and member of Blackfeet Tribe of Montana, filed a lawsuit against the head of the department on behalf of hundreds of thousands of fellow Indians. The plaintiffs claimed that government officials had cheated them out of billions of dollars in royalties over more than a century. The case slowly made its way through the federal court system, with several different trials, rulings, and appeals. When Henry Salazar was appointed Secretary of the Interior in the Obama administration, it became known as *Cobell v. Salazar.*

Under the terms of the settlement agreement, the U.S. government agreed to pay $3.4 billion to compensate the tribes for royalties owed from the land trusts. Each participant in the class-action lawsuit was

Wounded Knee occupation. As AIM faded in importance, Indians expressed wildly different opinions about the organization. Some praised the activists as proud defenders of Indian culture and sovereignty. Others condemned them as undisciplined, publicity-hungry thugs whose actions sometimes hurt the cause of Native Americans. Many Indians who disagreed with AIM tactics, though, acknowledge that Russell Means spoke accurately when he stated:

expected to receive a check for $1,000 plus additional money allocated under a formula. The deal also created an Indian Education Scholarship fund of up to $60 million to improve access to higher education for Indians. Obama issued a statement praising the settlement: "As a candidate, I heard from many in Indian country that the *Cobell* suit remained a stain on the nation-to-nation relationship I value so much. I pledged my commitment to resolving this issue, and I am proud that my administration has taken this step today."

Not everyone was pleased with the terms of the settlement. Some plaintiffs expressed disappointment that the monetary amount was lower than they believed was owed to them. They pointed out that independent sources had estimated unpaid royalties at between $6 billion and $10 billion, while their attorneys had come up with a figure of $58 billion. Still, Cobell acknowledged that the settlement would provide desperately needed financial assistance to struggling Indians. "There is little doubt this is significantly less than the full amount to which individual Indians are entitled," she stated. "Nevertheless, a large number of individual money account holders currently subsist in the direst poverty, and this settlement can begin to address that extreme situation and provide some hope and a better quality of life."

Sources: Capriccioso, Rob. "Obama Administration Moves to Settle Cobell." *Indian Country Today,* December 11, 2009. Available online at http://www.indiancountry today.com/home/content/79058262.html.
Cobell, Elouise. "Statement on Settlement," December 8, 2009. Available online at http://www.fcnl.org/issues/item.php?item_id=3809&issue_id=112.
"Settlement Reached in *Cobell v. Salazar,*" December 8, 2009. Available online at http://www.cobellsettlement.com/index.php.

Before AIM, Indians were dispirited, defeated and culturally dissolving. People were ashamed to be Indian. You didn't see the young people wearing braids or chokers or ribbon shirts in those days. Hell, I didn't wear 'em…. Then there was that spark at Alcatraz, and we took off. Man, we took a ride across this country. We put Indians and Indian rights smack dab in the middle of the public consciousness for the first time since the so-called Indian Wars [of the late 1800s].... [AIM] laid the groundwork for the next stage in regaining our sovereignty and self-determination as a nation, and I'm proud to have been a part of that.[7]

Growing Momentum for Indian Rights

By the mid-1970s it was clear that the fierce political protests that had begun a decade earlier had set in motion events that benefited Indian peoples across the country. During this period, for example, the U.S. Congress "passed more legislation relating to Indian education than it had approved during the prior two centuries,"[8] according to one scholar. These measures included the Elementary and Secondary Education Act of 1965, the Indian Education Act of 1972, the Indian Self-Determination and Education Act of 1975, Title XI of the Education Amendments of 1978, and the Tribally Controlled Community College Assistance Act of 1978. These works gave greater education opportunities to Indian children, authorized new programs about native cultures and languages, and gave Indian communities greater say in shaping and directing education programs for their youth. Similar strides were made in the realm of religious freedom with the passage of legislation such as the American Indian Religious Freedom Act of 1978 and the Religious Restoration Act of 1993.

During this same period, Indian peoples increasingly replaced militant protest actions with lawsuits and other legal strategies to press their claims. Indian interests were represented in many of these legal battles by native and white lawyers from the Native American Rights Fund (NARF), a non-profit organization founded in 1970 to provide legal services to Indian tribes, communities, and individuals across the country.

By the early 1980s, American Indian tribes had won milestone court decisions that confirmed native fishing and hunting rights, strengthened the sovereign status of Indian nations, improved native education and health care options, established new native rights over water and other natural resources on their reservations, and forced state and U.S. governments to pay up on long-ignored treaty obligations. These legal victories, observed historian Peter Nabokov, "were often of more lasting value than colorful protests."[9]

Media and popular culture representations of American Indians also underwent startling changes from the 1970s through the close of the 1990s.

Stereotypical portrayals of historical Indians as bloodthirsty savages and modern natives as irresponsible children finally gave way to books, films, and other media that showed the complexity and richness of various tribal cultures. Several college sports teams that had long used stereotypical Indian nicknames or mascots abandoned them in favor of less offensive team names and mascots (though many other schools and professional sports franchises refused similar requests from Indian groups). During this same time, Indian musicians, authors, artists, historians, and entrepreneurs made deep and lasting marks on the wider American society. Many of their works explained both the pride and sorrow that colored Indian life in modern America.

Ben Nighthorse Campbell, who is of Northern Cheyenne descent, served in the U.S. Senate from 1993 to 2005.

American Indians also made meaningful inroads into the world of U.S. politics during this era. Inspirational Indian leaders such as Wilma Mankiller became known far beyond reservation borders. In Colorado, meanwhile, a Northern Cheyenne lawmaker named Ben Nighthorse Campbell served his country as a member both of the U.S. House of Representatives (1987-1993) and the U.S. Senate (1993-2005). Prior to Campbell, the only American Indians who had ever served in Congress were Ben Reifel, a South Dakota representative of Lakota descent (1961-1971), and Charles Curtis, a lawmaker of mixed white and Kaw Indian ancestry who represented Kansas in the U.S. Senate from 1907 to 1929 (Curtis also served as vice president in the administration of Herbert Hoover from 1929 to 1933).

White Backlash against Indian Gains

These improvements did not solve all of the many economic, health, and social problems facing American Indians. To the contrary, Pine Ridge and

A 1980 photograph of impoverished Kickapoo Indians gathered around a water spigot in their village outside of Eagle Pass, Texas.

many other Indian communities still suffered from much higher rates of unemployment, poverty, alcoholism, obesity, infant mortality, and crime than were observed in the general U.S. population. Johnson Holy Rock, an Oglala Lakota resident of Pine Ridge, explained that "addressing what might be called our social and economic crisis on this reservation could be real difficult because this is something that has developed over almost a century and a half. These things cannot be changed with the flick of a wand."[10]

These troubles became even more acute on many reservations in the 1980s, when the administration of President Ronald Reagan made major cuts in job training initiatives, housing assistance programs, and health services for Indians as part of a wider campaign to reduce government spending. Yet despite the poor conditions that still prevailed in many Indian households in the 1970s and 1980s, tribal victories in Congress and in the nation's courtrooms aroused anger and discontent from some white Americans. These critics argued that American Indians were receiving too many benefits and acquiring too much independence from federal authority. They asserted that such "special treatment" was fundamentally anti-American. Some white hunters, fishermen, and property owners, angry over growing native fishing, hunting, and resource rights, even leveled the charge that "Uncle Sam is giving America back to the Indians."[11]

This complaint was ridiculed by Indians and their white supporters, some of whom openly wondered whether racism was a root cause of the uproar. Organizations and politicians dedicated to rolling back Indian hunting, fishing, and land-use rights rejected this charge. They insisted that they were engaged in legitimate campaigns to preserve fragile natural resources and the rights of all sportsmen. Whatever the blend of motivations for these protests, they had their desired effect. Political and public support for American Indian claims declined in many parts of the country by the late 1980s.

The Rise of Indian Casinos

This reversal of fortunes angered and disappointed many American Indians. Numerous tribes, however, were able to absorb this blow and make continued economic, health, and educational improvements to their communities. They were able to do so in part because of casino gambling, an economic development tool that improved the lives of tens of thousands of Indians in the 1980s and 1990s.

Indian casino gambling originated in 1979, when Seminole Indians in southern Florida opened the first for-profit bingo hall on their reservation. Other tribes quickly followed suit, and dozens of bingo hall operations were opened on reservations over the next few years. Legal challenges to these operations were filed by various states that opposed legalized gambling on tribal lands. But major federal court cases like *Seminole Tribe of Florida v. Butterworth* (1983) and *California v. Cabazon Band of Mission Indians* (1987) confirmed that states had no right to restrict gambling on Indian reservations if they allowed it elsewhere.

Within months of the U.S. Supreme Court's 6-3 *Cabazon* decision, gambling options on Indian reservations exploded. Eager to tap into the public's growing appetite for games of chance, tribes quickly expanded their operations. In 1988 Congress passed the Indian Gaming Regulatory Act (IGRA), which gave individual states limited regulatory authority over Indian gambling operations—but also greatly expanded the games that Indians could offer to patrons. Before long, huge Indian casinos were being built to accommodate slot machines, poker tables, roulette wheels, and many other forms of gambling machinery. "After the passage of the IGRA," wrote historian Christopher L. Miller, "Indian gambling became a high-flying growth industry."[12]

By 1999, Indian casino gambling operations were raking in an estimated $6 billion annually—about 10 percent of all gambling revenue in the United States. Among the tribes with gambling operations, household income was one-third higher than it had been a mere decade earlier. In 2005, nearly 400 casinos and gambling rooms on Indian lands generated total annual revenues of $22.6 billion—more than what the casinos of Las Vegas and Atlantic City, America's two largest gambling cities, brought in combined.[13]

These gambling operations have funneled desperately needed income into hundreds of American Indian communities. Gambling proceeds have been used to build new schools, fund new job training and health programs, construct new sewers, streets, and fire stations, and pay for many other social services. Gambling income has also enabled some tribes to invest in other industries, from auto manufacturing and hotel construction to golf course development and gas station chains. In 2006, for example, the Seminole Tribe of Florida announced that it was purchasing the entire Hard Rock Café restaurant chain.

About one-quarter of the American Indian tribes with gambling operations also distribute some of their gambling revenue to tribal members through regular payments. In most cases, payments range from small seasonal bonuses to checks large enough to help recipients cover monthly housing expenses or help with college tuition costs. But a handful of very small tribes—about a dozen out of the 562 federally recognized tribes in America—distribute hundreds of thousands of dollars a year in gambling income to individual tribal members. These highly publicized cases have contributed to a mistaken belief among some white Americans that *all* Indians are becoming millionaires thanks to the Indian casinos.[14]

Indian gaming has also attracted controversy for other reasons. Some critics—both inside and outside of Indian communities—have condemned gambling operations for promoting an immoral activity that hurts individuals and families who cannot afford the financial losses they sometimes incur. Indian casinos have also been criticized for alleged ties to organized crime and for draining the economic vitality of surrounding white communities.

A 2003 scene from inside a casino owned and operated by the Mille Lacs Band of Ojibwa Indians in Onamia, Minnesota.

Native casino operators hotly deny these charges, and some white observers have rushed to their defense as well. Scholar Peter Nabokov, for example, wrote that "Indians [have been] shocked to discover that not everyone applauded their ingenuity at succeeding economically on their own—as the white man had badgered them to do for over a century.... American Indian gold, silver, timber, and fur may have underwritten the European Renaissance, bankrolled Europe's educational and commercial systems, and built the vessels that carried colonialism around the earth, but how dare American Indians make a financial killing off the same greed that had seen them dispossessed of their lands and natural resources in the first place?"[15]

American Indians in the Twenty-First Century

As the various Indian nations of the United States entered the twenty-first century, they have looked back on the victories of the late twentieth century with a measure of satisfaction. Those victories have included court rulings that have fortified their sovereign status and legal rights, notable improvements in their financial circumstances, and increased recognition from the wider society that Indian cultures and heritages are worthy of respect and preservation.

To be sure, American Indians continue to face daunting obstacles in their quest for full equality in the United States. Many reservation lands have little commercial value, and tribes that do possess significant reserves of coal, uranium, natural gas, timber, or water often struggle to balance the economic benefits of resource development with their traditional high regard for environmental preservation. Poverty, obesity and chronic health problems, violent gang activity, alcoholism, teen suicide, and low education levels remain critical issues in many Indian communities. When photographer Aaron Huey visited the Pine Ridge Reservation in 2004 as part of a project to document U.S. poverty, he was confronted by levels of poverty and hopelessness that he termed "emotionally devastating … I'd call my wife late at night crying."[16] Grim conditions on some reservations have even prompted renewed interest in off-reservation boarding schools, where administrators now encourage instruction in Indian culture and customs—but in a tightly controlled environment far from the drug and alcohol abuse that afflicts many Indian communities.

Indians also remain politically under-represented in many parts of the West, and they still suffer from everyday discrimination. In the wake of the Indian gaming boom, some tribes have also had to sort out false applications for tribal membership from people seeking a share of the tribes' gambling earnings. In Connecticut, for example, the Mashuntucket Pequot people, who own and operate one of the United States' most profitable gambling resorts, experienced a 50 percent surge in the number of state residents claiming Indian blood.[17] Finally, American popular culture has entered the living rooms of Indian families in ways that threaten to blot out longstanding native traditions (see "One Indian's Perspective on Modern Society and Traditional Ways," p. 210).

Yet despite all of these problems and challenges, American Indian nations persevere. Indeed, numerous tribes say that they have comfortably integrated with the wider American society without losing sight of their distinctive cultural heritage (see "American Indians Take Stock on the Bicentennial of the Lewis and Clark Expedition," p. 213). In many parts of the country, the future for the American Indian looks brighter than it has looked in

116

Members of the 4-Wheel Warpony, a White Mountain Apache competitive skateboard team, honor their ancestors by posing in traditional 19th-century Apache scout garments.

well over a century. "Against all odds, over the course of two generations, Indian leaders achieved their objectives to a stunning degree," wrote historian Charles Wilkinson. "Native people raised the standard of living, made advances in health, housing and education, revitalized traditional practices, solidified treaty hunting and fishing rights, and expanded the tribal land base. Now tribal governments, not federal or state officials, made the great majority of decisions on the reservations.... Indian people have accomplished what would have been unthinkable in the dark days of the 1950s. They have created viable, permanent self-governed homelands."[18]

Notes

[1] Nabokov, Peter. *Native American Testimony: A Chronicle of Indian-White Relations from Prophecy to the Present, 1492-2000.* 1978. Revised ed. New York: Penguin Books, 1999, p. 356.

[2] Mankiller, Wilma, and Michael Wallis. *Mankiller: A Chief and Her People.* New York: St. Martin's Press, 2000, p. 192.

3 Quoted in Josephy, Alvin M., Jr. *Now that the Buffalo's Gone: A Study of Today's American Indians.* Norman: University of Oklahoma Press, 1984, p. 217.

4 Olson, James S., and Raymond Wilson. *Native Americans in the Twentieth Century.* Provo, UT: Brigham Young University Press, 1984, p. 172.

5 Churchill, Ward. "The Bloody Wake of Alcatraz: Political Repression of the American Indian Movement." In *American Nations: Encounters in Indian Country, 1850 to the Present.* Edited by Frederick Hoxie, Peter Mancall, and James H. Merrell. New York: Routledge, 2001, p. 383.

6 Anderson, Scott. "The Martyrdom of Leonard Peltier." *Outside,* July 1995. Available online at http://outside.away.com/magazine/0795/7f_leo1.html.

7 Quoted in "Indian Activism," *Alcatraz Is Not an Island.* 2005. PBS companion website to the television documentary produced by Independent Television Service (ITVS) and KQED. Available online at http://www.pbs.org/itvs/alcatrazisnotanisland/activism.html.

8 Iverson, Peter. *"We Are Still Here": American Indians in the Twentieth Century.* Wheeling, IL: Harlan Davidson, 1998, p. 160.

9 Nabokov, p. 385.

10 Quoted in Chapman, Serie L. *We, the People: Of Earth and Elders.* Vol. 2. Missoula, MT: Mountain Press Publishing, 2001, p. 351.

11 Quoted in Nichols, Roger L. *American Indians in U.S. History.* Norman: University of Oklahoma Press, 2003, p. 207.

12 Miller, Christopher L. "Coyote's Game: Indian Casinos and the Indian Presence in Contemporary America." In *American Indians in American History, 1870-2001: A Companion Reader.* Edited by Sterling Evans. Westport, CT: Praeger, 2002, p. 197.

13 "The Last Shall Be First: Indian Tribes and Casinos." *The Economist* (US), April 14, 2007, p. 29.

14 Wilkinson, Charles F. *Blood Struggle: The Rise of Modern Indian Nations.* New York: W.W. Norton, 2005, p. 344.

15 Nabokov, p. 441.

16 Quoted in Estrin, James. "Behind the Scenes: Still Wounded." *New York Times "Lens Blog,"* October 20, 2009. Available online at http://lens.blogs.nytimes.com/2009/10/20/behind-22/?scp=2&sq=Native%20American%20Wounded%20Knee&st=cse.

17 Evans, Sterling. *American Indians in American History: A Companion Reader.* Westport, CT: Praeger, 2002, p. 228.

18 Wilkinson, p. xiii.

BIOGRAPHIES

Big Foot (c. 1820-1890)
Chief of the Lakota Band Massacred at
Wounded Knee

Big Foot, also known as Sitanka, was born in the early 1820s in northwestern South Dakota. His Indian name was Hoh-pong-ge-le-skah, which means Spotted Elk. His father, Lone Horn, was chief of the Miniconjou, one of the seven subgroups of the American Indian people known as the Lakota or Teton Sioux. Big Foot had three brothers—Frog, Roman Nose, and Touch the Clouds—who also became leaders of Miniconjou bands. His extended family included several prominent members of other Lakota subgroups. He was a half-brother of Sitting Bull, the Hunkpapa spiritual leader, and a cousin of Crazy Horse, the Oglala war chief.

During his youth, when the Lakota subsisted primarily by hunting buffalo on the Great Plains, Big Foot developed a reputation as an accomplished horseman and hunter. He also became known as a skilled negotiator who was often called upon to settle disputes between different Lakota bands. His diplomatic skills were put to the test when he succeeded his father as chief of the Miniconjou in the mid-1870s.

Pushed onto a Reservation

Around this time, the discovery of gold in the Black Hills brought white prospectors and settlers streaming into the western half of South Dakota. This land had been set aside as a permanent reservation for the Lakota people under the Fort Laramie Treaty of 1868, however, and Big Foot and other Lakota leaders were determined to maintain control over it. When they refused to sell the Black Hills, the U.S. government tried to force the Lakota to abandon their nomadic existence on the plains and become farmers on small plots of reservation land. Sitting Bull and Crazy Horse responded with a campaign of armed resistance that became known as the Sioux Wars.

Big Foot and his band supported Sitting Bull and Crazy Horse in their fight to defend the Black Hills. The Lakota achieved a major victory in 1876 at the famous Battle of Little Bighorn, wiping out an entire regiment of the Seventh Cavalry under the command of Lieutenant Colonel George Armstrong Custer. In the end, though, they were no match for the U.S. Army's superior numbers and firepower. The Lakota were eventually forced to give up the Black Hills and live on reservations.

Big Foot and the Miniconjou were placed on the Cheyenne River Reservation in north-central South Dakota. Employing his diplomatic skills, the chief encouraged his people to follow the U.S. government's rules and coexist peacefully with the white settlers. The Miniconjou took up farming on the reservation and became one of the first groups to raise corn in accordance with federal standards. The land was not well-suited to agriculture, however, and they grew dependent upon government food rations to survive.

The Ghost Dance Brings Hope

Throughout the 1880s the Lakota struggled to adjust to reservation life while also trying to preserve important aspects of their language, culture, and traditions. This task was made ever more challenging by the U.S. government, which consistently failed to honor its treaty obligations and continued to chip away at the remaining Lakota territory. By 1889 the size of the Lakota reservations had been reduced to 20 percent of the land area that had been granted under the Fort Laramie Treaty. To make matters worse, the U.S. Congress also decreased the amount of money it provided for Indian rations, leaving many Lakota near starvation.

Big Foot traveled to Washington, D.C., to represent his people in negotiations with government officials. He demanded better living conditions on the reservation and urged white officials to build schools for Miniconjou children. His efforts did not produce results, however, and his people sunk further into hunger and despair.

In 1890 a new religious movement called the Ghost Dance swept through the Indian tribes of the western United States. It promised followers that if they performed a ritual dance, everything on earth would be restored to the way it was before the white men arrived. Thousands of desperate Lakota, including Big Foot and his people, eagerly adopted the Ghost Dance religion in hopes of improving their lives.

Ignoring reservation rules that prohibited traditional dancing, the Lakota combined the Ghost Dance religion with elements of their own belief system to create a more militant version of the dance than was practiced by some other tribes. Some Lakota believed that the white Ghost Shirts they wore while dancing had the power to protect them from harm, including knives and bullets. Although some reservation agents felt the dancing was harmless, others viewed it as a threat to their authority and tried to suppress it. A few agents grew so alarmed by the Indians' behavior that they sent urgent requests for military troops to protect them from an all-out uprising.

Killed at Wounded Knee

In November 1890 thousands of U.S. Army troops descended on South Dakota in an attempt to stop the Ghost Dance and restore order to the Lakota reservations. As part of this effort, several reservation agents decided to arrest prominent Lakota leaders who had supported the Ghost Dance movement. James McLaughlin, the agent at the Standing Rock Reservation, sent a tribal police force to arrest Sitting Bull on December 15. A fight broke out between police officers and Sitting Bull's followers, however, and the influential chief was killed in the confusion.

The death of Sitting Bull set off a chain of events that put Big Foot and his band in danger. Many of Sitting Bull's followers fled south to the Cheyenne River Reservation to seek the protection of Big Foot. Fearing for his own safety, Big Foot led a group of about 350 Miniconjou and Hunkpapa refugees further south. His destination was the Pine Ridge Reservation, where he hoped to help the Oglala chief Red Cloud negotiate a peaceful settlement to the Ghost Dance conflict and avoid further bloodshed.

Big Foot did not complete his 150-mile journey. On December 28 the Miniconjou were intercepted by about 500 troops of the Seventh Cavalry— the same unit that had been crushed in the Battle of Little Bighorn fourteen years earlier—at Wounded Knee Creek, about 20 miles away from the Pine Ridge agency. Big Foot, who was terribly ill with pneumonia, tied a white flag to his wagon and told the army's advance scouts that he intended to surrender. The Miniconjou set up camp near the creek, and the cavalry took up positions nearby.

The next morning, December 29, Colonel James W. Forsyth took charge of disarming and arresting the Indians. After ordering all of the Miniconjou to assemble in an open area near the creek, he asked Big Foot to hand over all of his weapons. When the chief only offered a few guns, Forsyth ordered his men to search the Miniconjou individually as well as their camp. The soldiers found additional guns hidden under blankets, in wagons, behind the flaps of tipis, and beneath people's clothing. As the search progressed and the pile of confiscated guns—which the Indians used for hunting—grew higher, the Indians became increasingly restless.

At one point a medicine man named Yellow Bird began performing the Ghost Dance in protest. Since the soldiers could not understand the medicine man's words, they worried that he was calling for the band's warriors to attack. The tense situation exploded into violence a few moments later, when a deaf Indian named Black Coyote responded defiantly to the soldiers' efforts to disarm him by holding his rifle over his head. During a scuffle over the gun, it went off.

The troops immediately opened fire on the assembled Indians. Big Foot was among the first to be killed. As soon as the shooting began, the Miniconjou women and children ran for their lives. Some were targeted by the Hotchkiss rapid-fire cannons perched on the hillside, while others were chased down and shot by soldiers on horseback. Some bodies were later found up to three miles away from the site of the original fight. Between 250 and 300 Lakota were killed in what became known as the Wounded Knee Massacre. Big Foot and 145 others were later buried in a mass grave at the site.

This tragic incident was the last major explosion of violence in four centuries of conflict between American Indians and white settlers. It became a powerful symbol of the terrible mistreatment of native peoples in the United States. Modern Lakota commemorate the anniversary of the event by participating in the annual Memorial Chief Big Foot ride. Riders on horseback begin at Standing Rock on December 15 and follow Big Foot's route to Wounded Knee. The ride concludes with a ceremony at the site of the massacre every December 29.

Sources:

"Big Foot, 1820?-1890." *Oregon Coast Magazine Online,* n.d. Available online at http://www.u-s-history.com/pages/h3793.html.

"Chief Big Foot." *IndigenousPeople.net,* 2009. Available online at http://www.indigenouspeople.net/bigfoot.htm.

"People: Big Foot." *The West,* PBS, 2001. Available online at http://www.pbs.org/weta/thewest/people/a_c/bigfoot.htm.

Crazy Horse (c. 1841-1877)
Lakota Warrior and Resistance Leader

Crazy Horse was born in the early 1840s in the Black Hills of South Dakota. His name was Tashunkewitko in the language of the American Indian people known as the Lakota or Teton Sioux. Literally translated, it meant a horse that had great mystical or holy powers. His father, also named Crazy Horse, was a respected medicine man among the Oglala, one of the seven Lakota subgroups. His mother, whose name is not known, came from the Brulé subgroup. She died when Crazy Horse was young. He and his older sister, Laughing One, and younger brother, Little Hawk, were raised mostly by an aunt named Gathers Her Berries.

Limited details are available about Crazy Horse's early life. People who knew him described him as a quiet, solitary, and somewhat strange young man. He was called Curly as a boy because he had wavy hair. Like most Lakota boys, Crazy Horse grew up riding horses and shooting at targets with a bow and arrow. According to legend, he became an expert hunter and fierce warrior at an early age. He supposedly killed his first buffalo by the age of ten, stole horses from the rival Crow Indians at thirteen, and led his first war party before reaching twenty. Among his people, however, Crazy Horse was also widely admired for his generosity. When he returned from a successful hunt, he typically distributed food to elderly people, widows, and children of the tribe.

Goes to War against the United States

Crazy Horse came of age around the time that the United States began rapidly expanding westward. Wagon trains full of white settlers traveled across the Great Plains, which had traditionally served as hunting grounds for the powerful Lakota nation. As the flow of settlers increased, growing white demand for land and other resources created conflict with the Indians. In 1865 the U.S. Army began building a series of forts along the Bozeman Trail to secure the area for white settlement. The Oglala chief Red Cloud and other Lakota leaders were determined to defend their territory and prevent the forts from being built. Crazy Horse was selected by tribal elders to be a "shirt-wearer," or protector of the Lakota people. He thus became one of the foremost warriors in the sustained military campaign that became known as Red Cloud's War (1865-68).

For more than two years, Red Cloud directed thousands of Lakota, Cheyenne, and Arapaho warriors in a coordinated series of attacks designed to disrupt the building of the forts. His war parties intercepted shipments of supplies, harassed construction workers, stole horses, stampeded livestock, and surrounded and besieged completed forts. It was the most cohesive and successful military action ever waged by an Indian nation against the United States. Crazy Horse played an important role in many of the raids and battles.

In 1866, for instance, Crazy Horse led a deadly ambush of U.S. troops in the hills surrounding Fort Phil Kearny in Wyoming. Early on the morning of December 21, a small group of soldiers left the fort to cut firewood. Crazy Horse and a handful of fellow warriors attacked the woodcutters, who sent up a call for help to the soldiers inside the fort. A special force of eighty men, led by Captain William J. Fetterman, rushed out of the fort to rescue them. Crazy Horse and his warriors immediately broke off the attack, but they taunted the soldiers as they rode away. Although Fetterman had been ordered not to engage or pursue the Indians, he took the bait and ordered his men to follow. Crazy Horse led the troops over a ridge to a place where 2,000 Lakota warriors waited. These forces quickly surrounded and killed Fetterman and all eighty of his men. This incident became known as the Fetterman Massacre among whites and as the Battle of 100 Slain among the Plains Indians.

Red Cloud's relentless military campaign eventually convinced the U.S. government to forge a peace agreement with the Lakota. Under the terms of the Fort Laramie Treaty of 1868, the U.S. Army agreed to abandon all of the forts along the Bozeman Trail. The U.S. government also granted the Lakota a permanent reservation of 60 million acres west of the Missouri River in South Dakota, as well as free access to hunting grounds in Wyoming and Montana. Although Crazy Horse did not sign the treaty, he was willing to follow the course set by Lakota leaders. Determined to stay as far away from white settlers as possible, he spent most of his time hunting along the Powder River in Wyoming.

In the relatively peaceful years that followed the signing of the Fort Laramie Treaty, Crazy Horse became involved in a personal scandal. For most of his life, he had been in love with Black Buffalo Woman. But she had chosen to marry his rival, a warrior named No Water. Although Lakota traditions allowed people to divorce their spouses and form new romantic partnerships, Crazy Horse and Black Buffalo Woman did not follow the tribe's rules of honorable conduct. Instead, they ran off together while No Water was away. No Water tracked the couple down and shot Crazy Horse in the face. The bullet entered below his nose and shattered his jaw, but he eventually recovered from the injury. Still, the violent incident nearly started a war among the different Lakota bands. Tribal elders were so dismayed by Crazy Horse's selfish actions that they stripped him of his status as a shirt wearer. Black Buffalo Woman returned to her husband, while Crazy Horse eventually married Black Shawl and had a daughter, They-Are-Afraid-of-Her.

In 1874 a U.S. Army expedition discovered gold in the Black Hills of South Dakota. White prospectors and settlers flooded into Lakota lands in violation of the Fort Laramie Treaty. The U.S. government offered to purchase the Black Hills, but the Lakota refused to sell and vowed to defend their territory. Crazy Horse fully supported the defiant stand taken by the Lakota leadership. "One does not sell the land on which people walk,"[1] he reportedly declared.

A short time later, Crazy Horse joined forces with Sitting Bull, a respected Lakota spiritual leader, and launched a series of attacks upon the white miners and railroad builders who encroached on their territory. They also skirmished with the U.S. Army troops sent to protect these business interests. During one legendary battle, witnesses claimed that Crazy Horse calmly rode back and forth in front of a line of soldiers firing rifles without ever being hit by a bullet.

The Battle of Little Bighorn

In early 1876 the U.S. government ordered Crazy Horse, Sitting Bull, and all other "non-treaty" Lakota (tribal groups that had not signed the 1868 Fort Laramie Treaty) to report to federal agencies on the reservation. White officials warned that anyone who failed to comply would be considered hostile and subject to attack by the U.S. Army. Crazy Horse ignored the order and became a leader of the Lakota resistance. Thousands of Lakota, as well as their Cheyenne and Arapaho allies, gathered along Rosebud Creek in Montana and prepared to fight.

The U.S. Army sent three main forces to South Dakota to subdue the Lakota. Crazy Horse encountered one of these forces, an infantry regiment under the command of General George Crook, on June 17, 1876. Leading a force of between 1,200 and 1,500 Lakota and Cheyenne warriors, Crazy Horse attacked Crook's troops early that morning. The Battle of the Rosebud raged all day until high casualties and low ammunition finally forced the general to retreat. Crook and his troops returned to their base camp, where they remained out of action for six weeks.

After turning back Crook's infantry, Crazy Horse and Sitting Bull moved their forces to the valley of the Little Bighorn River. An estimated 10,000 Indians, including 1,800 warriors, gathered there in huge camps that stretched for three miles. On the morning of June 25, around 700 soldiers of the U.S. Army's Seventh Cavalry, under the command of Lieutenant Colonel George Armstrong Custer, arrived in the area. Underestimating the strength of his adversary, Custer decided to attack immediately rather than wait for reinforcements.

Custer divided his troops into three groups. He assigned one column of cavalry to attack the Indian camp from the south and stationed a second column in the river valley to block off the Indians' best escape route. Meanwhile, Custer circled around the camp with a third column of cavalry and attacked from the north. When the first column of cavalry launched its attack, Crazy Horse quickly saddled his horse and prepared to join the battle. Just then, he noticed Custer's column approaching along a bluff directly across the river. Realizing that the enemy planned to attack from two sides at once, Crazy Horse led his warriors to the river to cut Custer off.

Crazy Horse prevented Custer's troops from crossing the river and trapped them on a ridge. Custer rallied his forces and tried to make a stand until help arrived. But Crazy Horse and his warriors advanced steadily from all sides. "We circled all around them—swirling like water round a stone," recalled Cheyenne Chief Two Moons, who rode with Crazy Horse. "We shoot, we ride fast, we shoot again."[2] By the time the clash ended, Custer and more than 260 of his men were dead. The Battle of Little Bighorn went down in history as one of the worst defeats the U.S. Army ever suffered in the Indian Wars.

Surrender of a Great Warrior

Following their victory over Custer, the Lakota who refused to go on the reservations were harassed relentlessly by large U.S. Army forces seeking revenge. Crazy Horse and his followers spent a rough winter of 1876-77 in the Badlands of South Dakota, where a shortage of buffalo and other food sources left them near starvation. These hardships finally convinced Crazy

Horse to surrender. On May 6, 1877, he led a procession of 1,000 people—including 300 warriors—into Fort Robinson in Nebraska. Crazy Horse was the last prominent Lakota chief to surrender except for Sitting Bull, who had taken his followers across the border into Canada. Crazy Horse laid down his arms without ever having been defeated in battle.

Although Crazy Horse was widely respected as a warrior, some Lakota leaders viewed him with envy or suspicion. They worried that he would cause trouble on the reservation and reduce their authority. In September 1877 Crazy Horse left the reservation without permission to take his sick wife to see her parents. His enemies spread a rumor that he had left in order to make war. General Crook issued an order for his arrest. Crazy Horse's friends urged him to report to army headquarters to explain his actions and reassure the general. When he arrived on September 5, however, tribal police officers grabbed him and started to take him to jail. Crazy Horse struggled with his captors, but they pinned his arms behind him. During the struggle, a soldier stabbed Crazy Horse in the abdomen with a bayonet. He died of his injuries.

Following Crazy Horse's death, his elderly parents took his body into the Badlands of South Dakota and hid it. The location of his grave remains unknown. In 1948 sculptor Korczak Ziolkowski convinced Oglala Chief Standing Bear to allow him to carve a memorial to Crazy Horse on the face of Thunderhead Mountain in the Black Hills. It depicts a Lakota warrior on horseback, pointing forward past the head of his mount. The completed work will be 563 feet high. The face of the warrior was dedicated in 1998. Since Crazy Horse refused to be photographed during his lifetime, the face symbolizes the proud heritage of all Lakota.

Sources:

Ambrose, Stephen E. *Crazy Horse and Custer: The Parallel Lives of Two American Warriors.* New York: Anchor Books, 1996.

"Crazy Horse: Story of a Brave Sioux Leader." *Brown Quarterly,* Winter 1999. Available online at http://brownvboard.org/brwnqurt/02-4/02-4c.htm.

Freedman, Russell. *The Life and Death of Crazy Horse.* New York: Holiday House, 1996.

McMurtry, Larry. *Crazy Horse: A Life.* New York: Viking Penguin, 1999.

"People: Crazy Horse." *The West,* PBS, 2001. Available online at http://www.pbs.org/weta/thewest/people/a_c/crazyhorse.htm.

Notes

[1] Quoted in Freedman, Russell. *The Life and Death of Crazy Horse.* New York: Holiday House, 1996, p. 97.

[2] Quoted in Freedman, p. 124.

George Armstrong Custer (1839-1876)
U.S. Cavalry Leader Killed in the Battle of Little Bighorn

George Armstrong Custer was born in New Rumley, Ohio, on December 5, 1839. His father, Emmanuel Custer, worked as a blacksmith. His mother, Maria Ward Kirkpatrick Custer, was a homemaker. George grew up in a large family, with four younger siblings in addition to six older half-siblings from his parents' first marriages. He spent part of his youth living with a favorite half-sister, Lydia Ann Kirkpatrick, and her husband in Monroe, Michigan.

Although he was a mediocre student, Custer's persistence and outgoing personality helped him gain an appointment to the prestigious U.S. Military Academy at West Point, New York. During his four years there, he earned a reputation as a practical joker who did the minimum amount of schoolwork possible. Custer graduated last in his class in June 1861. His fledgling military career almost ended a few days later when he failed to step in to stop a fight between two cadets, as school rules required. Custer faced a court martial and avoided punishment only because the Union Army was desperate for officers to fight in the Civil War (1861-65). Some of his classmates who had grown up in the South fought for the Confederate Army.

Custer was excited to put his military training to use to help the North defeat the rebellious South and reunite the nation. He had always felt a strong need to prove himself, and he viewed combat as an opportunity for glory. "When I was verging on manhood, my every thought was ambitious—not to be wealthy, not to be learned, but to be great," he once wrote. "I desired to link my name with acts and men, and in such a manner as to be a mark of honor—not only to the present, but to future generations."[1]

"Boy General" in the Civil War

Custer proved to be a bold and aggressive soldier. His outstanding horsemanship landed him a position in the cavalry—a division of the army that fought on horseback. Custer joined the Union's main fighting force, the Army of the Potomac, and participated in almost every major battle in the East. His courage and fighting skills impressed his superior officers, and he climbed rapidly through the military ranks. At the age of twenty-three, Custer achieved the rank of general and took command of a force of 2,500 men. Newspapers that tracked his daring exploits in battle called him the "Boy General."

Although Custer's cavalry units tended to suffer high casualty rates, his fearless and sometimes reckless charges made him famous. In 1863, as commander of the Michigan brigade, Custer played an important role in securing the Union victory at the Battle of Gettysburg. His unit protected the Union Army's left flank against a furious assault by Confederate troops under General Jeb Stuart.

In 1865 Custer's cavalry units proved vital to the Union's capture of Richmond, Virginia. He was even present when Confederate General Robert E. Lee surrendered at Appomattox Court House to end the Civil War. Afterward, Custer had high praise for his troops. "You have never lost a gun, never lost a color [flag], and never been defeated," he told them. "And, notwithstanding the numerous engagements in which you have borne a prominent part,... you have captured every piece of artillery which the enemy has dared to open upon you."[2]

Takes Command of the Seventh Cavalry

In 1864 Custer married Elizabeth (Libbie) Bacon, the daughter of a Michigan judge. Once the Civil War ended, he and many other career military men were assigned to the western frontier, where their job involved protecting white settlers on the Great Plains. In July 1866 Custer was appointed lieutenant colonel of the U.S. Army's Seventh Cavalry. The following year he received his introduction to an entirely new type of fighting in the Indian Wars. His new adversaries had a superior knowledge of the weather and terrain, and they fought with radically different tactics and goals than Custer had known before.

Custer's first western campaign, against the Southern Cheyenne Indians, did not go well. Faced with insubordinate troops and confusing orders, Custer deposited the Seventh Cavalry at a distant outpost and rode back east across Kansas on his own. Although he supposedly made the trip to meet with commanding officers and obtain supplies, he also took the opportunity to visit with his wife. General Winfield Hancock declared Custer absent without leave and had him arrested. He faced a court martial and was suspended from duty for a year. Custer claimed that the general had used him as a scapegoat to distract attention from his own failed Indian pacification strategy.

Upon returning to duty in 1868, Custer took the lead in another campaign against the Cheyenne. Responding to reports of Indian raids against white wagon trains, Custer and his troops followed some tracks to a Cheyenne village on the Washita River. Although the village sat on reservation land and flew a white flag of peace, Custer ordered an attack. The surprise charge killed more than 100 Indians, including the Cheyenne Chief Black Kettle.

After the Fort Laramie Treaty of 1868 brought temporary peace to the Great Plains, Custer and his regiment were ordered to Kentucky. He spent the next few years writing a series of popular articles about his frontier experiences for *Galaxy* magazine. Custer's tales of his exploits were published in book form as *My Life on the Plains* in 1874. Later that year he returned to the West and led an expedition into the Black Hills of South Dakota. Custer's massive wagon train included 700 soldiers of the Seventh Cavalry and 300 civilian surveyors, miners, geologists, and newspaper reporters. Soon after reaching its destination, the expedition turned up evidence of significant deposits of gold in the Black Hills.

Dies in the Battle of Little Bighorn

The discovery of gold in the Black Hills brought a rush of miners and speculators to the reservation lands that had been granted to the Lakota nation under the Fort Laramie Treaty. When the Lakota refused to sell the land, the U.S. government sent military troops to South Dakota to take it by force. In 1876 Custer and the Seventh Cavalry set out as part of a large U.S. Army mission to eliminate Lakota resistance.

In the meantime, thousands of Lakota prepared to defend the Black Hills with the help of Northern Cheyenne and Arapaho tribal members. By June 1876 an estimated 10,000 Indians, including 1,800 warriors, had gathered in huge camps that stretched for three miles along the Little Bighorn River in present-day Montana. Custer's cavalry reached the area on June 25, ahead of the supporting infantry units. Underestimating the number of Indians in the camp, Custer decided to attack immediately rather than wait for reinforcements.

Custer divided his troops into three groups. He assigned one column of cavalry, under the command of Major Marcus Reno, to attack the camp from the south. Meanwhile, he planned to circle around the camp with a second column of cavalry and attack from the north. He stationed the third group, under Captain Frederick Benteen, in the valley of the Little Bighorn to block off the Indians' best escape route.

Indians under the command of Sitting Bull turned back the initial attack by Reno's troops and chased the first wave of cavalry toward the river, where they were pinned down on a bluff. When Custer's forces arrived from the opposite direction, they were met by a large group of warriors led by Crazy Horse. The Indians trapped the cavalry in an indefensible position on a long ridge. The ensuing battle is often described as "Custer's last stand." By the time the clash ended, Custer and more than 260 of his men—including his brothers Tom and Boston—were dead. The Battle of Little Bighorn went down in history as one of the worst defeats the U.S. Army ever suffered in the Indian Wars.

Custer was initially buried on the battlefield along with his men. In 1877, however, his remains were moved to West Point, New York. Although Custer's final fight ended in a disastrous defeat, it also brought him the everlasting fame he craved. Many Americans had followed the daring exploits of the flamboyant military leader with great interest. In the years following his death, Custer became the subject of countless paintings, songs, and books. In fact, some sources claim that more books have been written about Custer than about any other figure in American history besides President Abraham Lincoln. Most of the early accounts portrayed him as a gallant military hero who fell victim to Indian treachery, but more recent biographies have described him as a vain and foolish cavalry commander.

Sources:

Ambrose, Stephen E. *Crazy Horse and Custer: The Parallel Lives of Two American Warriors.* New York: Anchor Books, 1996.

Anderson, Paul Christopher. *George Armstrong Custer: The Indian Wars and the Battle of Little Bighorn.* New York: Rosen Publishing, 2004.

"People: George Armstrong Custer." *The West,* PBS, 2001. Available online at http://www.pbs.org /weta/thewest/people/a_c/custer.htm.

Utley, Robert M. *Cavalier in Buckskin: George Armstrong Custer and the Western Military Frontier.* Norman: University of Oklahoma Press, 1988.

Notes

[1] Quoted in Ambrose, Stephen E. *Crazy Horse and Custer: The Parallel Lives of Two American Warriors.* New York: Anchor Books, 1996, p. 33.

[2] Custer, George Armstrong. "General Order, Appomattox Court House, 9 April 1865." Available online at http://www.georgearmstrongcuster.com.

Andrew Jackson (1767-1845)
U.S. President Who Signed the Indian Removal Act of 1830

Andrew Jackson was born in a log cabin in Waxhaw, a remote settlement of Scotch-Irish immigrants along the border of North Carolina and South Carolina, on March 15, 1767. His father died before he was born, and he lost his mother and two older brothers during the Revolutionary War (1775-1783). An orphan by the age of fifteen, Jackson received only a basic education in local schools. Still, he studied law and passed the bar exam in 1787.

The following year Jackson moved to Nashville, Tennessee, which was then on the western frontier of the rapidly growing United States. He built a successful law practice, served as a judge, and was elected to the U.S. House of Representatives when Tennessee became a state. In 1794 Jackson married Rachel Donelson Robards, the recently divorced daughter of a prominent Nashville family. In 1804 Jackson and his wife bought a mansion called The Hermitage. They also purchased African-American slaves to work in their household and cotton fields.

Becomes a War Hero

Known for his quick temper and pride, Jackson once killed a man in a duel for insulting his wife. In the 1810s he put his fighting spirit to use as a military leader. In 1814 he led a Tennessee militia force into Alabama to fight against the Creek Indians, who had killed hundreds of white settlers for encroaching on their territory. Jackson's victory over the Creek made an impression on other tribes in the southwestern United States. He helped negotiate treaties in which these tribes surrendered millions of acres of land in Tennessee, Alabama, Georgia, and Mississippi to the federal government.

Jackson also served as a major general in the U.S. Army during the War of 1812 (1812-1815). In January 1815 he commanded the successful defense of New Orleans against an assault by the British Navy. Jackson's ragtag army killed 2,000 well-armed British soldiers at a cost of only 13 lives on their own side. The impressive victory made Jackson a national war hero, even though it turned out that the war had officially ended two weeks earlier with the signing of the Treaty of Ghent.

In 1817 Jackson led a military effort to stop the Seminole Indians from conducting raids on American settlements from Florida, which was then controlled by Spain. Without formal permission, Jackson's troops conquered all of Florida. When Spain signed the territory over to the United States in an 1819 treaty, Jackson served as its first governor.

Elected President of the United States

Jackson's military exploits made him a serious candidate for the presidency in 1824. In this era before party conventions narrowed the field of nominees, he faced off against three other candidates. Although Jackson had the least experience in government of all the candidates, he was the best known nationally. The election results showed him ahead in the popular vote, with 43 percent, as well as in the electoral vote. Since Jackson had not achieved a majority, however, the election was decided in the U.S. House of Representatives. Fellow candidate Henry Clay withdrew from the race and threw his support behind John Quincy Adams, which enabled Adams to claim the presidency.

In 1828 Jackson launched another bid for the presidency. He based his campaign on the idea that political patronage and corruption had lifted Adams to office against the will of the people. By contrast, he presented himself as a self-made man who would democratize the federal government and restore power to ordinary citizens. He defeated Adams handily, earning 56 percent of the popular vote, to become the seventh president of the United States. The bitter election campaign took a toll on Rachel Jackson's health, though, and she died before her husband took office.

Jackson proved to be a controversial president who made numerous political enemies. He angered his opponents by expanding the executive power of the presidency and refusing to defer to Congress. In fact, he vetoed more bills passed by Congress than all of his predecessors combined. Some detractors claimed that Jackson behaved like a dictator or tyrant. His supporters, on the other hand, argued that the president stood up for the rights of average Americans against the interests of the wealthy elite. The strong differences of opinion about Jackson's policies caused his Republican Party to split into two competing factions. Jackson's supporters became known as the

Democratic Republicans or Democrats, while his opponents became known as the National Republicans or Whigs. Despite the controversy, Jackson retained his personal popularity and easily won reelection in 1832.

Jackson's second term in office was marked by major disagreements over federal authority and states' rights, North-South sectional rivalry, and the treatment of American Indians and African-American slaves. The president took a stand in favor of federal authority in 1832, when the state of South Carolina declared a federal tariff null and void and refused to collect it. Many states in the South disliked high federal tariffs on imported goods, which they felt helped manufacturers in the North at their expense. Jackson reacted to this challenge, known as the nullification crisis, by declaring the federal Union indivisible and threatening to use military force to make South Carolina collect the tariff. But Congress passed a law reducing the tariff before such action became necessary.

Pursues Indian Removal Policies

Although Jackson claimed to be a champion of the interests of ordinary people, his belief in equal protection did not extend to African Americans or Native Americans. As a Southern slave owner, he had no reservations about the institution of slavery. Debate over the issue intensified during his terms in office, contributing to a growing rift between the North and South. Jackson viewed the Northern abolitionist movement as a threat to national unity and promoted the adoption of "gag rules" to prevent the controversial topic from being discussed in Congress.

Jackson's legacy is also tainted by his policies toward Native Americans. From the moment he took office, he believed that all remaining tribes needed to be removed from the South to make way for white civilization. He thus pursued policies aimed at forcing all American Indians to relocate west of the Mississippi River. His chief weapon in this policy area was the Indian Removal Act of 1830. This sweeping legislation gave Jackson the power to create new Indian reservations west of the Mississippi, exchange those lands for tribal territory in the South, purchase Indian homes and other improvements made to the land, and pay the costs of transporting the Indians west. The Choctaw, Seminole, Creek, and Chickasaw tribes were all removed from the South over the next few years under the terms of this act, but the Cherokee people made a valiant stand against removal under the leadership of Chief John Ross.

The Cherokee considered themselves a sovereign nation—with their own roads, schools, written language, representative government, and constitution—and claimed jurisdiction over long-held territory in Georgia, Alabama, and Mississippi. When Georgia allowed white settlers to encroach upon Cherokee lands in violation of a federal treaty, Jackson sided with the state. He refused to recognize tribal sovereignty, arguing that the Cherokee were wards of the government in the states where they lived. He said that the Cherokee must move outside of existing state borders if they wanted to maintain a tribal government and hold territory.

The U.S. Supreme Court disagreed with Jackson's position. In *Worcester v. Georgia* (1832), the high court upheld the tribe's assertion that they were a sovereign nation and not subject to state authority. Chief Justice John Marshall wrote that the Cherokee Nation could only be removed if its leaders agreed in a formal treaty with the U.S. government. In 1835 Jackson convinced a small minority faction among the Cherokee to sign the Treaty of New Echota, which provided for the removal of the entire Cherokee Nation to a reservation in Oklahoma Territory.

Ross and other Cherokee leaders argued that the treaty was invalid, but Jackson ignored their protests. Following a heated debate, the U.S. Senate ratified it by a single vote. In 1838 federal troops moved to enforce the treaty. Around 13,000 Cherokee were rounded up and driven west, and an estimated 4,000 tribal members died of cold, starvation, or disease along the 1,000-mile forced march. This shameful episode in American history became known as the Trail of Tears.

By the time his Indian removal policies decimated the Cherokee Nation, Jackson had left office and retired to his Nashville cotton plantation. He kept a watchful eye on national politics and frequently sent letters of advice to his successor, Martin Van Buren. He also spent time arranging his personal papers and entertaining a stream of visitors. Jackson died at his home on June 8, 1845, at the age of 78.

Sources:

"Andrew Jackson." State Library of North Carolina, n.d. Available online at http://statelibrary.ncdcr.gov/nc/bio/public/jackson.htm.

"Andrew Jackson." The White House, n.d. Available online at http://www.whitehouse.gov/about/presidents/andrewjackson.

Remini, Robert V. *The Life of Andrew Jackson*. New York: Harper and Row, 1988.

Viola, Herman J. *Andrew Jackson*. New York: Chelsea House, 1986.

Wilentz, Sean. *Andrew Jackson*. New York: Macmillan, 2006.

Red Cloud (c. 1822-1909)
Lakota Chief and Resistance Leader

R ed Cloud was born around 1822 near the Platte River in Nebraska. His Indian name was Makhpiya-Luta in the language of the Lakota or Teton Sioux. His mother, Walks as She Thinks, was a member of the Oglala subgroup of Lakota. His father, a member of the Brulé subgroup whose name may have been Red Cloud, died when his son was very young. Red Cloud was raised in the family of his maternal uncle, Smoke, who was a chief among the Oglala.

Red Cloud grew up living in tipis, riding horses, and following the buffalo herds across the Great Plains. By the time he reached his teen years, he was known as a daring and talented horseman. Red Cloud often accompanied Oglala war parties in attacks on neighboring Crow, Pawnee, Ute, and Shoshone Indian tribes. His skills as a warrior enabled him to collect a large herd of horses. In 1841, during a dispute fueled by alcohol, Red Cloud killed a fellow Lakota named Bull Bear, who was the chief of a rival band. Although this incident created a rift between Bull Bear's band and Smoke's band, it also increased Red Cloud's prominence among his people.

Red Cloud's War

Red Cloud's reputation as a fierce warrior, along with his natural leadership skills, elevated him to a position as chief of the Oglala during the 1850s. Throughout this period, white miners, settlers, and soldiers encroached upon traditional Lakota territory in ever increasing numbers. By the 1860s vast wagon trains traveled the Bozeman Trail through the heart of Lakota land in Wyoming to reach gold deposits in Montana. When the U.S. Army started to build forts along the Bozeman Trail in 1865, Red Cloud and other Lakota leaders grew determined to defend their rapidly diminishing territory. "The Great Spirit ... raised me in this land and it belongs to me," Red Cloud declared. "The white man was raised over the water and his land is over there. Since they crossed the sea, I have given them room. There are now white people all about me. I have but a small spot of land left. The Great Spirit told me to keep it."[1]

For more than two years, Red Cloud led thousands of Lakota, Cheyenne, and Arapaho warriors in a coordinated series of attacks designed to disrupt the building of the forts. His war parties intercepted shipments of supplies, harassed construction workers, stole horses, stampeded livestock, and surrounded and besieged completed forts. Although Red Cloud rarely played a direct role in battles between the Indian forces and the U.S. Army troops, he proved to be an outstanding military strategist, logistical organizer, and inspirational leader. His campaign against the fort building, which became known as Red Cloud's War, was the most cohesive and successful military action ever waged by an Indian nation against the United States. In the second half of 1866 alone, Red Cloud's forces killed over 150 white soldiers and travelers, captured some 700 head of livestock, made more than 50 direct assaults on forts, and completely halted traffic on the Bozeman Trail.

Despite the fearsome effectiveness of Red Cloud's attacks, many U.S. Army leaders still dismissed the challenge they faced from the Lakota. They felt that Indians were too uncivilized to develop a comprehensive military strategy, so they believed that their superior training and equipment would eventually allow them to prevail. This attitude led to a disastrous defeat of U.S. soldiers at the hands of Red Cloud's warriors in December 1866. Red Cloud set up a carefully planned ambush in the hills surrounding Fort Phil Kearny in Wyoming, and the soldiers from the fort readily fell into his trap.

The commanding officer at Fort Phil Kearny was Colonel Henry B. Carrington, who adopted a fairly cautious approach toward the hostile Indians surrounding his outpost. Carrington realized that the 350 soldiers under his command were insufficient to defend the fort and protect wagon trains along a 100-mile stretch of the Bozeman Trail. But his chief tactical officer, Captain William J. Fetterman, grew impatient with Carrington's cautious approach. He argued that the army troops could easily wipe out the Indian forces with one major offensive. "Give me eighty men and I will ride through the entire Sioux nation!"[2] he was often heard to declare.

Early in the morning of December 21, a small group of soldiers left the fort to cut firewood. Red Cloud sent ten of his finest warriors, led by Crazy Horse, to attack the woodcutters. As expected, the woodcutters sent up a call for help to the soldiers inside the fort. A special force of eighty men, led by Fetterman, rushed out of the fort to rescue them. Crazy Horse and his warriors immediately broke off the attack, but they taunted the soldiers as they rode away. Although Carrington had issued specific instructions not to engage or pursue the Indians, Fetterman took the bait and ordered his men to follow. Crazy Horse led the pursuing troops over a ridge and into a trap where 2,000 Lakota warriors waited. Red Cloud's forces quickly surrounded and killed Fetterman and all eighty of his men, while losing only thirteen of their own warriors in the battle. Another group of soldiers arrived on the scene a short time later to find their comrades' bodies badly mutilated.

Signs the Fort Laramie Treaty of 1868

This incident, which became known as the Fetterman Massacre among whites and as the Battle of 100 Slain among the Plains Indians, sent shock waves through the United States. White settlers, miners, and political leaders were outraged and called for revenge. Some even demanded the total extermination of the Lakota. The U.S. Army fared somewhat better against Red Cloud's forces in 1867, but the Indians continued to disrupt the building of the forts and harass travelers along the Bozeman Trail. U.S. leaders offered to hold peace talks, but Red Cloud steadfastly refused to negotiate until all of the forts were abandoned.

In 1868 the U.S. government finally gave in to his demand. Under the terms of the Fort Laramie Treaty, the army agreed to withdraw its troops from all of the forts along the Bozeman Trail. The U.S. government also granted the Lakota a permanent reservation of 60 million acres west of the Missouri River in South Dakota, as well as free access to hunting grounds in Wyoming and Montana. Red Cloud refused to sign the treaty until his warriors had burned the empty forts to the ground. On November 4, 1868, the great chief finally lay down his arms and made peace with the United States.

Over the next few years, however, it became clear that U.S. leaders did not intend to honor the Fort Laramie Treaty. They insisted that Red Cloud and his people move to a reservation along the Missouri River, 300 miles from their traditional home and hunting grounds. They also tried to force the Oglala to become farmers and give up their religion and customs. Red Cloud traveled to Washington, D.C., to plead his case in person. "I have tried to get from the Great Father [the U.S. president] what is right and just," he explained. "I wish to know why Commissioners are sent out to us who do nothing but rob us and get the riches of this world away from us?"[3] Finally, in 1873, Red Cloud and his people settled on the Red Cloud Agency in Nebraska, northeast of Fort Laramie.

Peaceful Defender of Indian Rights

Peace between the Lakota and the U.S. government did not last long. In 1874 Lieutenant Colonel George Armstrong Custer led a military expedition into the Black Hills of South Dakota and discovered gold. Hopeful white prospectors and settlers streamed into the reservation lands set aside for the Lakota in violation of the treaty. When the Lakota refused to sell the land, the U.S. government sent military troops to subdue them. Red Cloud honored his pledge of peace and remained on the sidelines during the ensuing battles, which became known as the Sioux Wars. He thus did not take part in the 1876 Battle of Little Bighorn, when Lakota forces led by Sitting Bull and Crazy Horse killed a 260-man detachment of U.S. cavalry under the command of Custer.

Despite the Lakota victory in this historic battle, they were forced to give up the Black Hills later that year, and by 1889 they had lost 80 percent of their original reservation. Throughout this period, Red Cloud waged a diplomatic fight to preserve Lakota autonomy, dignity, and culture. He also established himself as a persistent critic of government policies that harmed his people. After moving to the newly created Pine Ridge Agency in 1878, for instance, Red Cloud launched a campaign of peaceful resistance against federal agent Valentine T. McGillycuddy, who was appropriating Indian rations for his own use. Red Cloud repeatedly argued his case before U.S. leaders and eventually succeeded in forcing McGillycuddy's dismissal.

In 1890 a revolutionary new religious movement called the Ghost Dance swept through the Indian tribes of the western United States. It promised followers that everything in the world would be restored to the way it was before the white man arrived, with plentiful land and game, if they performed a ritual dance. Red Cloud viewed the movement with suspicion and did not endorse it, although it attracted followers from among his people. The agent in charge of Pine Ridge, Daniel Royer, grew alarmed by the Ghost Dance and demanded federal troops to restore order on the reservation and protect nearby white settlers. Mounting tensions surrounding the Ghost Dance led to the death of Sitting Bull and the massacre of around 250 Lakota men, women, and children by U.S. cavalry troops at Wounded Knee Creek, about twenty miles from Pine Ridge.

Following the tragic incident at Wounded Knee in December 1890, most Lakota ceased their resistance and resigned themselves to reservation life. The elderly Red Cloud lost his eyesight and some of his power as he aged, although he continued to exert influence in tribal matters. In the early 1900s he was baptized as a Christian. Red Cloud died at Pine Ridge on December 10, 1909.

Sources:

Lazar, Jerry. *Red Cloud: Sioux War Chief.* New York: Chelsea House, 1995.

Olson, James C. *Red Cloud and the Sioux Problem.* Lincoln: University of Nebraska Press, 1965.

"People: Red Cloud." *The West,* PBS, 2001. Available online at http://www.pbs.org/weta/thewest /people/i_r/redcloud.htm.

"Red Cloud." *Biography,* n.d. Available online at http://www.biography.com/articles/Red-Cloud -9453402.

Notes

[1] Quoted in Lazar, Jerry. *Red Cloud: Sioux War Chief.* New York: Chelsea House, 1995, p. 56.

[2] Quoted in Lazar, p. 15.

[3] Quoted in Lazar, p. 78.

John Ross (1790-1866)
Cherokee Chief during the Trail of Tears

John Ross was born on October 4, 1790, in Turkeytown, Alabama. His father, Daniel Ross, was a Scottish trader. His mother, Mary Ross, was part Scottish and part Cherokee Indian. John was the third of their nine children. His family had lived among the Cherokee and operated trading posts in tribal territory since before the American Revolution (1775-1783). Although John was only one-eighth Cherokee by blood, he grew up as a full-fledged member of the Cherokee Nation. As a boy he was known by the Indian name Tsan Usdi, meaning "Little John." As an adult he acquired the name Guwisguwi, after a rare migratory bird.

Ross spent much of his youth near Lookout Mountain along the Tennessee-Georgia border. This region was on the remote western frontier of the United States at that time. He was educated by a private tutor and also attended a preparatory academy at Kingston, Tennessee, for a few years. Although he learned to speak English and fit into white society, he maintained close ties to the Cherokee and followed many Indian customs.

Ross joined the U.S. Army during the War of 1812 (1812-1815), in which the United States faced Great Britain and allied Indian tribes. He fought alongside a number of famous Americans—including Davy Crockett, Sam Houston, and future president Andrew Jackson—against the Creek Indians in the decisive Battle of Horseshoe Bend. When the war ended, Ross established a ferry service and trading post at Ross Landing, Tennessee, which later became Chattanooga. He also worked as a federal postmaster and served as a translator and liaison for white missionaries and settlers. Ross married a Cherokee woman, Quatie Martin, and started a family during these years.

Elected Principal Chief of the Cherokee Nation

Throughout the early years of Ross's life, the Cherokee were one of the most powerful Indian tribes of the Southeast. They possessed a large territory encompassing southern Tennessee, northern Alabama, northern Georgia, and western North Carolina. With the Louisiana Purchase of 1803, however, the United States gained a huge swath of new land west of the Mississippi River. The U.S. government decided to move the Cherokee and all other eastern Indian tribes into this territory in order to open the lands east of the Mississippi for white settlement. As the pressure to relocate mounted, the Cherokee tried to forestall it by adopting many of the "civilized" ways of white society. They took up farming, established schools and businesses, developed a written language, and published a tribal newspaper.

In the early 1820s the Cherokee took steps to become a sovereign nation by adopting a constitution and forming a representative government. This bold step angered officials in the state of Georgia. They argued that the Cherokee were subject to state law and should not be granted any special status or privileges. Georgia Governor George M. Troup, for instance, insisted that "a state of things so unnatural and fruitful of evils as an independent government of a semi-barbarous people existing within the limits of a state could not long continue."[1]

But the Cherokee persisted in forming their own government and held an election in 1828. By this time Ross was one of the wealthiest, most prominent, and widely respected members of the tribe. The Cherokee people elected him as the first principal chief of the Cherokee Nation. He went on to be elected to ten consecutive four-year terms of office.

Leads the Fight against Removal

Ross took office in the same year that Andrew Jackson became president of the United States. Jackson was convinced that the remaining Indian tribes of the Southeast should be pushed out to make way for white civilization. In 1830 he convinced Congress to pass the Indian Removal Act. This sweeping legislation gave Jackson the power to create new Indian reservations west of the Mississippi, exchange those lands for tribal territory in the Southeast, purchase Indian homes and other improvements made to the land, and pay the costs of transporting the Indians west.

Ross led the Cherokee Nation's valiant effort to avoid forced removal to the West. The chief lobbied U.S. leaders in Washington, D.C., published letters and gave interviews to newspapers across the country, and launched a determined legal battle in federal court. In 1832 Georgia organized a land lottery to divide Cherokee territory among white settlers and business interests.

Ross challenged Georgia's attempt to confiscate Cherokee land in two historic cases before the U.S. Supreme Court, *Cherokee Nation v. Georgia* (1831) and *Worcester v. Georgia* (1832). In the first case, the Court ruled that it did not have jurisdiction over Indian tribes. In the second, however, the Court reversed itself and upheld the tribe's assertion that they were a sovereign nation and not subject to state authority.

In explaining the court's decisions, Chief Justice John Marshall wrote that the Cherokee Nation "is a distinct community occupying its own territory … in which the laws of Georgia can have no force." Therefore, he found that "the Indians possessed a full right to the lands they occupied until that right should be extinguished by the United States with their consent."[2] In other words, the Court ruled that the Cherokee Nation could only legally be removed from Georgia if its elected leaders agreed to such a move in a formal treaty with the U.S. government. Unfortunately for the Cherokee, Georgia simply ignored the Court's ruling, and Jackson made no effort to enforce it. The state claimed Ross's 200-acre plantation and evicted his family from the property in 1834.

In 1835 Jackson convinced a small minority faction among the Cherokee to sign the Treaty of New Echota, which provided for the removal of the entire Cherokee Nation to a federal reservation in Oklahoma Territory. The signers believed that removal was inevitable and wanted to get the best possible terms for the tribe. Ross and other Cherokee leaders argued that the treaty was invalid. They pointed out that the signers did not have the authority to enter into a treaty on behalf of the Cherokee Nation. Ross then collected nearly 16,000 signatures to prove that the vast majority of Cherokee opposed the treaty. Since the treaty furthered the cause of Indian removal, though, Jackson pressured the U.S. Senate to ratify it. Following a heated debate, it passed by a single vote on May 23, 1836.

Travels the Trail of Tears

In May 1838 federal troops under the command of General Winfield Scott began rounding up the Cherokee people and driving them westward. They were forced to make the 1,000-mile forced march under extremely difficult conditions. Of the 13,000 Cherokee who started the journey, an estimated 4,000 died of disease, exposure, starvation, or exhaustion along the way. Ross's wife, Quatie, was among the tribal members who succumbed. This shameful episode in American history became known as the Trail of Tears.

Once they reached Oklahoma Territory, the Cherokee started over with Ross as their leader. He immediately moved to reunite the demoralized and divided tribe. In 1839 the various factions came together to draw up a new constitution and form the United Cherokee Nation. Two years later a new capital was established in Tahlequah. By the 1850s the Cherokee Nation once again had its own roads, businesses, newspaper, and public school system. Ross married a Quaker woman named Mary Brian Stapler during these years.

During the 1860s the Cherokee Nation struggled to remain neutral during the Civil War. Under pressure from the surrounding states, Ross eventually ended up signing a treaty with the Confederacy. By doing so, he repudiated all treaties formerly signed between the Cherokee Nation and the U.S. government. Ross spent the war years in Washington, D.C., with his family. He met with President Abraham Lincoln to explain the decision to end Cherokee neutrality. After the war ended in a Union victory in 1865, Ross worked to secure permanent land rights for his people by forging a new treaty with the United States. He signed the Treaty of 1866 shortly before he died on August 1.

The respected chief was laid to rest near his home in Park Hill, Oklahoma. The Cherokee Nation passed a formal resolution honoring Ross for his decades of tireless service. "He never faltered in supporting what he believed to be right," it read. "He never sacrificed the interests of his nation to expediency. He never lost sight of the welfare of his people. For them he labored daily for a long life, and upon them he bestowed his last expressed thoughts."[3]

Sources:

"Chief John Ross." Library of Congress, American Memory Collection, October 3, 2007. Available online at http://memory.loc.gov/ammem/today/oct03.html.

"John Ross: Chief of the Cherokee." Georgia Tribe of Eastern Cherokee, n.d. Available online at http://www.georgiatribeofeasterncherokee.com/chiefjohnross.htm.

Koestler-Grack, Rachel A. *Chief John Ross*. New York: Heinemann, 2004.

Meserve, John Bartlett. "Chief John Ross." *Chronicles of Oklahoma*, December 1935, p. 423. Available online at http://digital.library.okstate.edu/Chronicles/v013/v013p421.html.

Moulton, Gary E. *John Ross: Cherokee Chief*. Athens: University of Georgia Press, 1978.

Notes

[1] Quoted in Meserve, John Bartlett. "Chief John Ross." *Chronicles of Oklahoma*, December 1935, p. 423. Available online at http://digital.library.okstate.edu/Chronicles/v013/v013p421.html.

[2] "Cherokee Nation v. State of Georgia," 1831. Available online at http://www.mtholyoke.edu/acad/intrel/cherokee.htm.

[3] Quoted in "John Ross: Chief of the Cherokee." Georgia Tribe of Eastern Cherokee, n.d. Available online at http://www.georgiatribeofeasterncherokee.com/chiefjohnross.htm.

Sitting Bull (1831-1890)
Lakota Chief and Holy Man

Sitting Bull, or Tatanka Iyotake, was born in March 1831 along the banks of the Grand River in South Dakota. He was a member of the American Indian people known as the Lakota or Teton Sioux. Sitting Bull's father, Jumping Bull, was a well-known warrior among the Hunkpapa, one of seven Lakota subgroups. Sitting Bull's mother was called Mixed Day when he was born, but she became known as Her-Holy-Door once her son emerged as a great chief of the Lakota.

Sitting Bull's childhood name was Slow, because he was a bit awkward and a slow runner. According to Indian tradition, he kept this name until he earned a better one. Legend has it that he became known as Sitting Bull after he wrestled a buffalo calf to the ground in a boys' game that imitated a buffalo hunt.

As a young man, Sitting Bull gained a reputation as a bold and courageous warrior. He got his first taste of battle at the age of fourteen, when he took part in a raid on the neighboring Crow Indian tribe. But Sitting Bull also impressed his people by showing mercy and compassion. In 1857 he prevented fellow Lakota warriors from harming a young boy from the Assiniboine tribe who continued to fight bravely after his family was killed. Sitting Bull adopted the boy as a brother and took responsibility for raising him.

In the mid-1860s the Lakota went to war to defend their traditional territory against a steadily growing invasion of white hunters, settlers, and soldiers. Sitting Bull faced off against U.S. Army troops in a number of fights, including the Battle of Killdeer Mountain and the Battle of the Badlands. His courage in battle became legendary. During one fight, he supposedly sat in the open and casually smoked a pipe while enemy bullets flew all around him.

Head Chief of the Lakota Nation

In 1867, at the age of thirty-six, Sitting Bull became head chief of the Lakota. He achieved this rank not only because of his bravery in battle, but also because of his growing reputation for fairness, generosity, and spiritual wisdom. One year later, several major Lakota bands signed the Fort Laramie Treaty of 1868. This treaty gave the Lakota a permanent reservation of 60 million acres—or about 93,000 square miles—west of the Missouri River in South Dakota. They also received hunting access to a large area of unceded Indian territory outside of the reservation.

Sitting Bull was skeptical about the treaty and refused to sign, but he was willing to abide by its terms as long as the U.S. government kept its promise not to build roads, forts, or settlements in the area set aside as the Great Sioux Reservation. In 1874, however, Lieutenant Colonel George Armstrong Custer led a government expedition into the Black Hills of South Dakota—along the western edge of the reservation—in violation of the treaty. They discovered gold, which sent a flood of white prospectors rushing into the area. The U.S. government offered to purchase the Black Hills, but the Lakota refused to sell and vowed to defend their territory. "We want no white men here," Sitting Bull declared. "The Black Hills belong to me. If the whites try to take them, I will fight."[1]

The U.S. government responded by ordering all tribal members to report to the reservation by January 31, 1876. Anyone who failed to comply would be considered hostile and subject to attack by the U.S. Army. Sitting Bull ignored the order and led his people to a camp near Rosebud Creek in Montana. Thousands of Lakota, as well as their Cheyenne and Arapaho allies, gathered at the site and prepared to protect their land and way of life. "We are an island of Indians in a lake of whites," Sitting Bull announced. "We must stand together, or they will rub us out separately. These soldiers have come shooting; they want war. All right, we'll give it to them!"[2]

The Battle of Little Bighorn

In preparation for the coming battles, Sitting Bull led his people in the sun dance, prayed to the Great Spirit, and slashed his arms 100 times as a form of sacrifice. After completing these rituals, Sitting Bull said that he had experienced a mystical vision of army soldiers falling into the Indian camp like grasshoppers from the sky. His vision inspired the Lakota on June 17, when they defeated a force led by General George Crook in the Battle of the Rosebud.

The Lakota and their allies then moved to the valley of the Little Bighorn River. An estimated 10,000 Indians, including 1,800 warriors, gathered there in huge camps that stretched for three miles. On the morning of June 25, 1876, Custer led an estimated 700 soldiers of the U.S. Army's Seventh Cavalry toward the Little Bighorn. Custer divided his troops into three groups. He assigned one column of cavalry to attack the Indian camp from the south and stationed another column in the river valley to block off the Indians' best escape route. Meanwhile, Custer circled around the camp with a third column of cavalry and attacked from the north.

Sitting Bull and his forces fended off the initial attack, then pursued Custer's forces and trapped them on a ridge. By the time the clash ended, Custer and more than 260 of his men were dead. The Battle of Little Bighorn went down in history as one of the worst defeats the U.S. Army ever suffered in the Indian Wars. Among white Americans, though, Custer's disastrous defeat was widely interpreted as a massacre of heroic American soldiers by hostile savages. From that time on, Sitting Bull and other Indians who refused to go on the reservations were harassed relentlessly by large U.S. Army forces seeking revenge.

Most other Indian leaders surrendered within a year, but Sitting Bull escaped capture by leading 2,000 of his followers across the border into Canada. They received only a lukewarm welcome from Canadian officials, however, and struggled to support themselves. After four years, Sitting Bull finally led his hungry and discouraged people back to the United States. He surrendered on July 19, 1881, at Fort Buford in Montana.

Settles on the Reservation

Sitting Bull spent the next two years in a military prison at Fort Randall on the Missouri River. On May 10, 1883, he was allowed to rejoin his people at the Hunkpapa reservation at Standing Rock, along the border between North Dakota and South Dakota. He and about 250 followers lived in cabins along the Grand River and maintained a degree of independence. Although Sitting Bull kept livestock and did some farming, he also refused to give up many of his people's traditions and customs. His defiant attitude kept him at odds with Major James McLaughlin, the agent in charge of Standing Rock.

In 1885 Sitting Bull was allowed to leave the reservation in order to tour the United States as part of William "Buffalo Bill" Cody's famous Wild West

Show. He earned $50 per week for his appearances, plus whatever he received for signing autographs and posing for pictures. He even met U.S. President Grover Cleveland during one stop on the tour. But Sitting Bull disliked all the attention and found it difficult to understand white society.

In 1889 a U.S. government commission headed by Crook came to the Great Sioux Reservation. They presented an "allotment" proposal to distribute a plot of reservation land to the head of each Lakota family. Once all of the eligible Lakota tribal members had claimed their allotments, the government planned to sell off any "surplus" reservation land to white homesteaders and railroad builders. Sitting Bull stood firmly opposed to this arrangement, which would reduce the total land area set aside for the Lakota by nine million acres. But Crook managed to convince three-quarters of eligible Lakota voters to approve the plan. Upon learning that his fellow Indians had agreed to break up the reservation, a disgusted Sitting Bull said, "There are no Indians left but me!"[3]

The Ghost Dance Controversy

In the fall of 1890 a new religious movement called the Ghost Dance swept through the Indian tribes of the western United States. According to this movement, followers who performed a ritual dance would be rewarded with a world free of white people and abundant with buffalo and other game. Suffering from hunger, despair, and the destruction of their culture and way of life, the Lakota eagerly grasped at the ray of hope it offered. Although Sitting Bull harbored some doubts about the movement, he set his personal feelings aside and allowed his followers to learn the Ghost Dance. When McLaughlin ordered the dancing to stop, Sitting Bull grew determined to protect his people's right to practice the new religion. The situation soon escalated into a tense standoff between the two strong-willed men. McLaughlin eventually decided that he needed to arrest Sitting Bull in order to prevent an all-out uprising on the reservation.

Early on the morning of December 15, 1890, McLaughlin sent a 43-member tribal police force under the command of Captain Henry Bull Head to Sitting Bull's cabin. The officers woke up the influential chief and convinced him to accompany them to the Standing Rock agency. By the time Sitting Bull was dressed and ready to go, however, his followers had gathered outside the cabin. As the angry crowd surrounded the police officers, shots were fired. The resulting clash took the lives of Sitting Bull and eight of his followers, including his teenage son Crowfoot, as well as six reservation police officers.

The death of Sitting Bull sent shock waves through the Lakota Nation. Fearing for their lives, thousands of Lakota fled their reservations. One of these bands, a Miniconjou Lakota group led by Chief Big Foot, was massacred by U.S. Army troops near Wounded Knee Creek on December 29, 1890. This tragic incident marked the end of armed conflict between the Lakota and the U.S. government. Sitting Bull is remembered as the last of the great chiefs who mounted a fierce resistance to white domination. He was initially buried at Fort Yates in North Dakota. In 1953 the Lakota Nation moved his remains to Mobridge, South Dakota, and erected a monument honoring his life and legacy.

Sources:

Bernotas, Bob. *Sitting Bull: Chief of the Sioux.* New York: Chelsea House, 1991.

"People: Sitting Bull." *The West,* PBS, 2001. Available online at http://www.pbs.org/weta/thewest /people/s_z/sittingbull.htm.

Utley, Robert M. *The Lance and the Shield: The Life and Times of Sitting Bull.* New York: Holt, 1993.

Vestal, Stanley. *Sitting Bull: Champion of the Sioux.* Norman: University of Oklahoma Press, 1989.

Notes

[1] Quoted in Bernotas, Bob. *Sitting Bull: Chief of the Sioux.* New York: Chelsea House, 1991, p. 42.

[2] Quoted in Bernotas, p. 59.

[3] Quoted in Bernotas, p. 95.

Wovoka (c. 1856-1932)
Paiute Prophet Who Created the Ghost Dance Religion

W ovoka, also known as Jack Wilson, was born near Yerington, Nevada, around 1856. His name means "Woodcutter" in the language of the Northern Paiute Indians. Limited information is available about Wovoka's early life. His father was known variously as Numu-tibo'o, Tavid, or Tavibo, and he was a Paiute medicine man and warrior. His mother's name was Tiya. Wovoka was believed to be the oldest of their four sons.

Some accounts claim that Wovoka was orphaned as a teenager, while others say that his parents lived into the twentieth century. In any case, around the age of fourteen Wovoka went to live with the family of a local white rancher, David Wilson. It was here that he learned to speak English and became known as Jack Wilson. He also trained to be a woodcutter. Around the age of twenty Wovoka married a Paiute woman named Tumm, who became known as Mary Wilson. They eventually had three daughters.

Throughout his youth, Wovoka was exposed to a broad spectrum of religious influences. He learned about Christianity from the Wilson family. They were devout Presbyterians who read the Bible every day. He also came into frequent contact with Christian missionaries and Mormon settlers in the region where he lived. Finally, Wovoka learned about traditional Paiute religious beliefs and mysticism from his father.

By the time he reached adulthood, Wovoka was presenting himself as a man with mystical gifts. Many fellow Indians came to see him as someone who possessed great spiritual powers and a gift for prophecy. Followers claimed that he could predict future events, control the weather, stop bullets in midair, and even raise people from the dead.

Mystical Vision Launches the Ghost Dance

On New Year's Day 1889, a total eclipse of the sun occurred in the western United States. As this unusual and startling event unfolded, Wovoka became terribly ill with what may have been scarlet fever. He became delirious and fell unconscious. During this period, Wovoka said that he experienced a powerful dream or vision, which he interpreted as a spiritual prophecy. According to Wovoka's vision, God wanted the Indians to live peacefully together and perform a ritual dance. If they did so, God would reward them in the spring of 1891 by restoring everything in the world to the way it was before the white man arrived.

Wovoka told his followers that God planned to cover the land with 30 feet of rich soil. All the white people would be buried underneath, and only the Indians would survive. The fresh earth would be planted with trees and grasses, and vast herds of buffalo and horses would thrive there once again. All of the Indians' ancestors would come back to life, and the people would be free to ride, hunt, practice their traditional religion, and follow their ancient customs. Word of Wovoka's vision traveled quickly through the Indian tribes of the West. It held a great deal of appeal for thousands of hungry and desperate people who had been pushed onto reservations and forced to give up their traditional way of life. "Wovoka's message of hope spread like wildfire among the demoralized tribes,"[1] noted one historian.

Although Indians across the West eagerly adopted Wovoka's teachings, white authorities generally dismissed him as a lunatic or denounced him as a fraud. Some critics claimed that Wovoka falsely presented himself as a messiah sent to save the Indian people. Others argued that he was a dangerous troublemaker who wanted to incite an Indian uprising. But his friend and business partner Ed Dyer insisted that Wovoka was a peaceful man with good intentions. "I was thoroughly convinced that Jack Wilson had at no time attempted deliberately to stir up trouble," he stated. "He never advocated violence. Violence was contrary to his very nature. Others seized upon his prophecies and stunts, and made more of them than he intended.... In a way, once started, he was riding a tiger. It was difficult to dismount."[2]

The Wounded Knee Massacre

In the fall of 1889 Lakota leaders in South Dakota sent a delegation to Nevada to see Wovoka and learn more about the new religion. The delegates returned full of excitement and taught the Ghost Dance to their people. Like many other tribes, the Lakota adapted Wovoka's core message—which incorporated elements from various religious traditions—to their own beliefs and circumstances. The Lakota practiced a more militant version of the new religion than some other groups. For instance, Lakota followers believed that the sacred "ghost shirts" they wore while dancing had the power to protect them from harm, including bullets. This conviction inspired some Lakota dancers to stand up to federal agents and Indian police officers.

As the Ghost Dance took hold on the Lakota reservations, many white people in South Dakota expressed concern. Some reservation agents felt the dancing was harmless and chose to ignore it, but others viewed it as a threat to their authority and tried to suppress it. A few agents grew so alarmed by the Indians' behavior that they requested additional military troops for protection.

In November 1890 thousands of U.S. Army troops descended on South Dakota in an attempt to stop the Ghost Dance and restore order to the Lakota reservations. As part of this effort, several reservation agents decided to arrest prominent Lakota leaders. James McLaughlin, the agent at the Standing Rock Reservation, sent a tribal police force to arrest Sitting Bull on December 15. A fight broke out between police officers and Sitting Bull's followers, and the influential chief was killed in the confusion.

The death of Sitting Bull instilled fear among the Lakota, and many people fled the reservations. A band of about 350 Miniconjou Lakota led by Chief Big Foot was intercepted by about 500 troops of the Seventh Cavalry near Wounded Knee Creek on December 28, 1890. The next morning, Colonel James Forsyth ordered his men to surround the Indians and confiscate their weapons. During the attempt to disarm the Miniconjou, a scuffle broke out. The soldiers opened fire on the gathered Indians, then chased down many of those who fled the carnage. Between 250 and 300 Lakota were killed in what became known as the Wounded Knee Massacre.

An Influential Religious Leader

In the wake of the shocking tragedy at Wounded Knee, most Indians gave up the Ghost Dance and resigned themselves to the realities of reservation life. Although Wovoka's prophecy was not fulfilled, he remained a famous and influential medicine man for the rest of his life. He went on lengthy tours of reservations in Wyoming, Montana, Kansas, and Oklahoma, during which he often received cash and gifts. He also launched a successful mail-order business selling hats, clothing, feathers, paint, and other items to his many admirers. Even though his fame brought financial rewards, Wovoka continued to live a humble life. He lived in a simple, two-room cabin on the Walker Lake Reservation in Nevada, where visitors noted that he slept and ate on the floor.

By most accounts, Wovoka retained his faith in his spiritual powers until he died from prostate disease on September 29, 1932. Many fellow Paiute tribal members believed so strongly in his supernatural abilities that they expected him to rise from the dead. Since his death, historians have noted that Wovoka's vision had a lasting impact on Native Americans throughout the West. In fact, some credit him for contributing to the development of a shared Indian identity that crossed tribal boundaries. In his book *Native American Prophecies*, Scott Peterson argues that if Wovoka had not "set a date for the apocalypse … the Ghost Dance, with its vision of a brighter tomorrow, might still very well be a vital force in the world today."[3]

Sources:

Boring, Mel. *Wovoka: The Story of an American Indian*. Minneapolis: Dillon Press, 1981.

Hittman, Michael. *Wovoka and the Ghost Dance*. Lincoln: University of Nebraska Press, 1997.

"Wovoka Biography." *Encyclopedia of World Biography*, n.d. Available online at http://www.ghost dance.us/history/history-wovokaewb.html.

"Wovoka (Jack Wilson)." *The West,* PBS, 2001. Available online at http://www.pbs.org/weta/thewest /people/s_z/wovoka.htm.

Notes

[1] Peterson, Scott. *Native American Prophecies*. St. Paul, MN: Paragon House, 1990, p. 91.

[2] Quoted in Hittman, Michael. *Wovoka and the Ghost Dance*. Lincoln: University of Nebraska Press, 1997, p. 21.

[3] Peterson, p. 126.

PRIMARY SOURCES

Tecumseh Calls for Indian Unity against the White Invaders

As American settlers moved steadily westward in the early nineteenth century, some Indian tribes refused to give way without a fight. One of the most formidable native resistance movements was led by Tecumseh, a Shawnee warrior who worked tirelessly to unite Midwestern tribes against white incursions. The following excerpt provides an account of Tecumseh's effort to recruit Osage bands to his side in the struggle against the Americans. It provides valuable insight into Tecumseh's motivations and dedication to his cause.

The author of this excerpt is John D. Hunter, who clearly admired Tecumseh. Kidnapped from a frontier community as an infant, he spent his childhood and youth living with various Midwestern tribes. He returned to white society at about age nineteen in 1816. After learning to read and write English, Hunter published a popular account of his early life with the Indians, called Memoirs of a Captivity Among the Indians of North America, *in 1824.*

I wish it was in my power to do justice to the eloquence of this distinguished man: but it is utterly impossible. The richest colours, shaded with a master's pencil, would fall infinitely short of the flowing finish of the original. The occasion and subject were peculiarly adapted to call into action all the powers of genuine patriotism; and such language, such gestures, and such feelings and fulness of soul contending for utterance, were exhibited by this untutored native of the forest in the central wilds of America, as no audience, I am persuaded, either in ancient or modern times ever before witnessed....

The unlettered Tecumseh gave extemporaneous utterance only to what he felt; it was a simple, but vehement narration of the wrongs imposed by the white people on the Indians, and an exhortation for the latter to resist them.... This discourse made an impression on my mind, which, I think, will last as long as I live. I cannot repeat it *verbatim,* though if I could, it would be a mere skeleton, without the rounding finish of its integuments: it would only be the shadow of the substance; because the gestures, and the interest and feelings excited by the occasion, and which constitute the essentials of its character, would be altogether wanting. Nevertheless, I shall, as far as my recollection serves, make the attempt....

When the Osages and distinguished strangers had assembled, Tecumseh arose; and after a pause of some minutes, in which he surveyed his audience in a very dignified, though respectfully complaisant and sympathizing manner, he commenced as follows:

"*Brothers,* — We all belong to one family; we are all children of the Great Spirit; we walk in the same path; slake our thirst at the same spring; and now affairs of the greatest concern lead us to smoke the pipe around the same council fire!

"*Brothers,* — We are friends; we must assist each other to bear our burdens. The blood of many of our fathers and brothers has run like water on the ground, to satisfy the avarice of the white men. We, ourselves, are threatened with a great evil; nothing will pacify them but the destruction of all the red men.

"*Brothers,* — When the white men first set foot on our grounds, they were hungry; they had no place on which to spread their blankets, or to kindle their fires. They were feeble; they could do nothing for themselves. Our fathers commiserated their distress, and shared freely with them whatever the Great Spirit had given his red children. They gave them food when hungry, medicine when sick, spread skins for them to sleep on, and gave them grounds, that they might hunt and raise corn.

"*Brothers,* — The white people are like poisonous serpents: when chilled they are feeble and harmless; but invigorate them with warmth, and they sting their benefactors to death. The white people came among us feeble; and now we have made them strong, they wish to kill us, or drive us back, as they would wolves and panthers.

"*Brothers,* — The white men are not friends to the Indians: at first, they only asked for land sufficient for a wigwam; now, nothing will satisfy them but the whole of our hunting grounds, from the rising to the setting sun.

"*Brothers,* — The white men want more than our hunting grounds; they wish to kill our warriors; they would even kill our old men, women, and little ones.

"*Brothers,* — Many winters ago, there was no land; the sun did not rise and set: all was darkness. The Great Spirit made all things. He gave the white people a home beyond the great waters. He supplied these grounds with game, and gave them to his red children; and he gave them strength and courage to defend them.

"*Brothers,* — My people wish for peace; the red men all wish for peace: but where the white people are, there is no peace for them, except it be on the bosom of our mother.

"*Brothers,* — The white men despise and cheat the Indians; they abuse and insult them; they do not think the red men sufficiently good to live. The red men have borne many and great injuries; they ought to suffer them no longer. My people will not; they are determined on vengeance; they have taken up the tomahawk; they will make it fat with blood; they will drink the blood of the white people.

"*Brothers,* — My people are brave and numerous; but the white people are too strong for them alone. I wish you to take up the tomahawk with them. If we all unite, we will cause the rivers to stain the great waters with their blood.

"*Brothers,* — If you do not unite with us, they will first destroy us, and then you will fall an easy prey to them. They have destroyed many nations of red men because they were not united, because they were not friends to each other.

"*Brothers,* — The white people send runners amongst us; they wish to make us enemies, that they may sweep over and desolate our hunting grounds, like devastating winds, or rushing waters.

"*Brothers,* — Our Great Father [the king of England], over the great waters, is angry with the white people, our enemies. He will send his brave warriors against them; he will send us rifles, and whatever else we want—he is our friend, and we are his children.

"*Brothers,* — Who are the white people that we should fear them? They cannot run fast, and are good marks to shoot at: they are only men; our fathers have killed many of them: we are not squaws, and we will stain the earth red with their blood.

"*Brothers,* — The Great Spirit is angry with our enemies; he speaks in thunder, and the earth swallows up villages, and drinks up the Mississippi. The great waters will cover their lowlands; their corn cannot grow; and the Great Spirit will sweep those who escape to the hills from the earth with his terrible breath.

"*Brothers,* — We must be united; we must smoke the same pipe; we must fight each other's battles; and more than all, we must love the Great Spirit: he is for us; he will destroy our enemies, and make all his red children happy."

Source: Hunter, John D. *Memoirs of a Captivity among the Indians of North America.* London: Longman, Hurst, 1823, pp. 43-48.

Andrew Jackson Praises Indian Removal

When Andrew Jackson became America's seventh president in March 1829, he immediately made Indian removal one of his main policy goals. He believed that the eastern tribes posed an unacceptable obstacle to U.S. geographic and economic expansion, and he worked closely with Congress to pass legislation that would push native tribes west of the Mississippi River. In 1830 Jackson signed the Indian Removal Act, which gave him the authority to open up Indian lands in the Southeast to white settlement—and forcibly relocate any tribes that were in the way.

In the following excerpt from Jackson's December 6, 1830, State of the Union address to Congress, the president describes Indian removal as one of his administration's greatest accomplishments. He frames this undertaking, which devastated dozens of tribes during the 1830s and 1840s, as a righteous one. In addition, Jackson ridicules Indian complaints about the policy as childish and selfish—even though white greed for new land formed the very foundation of the Indian Removal Act.

It gives me pleasure to announce to Congress that the benevolent policy of the Government, steadily pursued for nearly 30 years, in relation to the removal of the Indians beyond the white settlements is approaching to a happy consummation. Two important tribes have accepted the provision made for their removal at the last session of Congress, and it is believed that their example will induce the remaining tribes also to seek the same obvious advantages.

The consequences of a speedy removal will be important to the United States, to individual States, and to the Indians themselves.... It puts an end to all possible danger of collision between the authorities of the General and State Governments on account of the Indians. It will place a dense and civilized population in large tracts of country now occupied by a few savage hunters. By opening the whole territory between Tennessee on the north and Louisiana on the south to the settlement of the whites it will incalculably strengthen the southwestern frontier and render the adjacent States strong enough to repel future invasions without remote aid. It will relieve the whole State of Mississippi and the western part of Alabama of Indian occupancy, and enable those States to advance rapidly in population, wealth, and power. It will separate the Indians from immediate contact with settlements of whites; free them from the power of the States; enable them to pursue happiness in their own way and under their own rude institutions; will retard the progress of decay, which is lessening their numbers, and perhaps cause them gradually, under the protection of the Government and through the influence of good counsels, to cast off their savage habits and become an interesting, civilized, and Christian community. These consequences, some of them so certain and the rest so probable, make the complete execution of the plan sanctioned by Congress at their last session an object of much solicitude.

Toward the aborigines of the country no one can indulge a more friendly feeling than myself, or would go further in attempting to reclaim them from their wandering habits and make them a happy, prosperous people. I have endeavored to impress upon them my own solemn convictions of the duties and powers of the General Government in relation to the State authorities. For the justice of the laws passed by the States within the scope of their reserved powers, they are not responsible to this Government. As individuals we may entertain and express our opinions of their acts, but as a Government we have as little right to control them as we have to prescribe laws for other nations.

With a full understanding of the subject, the Choctaw and the Chickasaw tribes have with great unanimity determined to avail themselves of the liberal offers presented by the act of Congress, and have agreed to remove beyond the Mississippi River. Treaties have been made with them, which in due season will be submitted for consideration. In negotiating these treaties they were made to understand their true condition, and they have preferred maintaining their independence in the Western forests to submitting to the laws of the States in which they now reside. These treaties, being probably the last which will ever be made with them, are characterized by great liberality on the part of the Government. They give the Indians a liberal sum in consideration of their removal, and comfortable subsistence on their arrival at their new homes. If it be their real interest to maintain a separate existence, they will there be at liberty to do so without the inconveniences and vexations to which they would unavoidably have been subject in Alabama and Mississippi.

Humanity has often wept over the fate of the aborigines of this country, and philanthropy has been long busily employed in devising means to avert it, but its progress has never for a moment been arrested, and one by one have many powerful tribes disappeared from the earth. To follow to the tomb the last of his race and to tread on the graves of extinct nations excite melancholy reflections. But true philanthropy reconciles the mind to these vicissitudes as it does to the extinction of one generation to make room for another. In the monuments and fortifications of an unknown people, spread over the extensive regions of the West, we behold the memorials of a once powerful race, which was exterminated or has disappeared to make room for the existing savage tribes. Nor is there anything in this which, upon a comprehensive view of the general interests of the human race, is to be regretted. Philanthropy could not wish to see this continent restored to the condition in which it was found by our forefathers. What good man would prefer a country covered with forests and ranged by a few thousand savages to our extensive Republic, studded with cities, towns, and prosperous farms, embellished with all the improvements which art can devise or industry execute, occupied by more than 12,000,000 happy people, and filled with all the blessings of liberty, civilization, and religion?

The present policy of the Government is but a continuation of the same progressive change by a milder process. The tribes which occupied the countries now constituting the Eastern States were annihilated or have melted away to make room for the whites. The waves of population and civilization are rolling to the westward, and we now propose to acquire the countries occupied by the red men of the South and West by a fair exchange, and, at the expense of the United States, to send them to a land where their existence may be prolonged and perhaps made perpetual.

Doubtless it will be painful to leave the graves of their fathers; but what do they more than our ancestors did or than our children are now doing? To better their condition in an unknown land our forefathers left all that was dear in earthly objects. Our children by thousands yearly leave the land of their birth to seek new homes in distant regions. Does Humanity weep at these painful separations from every thing, animate and inanimate, with which the young heart has become entwined? Far from it. It is rather a source of joy that our country affords scope where our young population may range unconstrained in body or in mind, developing the power and faculties of man in their highest perfection.

These remove hundreds and almost thousands of miles at their own expense, purchase the lands they occupy, and support themselves at their new homes from the moment of their arrival. Can it be cruel in this Government when, by events which it can not control, the Indian is made discontented in his ancient home to purchase his lands, to give him a new and extensive territory, to pay the expense of his removal, and support him a year in his new abode? How many thousands of our own people would gladly embrace the opportunity of removing to the West on such conditions! If the offers made to the Indians were extended to them, they would be hailed with gratitude and joy.

And is it supposed that the wandering savage has a stronger attachment to his home than the settled, civilized Christian? Is it more afflicting to him to leave the graves of his fathers than it is to our brothers and children? Rightly considered, the policy of the General Government toward the red man is not only liberal, but generous. He is unwilling to submit to the laws of the States and mingle with their population. To save him from this alternative, or perhaps utter annihilation, the General Government kindly offers him a new home, and proposes to pay the whole expense of his removal and settlement.

In the consummation of a policy originating at an early period, and steadily pursued by every Administration within the present century—so just to the States and so generous to the Indians—the Executive feels it has a right to expect the cooperation of Congress and of all good and disinterested men. The States, moreover, have a right to demand it. It was substantially a part of the compact which made them members of our Confederacy. With Georgia there is an express contract; with the new States an implied one of equal obligation. Why, in authorizing Ohio, Indiana, Illinois, Missouri, Mississippi, and Alabama to form constitutions and become separate States, did Congress include within their limits extensive tracts of Indian lands, and, in some instances, powerful Indian tribes? Was it not understood by both parties that the power of the States was to be coextensive with their limits, and that with all convenient dispatch the General Government should extinguish the Indian title and remove every obstruction to the complete jurisdiction of the State governments over the soil? Probably not one of those States would have accepted a separate existence—certainly it would never have been granted by Congress—had it been understood that they were to be confined for ever to those small portions of their nominal territory the Indian title to which had at the time been extinguished.

It is, therefore, a duty which this Government owes to the new States to extinguish as soon as possible the Indian title to all lands which Congress themselves have included within their limits....

Source: Jackson, Andrew. "Second Annual Message." *The Statesmanship of Andrew Jackson as Told in His Writings and Speeches.* Edited by Francis Newton Thorpe. New York: Tandy Thomas, 1909, pp. 110-15. Available online at *A Century of Lawmaking for a New Nation: U.S. Congressional Documents and Debates, 1774-1875*, Library of Congress American Memory page, http://memory.loc.gov/cgi-bin/ampage?collId=llrd&fileName=010/llrd010.db&recNum=438.

Cherokee Chief John Ross Denounces Indian Removal Policies

During the 1830s President Andrew Jackson's Indian removal policies pushed most Indians of the American Southeast to reservations thousands of miles to the west. This dislocation took place despite the best efforts of Indian leaders like John Ross, chief of the Cherokee nation in Georgia. During the early 1830s Ross and the Cherokee won several key legal victories in U.S. courts to check the Jackson administration's efforts to pry them loose from their homelands. But in December 1835, a small minority of Cherokee representatives signed the Treaty of New Echota. Under the terms of this treaty, the Cherokee accepted U.S. government terms for removal of the entire nation from its long-held lands in the East to a reservation in the Oklahoma Territory.

In this September 28, 1836, letter composed by Ross, the Cherokee chief argues that the Treaty of New Echota was completely fraudulent. But despite his legitimate protests, the U.S. government used the treaty to round up the Cherokee people of Georgia and force them west to reservations in modern-day Oklahoma. This grim journey, which claimed the lives of an estimated 4,000 Cherokee, became known as the "Trail of Tears."

I t is well known that for a number of years past we have been harassed by a series of vexations, which it is deemed unnecessary to recite in detail, but the evidence of which our delegation will be prepared to furnish. With a view to bringing our troubles to a close, a delegation was appointed on the 23rd of October, 1835, by the General Council of the nation, clothed with full powers to enter into arrangements with the Government of the United States, for the final adjustment of all our existing difficulties. The delegation failing to effect an arrangement with the United States commissioner, then in the nation, proceeded, agreeably to their instructions in that case, to Washington City, for the purpose of negotiating a treaty with the authorities of the United States.

After the departure of the Delegation, a contract was made by the Rev. John F. Schermerhorn, and certain individual Cherokees, purporting to be a "treaty, concluded at New Echota, in the State of Georgia, on the 29th day of December, 1835, by General William Carroll and John F. Schermerhorn, commissioners on the part of the United States, and the chiefs, headmen, and people of the Cherokee tribes of Indians." A spurious Delegation, in violation of a special injunction of the general council of the nation, proceeded to Washington City with this pretended treaty, and by false and fraudulent representations supplanted in the favor of the Government the legal and accredited Delegation of the Cherokee people, and obtained for this instrument, after making important alterations in its provisions, the recognition of the United States Government. And now it is presented to us as a treaty, ratified by the Senate, and approved by the President [Andrew Jackson], and our acquiescence in its requirements demanded, under the sanction of the displeasure of the United States, and the threat of summary compulsion, in case of refusal. It comes to us, not through our legitimate authorities, the known and usual medium of communication between the Government of the United States and our nation, but through the agency of a complication of powers, civil and military.

By the stipulations of this instrument, we are despoiled of our private possessions, the indefeasible property of individuals. We are stripped of every attribute of freedom and eligibility for legal self-defence. Our property may be plundered before our eyes; violence may be committed on our persons; even our lives may be taken away, and there is none to regard our complaints. We are denationalized; we are disfranchised. We are deprived of membership in the human family! We have neither land nor home, nor resting place that can be called our own. And this is effected by the provisions of a compact which assumes the venerated, the sacred appellation of treaty.

We are overwhelmed! Our hearts are sickened, our utterance is paralized, when we reflect on the condition in which we are placed, by the audacious practices of unprincipled men, who have managed their stratagems with so much dexterity as to impose on the Government of the United States, in the face of our earnest, solemn, and reiterated protestations.

The instrument in question is not the act of our Nation; we are not parties to its covenants; it has not received the sanction of our people. The makers of it sustain no office nor appointment in our Nation, under the designation of Chiefs, Head men, or any other title, by which they hold, or could acquire, authority to assume the reins of Government, and to make bargain and sale of our rights, our possessions, and our common country. And we are constrained solemnly to declare, that we cannot but contemplate the enforcement of the stipulations of this instrument on us, against our consent, as an act of injustice and oppression, which, we are well persuaded, can never knowingly be countenanced by the Government and people of the United

States; nor can we believe it to be the design of these honorable and high-minded individuals, who stand at the head of the Govt., to bind a whole Nation, by the acts of a few unauthorized individuals. And, therefore, we, the parties to be affected by the result, appeal with confidence to the justice, the magnanimity, the compassion, of your honorable bodies, against the enforcement, on us, of the provisions of a compact, in the formation of which we have had no agency.

In truth, our cause is your own; it is the cause of liberty and of justice; it is based upon your own principles, which we have learned from yourselves; for we have gloried to count your [George] Washington and your [Thomas] Jefferson our great teachers; we have read their communications to us with veneration; we have practised their precepts with success. And the result is manifest. The wildness of the forest has given place to comfortable dwellings and cultivated fields, stocked with the various domestic animals. Mental culture, industrious habits, and domestic enjoyments, have succeeded the rudeness of the savage state.

We have learned your religion also. We have read your Sacred books. Hundreds of our people have embraced their doctrines, practised the virtues they teach, cherished the hopes they awaken, and rejoiced in the consolations which they afford. To the spirit of your institutions, and your religion, which has been imbibed by our community, is mainly to be ascribed that patient endurance which has characterized the conduct of our people, under the laceration of their keenest woes. For assuredly, we are not ignorant of our condition; we are not insensible to our sufferings. We feel them! We groan under their pressure! And anticipation crowds our breasts with sorrows yet to come. We are, indeed, an afflicted people! Our spirits are subdued! Despair has well nigh seized upon our energies! But we speak to the representatives of a Christian country; the friends of justice; the patrons of the oppressed. And our hopes revive, and our prospects brighten, as we indulge the thought. On your sentence, our fate is suspended; prosperity or desolation depends on your word. To you, therefore, we look! Before your august assembly we present ourselves, in the attitude of deprecation, and of entreaty. On your kindness, on your humanity, on your compassion, on your benevolence, we rest our hopes. To you we address our reiterated prayers. Spare our people! Spare the wreck of our prosperity! Let not our deserted homes become the monuments of our desolation! But we forbear! We suppress the agonies which wring our hearts, when we look at our wives, our children, and our venerable sires! We restrain

168

the forebodings of anguish and distress, of misery and devastation and death, which must be the attendants on the execution of this ruinous compact.

In conclusion, we commend to your confidence and favor, our well-beloved and trust-worthy brethren and fellow-citizens, John Ross, Principal Chief, Richard Taylor, Samuel Gunter, John Benge, George Sanders, Walter S. Adair, Stephen Foreman, and Kalsateehee of Aquohee, who are clothed with full powers to adjust all our existing difficulties by treaty arrangements with the United States, by which our destruction may be averted, impediments to the advancement of our people removed, and our existence perpetuated as a living monument, to testify to posterity the honor, the magnanimity, the generosity of the United States. And your memorialists, as in duty bound, will ever pray.

[Signed by Ross, George Lowrey, Edward Gunter, Lewis Ross, thirty-one members of the National Committee and National Council, and 2,174 others.]

Source: John Ross. "Letter from John Ross, Principal Chief of the Cherokee Nation of Indians, in Answer to Inquires from a Friend Regarding the Cherokee Affairs with the United States." Washington, D.C., 1836, pp. 22–24. Also available in *The Papers of Chief John Ross: Vol. 1, 1807-1839*. Edited by Gary E. Moulton. Norman: University of Oklahoma Press, 1985; and online at *Cherokee Nation,* http://www.cherokee.org /Culture/162/Page/default.aspx.

A Cheyenne Recalls the Deadly Impact of Cholera on His Tribe

European diseases brought over to North America by white settlers had a catastrophic impact on Indian tribes across the continent. Cholera, smallpox, measles, tuberculosis, and other diseases for which Indians had no immunity wiped out entire villages, and these losses made it much harder for native communities to resist the incursions of white settlers and soldiers. This account of a cholera epidemic that ripped through the Great Plains tribes in 1849 was written by George Bent, a well-known frontier trader of mixed white and Cheyenne descent.

In '49, the emigrants brought the cholera up the Platte Valley, and from the emigrant trains it spread to the Indian camps. "Cramps" the Indians called it, and they died of it by the hundreds. On the Platte whole camps could be seen deserted with the tepees full of dead bodies, men, women, and children.

The Sioux and Cheyennes, who were nearest to the road [wagon train route], were the hardest hit, and from the Sioux the epidemic spread northward clear to the Blackfeet, while from the Cheyennes and Arapahoes it struck down into the Kiowa and Comanche country and created havoc among their camps.

Our tribe suffered very heavy loss; half of the tribe died, some old people say. A war party of about one hundred Cheyennes had been down the Platte, hunting for the Pawnees, and on their way home they stopped in an emigrant camp and saw white men dying of cholera in the wagons. When the Cheyennes saw these sick white men, they rushed out of the camp and started for home on the run, scattering as they went; but the terrible disease had them already in its grip, and many of the party died before reaching home, one of my Indian uncles and his wife dying among the first.

The men in the war party belonged to different camps, and when they joined these camps, they brought the cholera with them and it was soon raging in all the villages. The people were soon in a panic. The big camps broke up into little bands and family groups, and each little party fled from the rest.

[My] grandmother and stepmother, Yellow Woman, took the children that summer out among the Cheyennes, and they went to the Canadian, I think, where the Kiowas and Comanches were to make medicine. During the medicine dance an Osage visitor fell down in the crowd with cholera cramps. The Indians broke camp at once and fled in every direction, the Cheyennes north toward the Arkansas. They fled all night and halted on the Cimarron.

Here a brave man whose name I have forgotten—a famous warrior—mounted his war horse with his arms and rode through the camp shouting, "If I could see this thing [cholera], if I knew where it was, I would go there and kill it!" He was taken with the cramps as he rode, slumped over on his horse, rode slowly back to his lodge, and fell to the ground. The people then broke camp in wild fright and fled north through the big sand hills all that night.

Source: Hyde, George. *Life of George Bent: Written from His Letters.* Edited by Savoie Lottinville. Norman: University of Oklahoma Press, 1968, pp. 95-97.

Negotiating the Fort Laramie Treaty of 1868

During the 1850s and 1860s, U.S. government officials negotiated a number of treaties with Great Plains tribes to defuse rising white-Indian tensions and violence. Many of these treaties fell apart fairly quickly, primarily due to white violations of treaty terms. In the late 1860s, though, a government commission issued a report that harshly criticized the behavior of the U.S. government and white settlers, condemned conditions on Indian reservations, and urged federal authorities to craft—and honor—a comprehensive new treaty with the Lakota nation, the most powerful tribe on the Great Plains.

A short time later, U.S. negotiators convinced many Lakota bands to sign the Fort Laramie Treaty of 1868. Under this agreement, the Lakota were to receive financial aid and "permanent" possession of large swaths of land that they had long used. In addition, white authorities promised to abandon military forts they had built along the Bozeman Trail, a popular pioneer route to the west, and keep prospectors and settlers off Lakota lands. But the tribal leaders who signed the 1868 treaty nonetheless did so only under pressure, as white officials repeatedly issued dark warnings about the capacity of the United States to crush uncooperative tribes.

The following is an excerpt from the treaty council held at Fort Laramie on April 28, 1868. The speakers are U.S. Army General John B. Sanborn, General William S. Harney, and Iron Shell, a Brulé Lakota chieftain. Iron Shell expresses doubt about the trustworthiness of the whites throughout this meeting, but he eventually signs the agreement. As it turns out, his skepticism is well-founded; within a few years, lands set aside in the treaty for exclusive Lakota use were being overrun by white settlers, gold prospectors, and soldiers.

General Sanborn: We … offer you peace to save your nations from destruction. We speak the truth. But the truth is often unwelcome and grates harshly upon the ear. You will not believe me when I tell you that you cannot protect yourselves from the white people. You will not believe me when I tell you that this military officer now here, a commissioner to meet you, had to use his authority to keep a great body of whites out of your country last year. You will not believe me when I tell you that the white soldiers whom you were killing and trying to kill last year were driving back the whites from your country and trying to save the country for you and to prevent your destruction. But all this is true, and you must have the protec-

---

tion of the President of the United States and his white soldiers or disappear from the earth.

We want you to see this yourselves, and not be compelled to believe it because we say so. That you may see how the case stands we request you to send some of your chiefs and braves to Washington now. Any of your friends among the whites that you desire may go along with you. You will then see and know what we know, and can determine what course it is best for your nations to take. You do not see the white soldiers when they are fighting the whites and keeping them out of your country, but only when they resist your attacks made upon them when marching along the road. The questions between you and the whites must soon be finally and forever settled.

If you continue to fight the whites you can not expect the President nor your friends among them to protect you in your country from those who are waiting to go there in large numbers. If you continue at war your country will soon be all overrun by white people. Military posts will be located on all the rivers. Your game and yourselves will be destroyed. This is the last effort of the President to make peace with you and save for you a country and home.

We therefore propose that you now make a treaty by which you can and will abide. By this treaty we will agree to protect you from the inroads of our people and keep them out of a portion of your present country described in the treaty. We shall agree to furnish you supplies in clothing and other useful articles while you continue to roam and hunt. We shall agree to furnish cattle, horses, cows, and implements to work the ground to each of your people as may at any time settle down and build a home and wish to live like the whites. Under this treaty you can roam and hunt while you remain at peace and game lasts; and when the game is gone you will have a home and means of supporting yourselves and your children. But you must understand that if peace is not now made all efforts on our part to make it are at an end.

We ask you now to consider this matter with the understanding of men and not with the malice of children; and when you reply speak your whole thoughts and feelings. If there are any here who do not design to remain at peace, we do not want them to sign any treaty. If there are any here who design to disturb the railroads or any of the ranches or white people south of the Platte River, we do not want them to sign any treaty, for such acts repeated will force the President to send soldiers into your country and to make war. But all who now conclude to make peace and abide by it, who intend to meet the whites in a friendly manner, and receive aid and protection from the President, we now request to sign the treaty tomorrow morning at 10 o'clock. This is all that we have been told to say to you.

General Harney: I am afraid you do not understand why we want to make peace. Perhaps you think we are afraid. You can not be such fools as that, I hope. We do not want to go to war with you because you are a small nation, a handful compared with us, and we want you to live. If we go to war we shall send out to meet you a large army. Suppose you kill the whole army, we have another to send in its place. A great many of you will be killed and you have nobody to take their places. We are kind to you here. You have true hearts and we want you to live. We have not been making war with you. You are at war with us. We have not commenced yet. I hope you will not drive us to war.

Iron Shell (Brulé): I am getting to be an old man. The talk you have just made is what I have always gone by since I was a young man. When I was about 30 years old I joined the sensible men and have been with them ever since. When I was a young man I looked for nothing good, but everything that was bad. I was out hunting buffalo, and I heard that there were some good men here waiting to see me and I came in. I heard that General Harney had left the warpath and was ready for peace, so I came in.

My father and grandfather used to be with the whites, and I have been with them, too. We used to treat them well, I do not recollect that there was any war while we were with the whites. We used to take pity on one another and did nothing bad to each other while we were together. I know that the whites are like the grass on the prairie. Anybody that takes anything from the whites must pay for it. You have come into my country without my consent and spread your soldiers all over it. I have looked around for the cause of the trouble and I can not see that my young men were the cause of it. All the bad things that have been done, you have made the road for it. That is the truth. I love the whites. You whites went all over my country, killing my young men, and disturbing everything in my country. My heart is not made out of rock, but of flesh, but I have a strong heart. All the bad deeds that have been done I have had no hand in, neither have any of our young men.

I want to hear you give us good advice. I came here for that purpose. We helped you to stop this war between us and the whites. You have put us in misery; also these old traders whom the war has stopped. We want you to set us all right and put us back the same as in old times.

We want you to take away the forts from the country. That will leave big room for the Indians to live in. If you succeed about the forests all the game will come back and we will have plenty to eat. If you want the Indian to live do that and we will have a chance to live. One above us has created all of us, the whites the same as the Indians, and he will take pity on us. Our God has put us on earth to live in the way we do, to live on game. Our great father we depend on at Washington. We do not deliberate for ourselves, and we want him to take pity on us. Do you think that our God is for us the same as for the whites? I have prayed to God and asked him to make me succeed, and He has allowed it to me. I succeeded often. Your commissioners want to make peace and take pity on the Indians. Take away all these things if you intend to make peace, and we will live happy and be at peace. All we have is the land and the sky above. This war has set an example to our young men to make war on the whites. If it had not been for that we should have been at peace all the time....

I have listened to your advice, General Sanborn, and I told the others to listen to you. You sent messengers to us last winter and we have come in to you....

Our country is filling up with whites. Our great father has no sense; he lets our country be filled up. That is the way I think sometimes. Our great father is shutting up on us and making us a very small country. That is bad. For all that I have a strong heart. I have patience and pass over it, although you come over here and get all our gold, minerals, and skins. I pass over it all and do not get mad. I have always given the whites more than they have given me.

Yesterday you tell us we would have a council and last night I did not sleep; I was so glad. Now, I would like you to pick some good sensible young men, from one to four, and send them out, men who can be depended upon. I name Blue Horse, myself, and I want him to pick the others. We have been speaking very well together, and I am glad we get along so smoothly. The last thing I have to ask you about are the forts. This is sufficient and all right. We have got through talking. Give us our share of the goods and send them over to our village. We want to get back immediately as our children are crying for food. What you are doing with the Brulés will be a good example to the others. It will encourage them. We do not want to stay here and loaf upon you.

General Harney: We know very well that you have been treated very badly for years past. You have been cheated by everybody, and everybody has told lies to you, but now we want to commence anew. You have killed our people and have taken enough of our property and you ought to be satisfied.

It is not the fault of your great father in Washington. He sends people out here that he thinks are honest, but they are people who cheat you and treat you badly. We will take care that you shall not be treated so any more. We will begin to move the forts as soon as possible. They will be removed as soon as the treaty is made with all the Indians....

Iron Shell: I will always sign any treaty you ask me to do, but you have always made away with them, broke them. The whites always break them, and that is the way that war has come up.

[The treaty was here signed by the chiefs and head soldiers of the Brulés.]

Source: "Council with the Brulé Sioux, April 28, 1868." From *Proceedings of the Great Peace Commission of 1867-1868*. Vine Deloria Jr. and Raymond DeMallie, intro. Washington, DC: Institute for the Development of Indian Laws, 1975, pp. 106-09.

Eyewitness Recollections of the Battle of Little Bighorn

On June 25, 1876, U.S. Army General George Armstrong Custer and more than 260 cavalrymen under his command were slain by Lakota, Cheyenne, and Arapaho warriors at the Battle of Little Bighorn in present-day Montana. This famous battle ranked as the worst defeat that the U.S. Army suffered in the so-called Indian Wars of the nineteenth century. In the following selection, Indian eyewitnesses offer their recollections of the events at Little Bighorn.

Antelope Woman (Cheyenne): The band of Cheyennes that I lived with had about forty family lodges. In the last part of the winter we camped on the west side of Powder River, not far above the mouth of Little Powder River. Soldiers came early one morning in March 1876. They got between our camp and our horse herds, so that all of us had to run away on foot. Not many of our people were killed, but our tepees and everything in them were burned. Three days later, all of us walking, we arrived at the camp of Crazy Horse, the Oglala Sioux chief.

The Oglalas gave us food and shelter. After a few days the two bands went northward and found the Hunkpapa Sioux, where Sitting Bull was chief. The leaders of the three tribes decided that all of us should travel together for the spring and summer hunting.

We moved from place to place as the grass came up. Because Indians kept coming from the Dakota reservation, our three bands grew larger and larger. Other tribal bands joined us. Miniconjou Sioux, Blackfeet Sioux, Arrows All Gone [Sans Arc] Sioux—all came with us. There were then six separate camp circles, each having its own chiefs, wherever we camped. In some of the other camps there were small bands of other Sioux—the Burned Thigh, the Assiniboine, and some Waist and Skirt people.

All of us traveled together to the west side of the lower Powder River, on west across the Tongue River, and then to the Rosebud valley where the grass was high and our ponies became strong. Our men killed many buffalo, and we women tanned the hides and dried the meat as we moved from place to place up the Rosebud.

White Man Runs Him (Crow, a scout in Custer's cavalry unit): The scouts with General Custer were all Crows and Arikaras. Mitch Bouyer, a half-blood Sioux, was Chief of Scouts. The Crow scouts were Half Yellow Face, White Swan, Goes Ahead, Hairy Moccasin, Curly, and I, White Man

177

Runs Him. I was one of the oldest of the scouts and did most of the advance scouting. I knew this country very well.

On June 24 we were camped at a place just below where Busby is now. Hairy Mocassin, Goes Ahead, and I took some soldiers' horses and rode to a high point on the divide between the Rosebud and the Little Horn. This place was used by the Crows as a lookout during campaigns, and from it you could see for miles around. In this hill was a pocket where horses could be hidden.

As soon as it became light enough to see, we could make out smoke from the Sioux camp down in the Little Horn Valley and could see some white horses on the other side of the Little Horn River. The soldiers had marched during the night and were now camped a little below us on Davis Creek. We could see the smoke of their campfires as they cooked breakfast. In a little while we saw the soldiers come marching up, and [Lieutenant Colonel George Armstrong] Custer stopped opposite to our lookout. I went down and told him about the smoke we had seen from the Sioux camp. This was about six o'clock in the morning.

Custer came up the hill far enough to see over and down the valley. When he saw the Sioux village, he said, "These people are very troublesome and bother the Crows and white people. I am going to teach them a lesson today. I will whip them, and you Crows may then live in peace."

We scouts thought there were too many Indians for Custer to fight. There were camps and camps and camps. One big camp was in a circle near the western hills. I would say there were between four thousand and five thousand warriors, maybe more, I do not know. It was the biggest Indian camp I have ever seen.

Red Horse (Miniconjou): I was one of the chiefs of the council, and my lodge was pitched in the center of the camp. On the day of the attack, I and four women were out about a mile from camp digging wild turnips. Suddenly one of the women called my attention to a cloud of dust rising a short distance away. I soon saw that the soldiers were charging the camp.

We ran for the camp, and when I got there I was sent for at once to come to the council lodge. I found many of the council men already there when I arrived. We had no time to talk about what action we should take. We came out of the council lodge and called in all directions: Young men—mount horses and take guns; go fight the soldiers. Women and children—mount horses and go, get out of the way.

178

The day was hot. The soldiers came on the trail made by the Sioux camp in moving, and crossed the Little Bighorn River above where the Sioux crossed, and attacked the lodges of the Hunkpapas, farthest up the river.

Antelope Woman: In all the camps, as I went through them, there was great excitement. Old men were helping the young warriors in dressing and painting themselves for battle. Some women were bringing horses from the horse herd. Other women were working fast taking down their tepees. A few were loading horses with tepees and gear, while others were carrying heavy burdens on their backs. Many were taking away nothing, leaving their tepees and everything in them, running away with their children and only small packs in their hands. I saw a Sioux woman standing in one spot, jumping up and down screaming because she could not find her small son.

White Man Runs Him: Custer and his brother went to the right of us and halted on a small hill. His troops were moving forward below him. Custer turned around as he reached the top of the hill and waved his hat, and the soldiers at the bottom of the hill waved their hats and shouted. Custer then proceeded on up the ridge and his men followed. They were moving rapidly, and the scouts were forced to gallop their ponies sometimes to keep up with them. At a certain point on the ridge they turned to the right and rode down a coulee in a northern direction.

The scouts took up a position on the high bluffs, where we could look down into the Sioux camp. As we followed along on the high ground, Custer had come down Medicine Tail Creek and was moving toward the river. The Indians saw him there, and all began running that way. There were thousands of them. Custer tried to cross the river at the mouth of Medicine Tail Creek, but was unable to do so. This was the last we saw Custer.

Mitch Bouyer said to us, "You scouts need go no farther. You have guided Custer here, and your work is finished, so you had better go back to the pack train and let the soldiers do the fighting." Mitch Bouyer said that he was going down to join Custer, and turning his horse, he galloped away. That is the last time we saw Mitch Bouyer. He was killed with Custer over on the ridge.

Wooden Leg (Cheyenne): Bows and arrows were in use much more than guns. An Indian using a gun had to jump up and expose himself long enough to shoot. From their hiding places, Indians could shoot arrows in a high and long curve, to fall upon the soldiers or their horses. The arrows falling upon the horses stuck in their backs and caused them to go plunging here and there, knocking down the soldiers. The ponies of our warriors who were creeping along the gulches had been left farther back. Some of them were let loose, dragging their ropes, but most of them were tied to sagebrush. The Indians all the time could see where the soldiers were on the ridge, but the soldiers could not see our warriors crawling in the gullies through the sagebrush.

After this time of slow fighting, about forty of the soldiers came galloping from the east part of the ridge down toward the river, toward where most of the Cheyennes and many Oglalas were hidden. The Indians ran back to a deep gulch. The soldiers stopped and got off their horses when they arrived at a low ridge where the Indians had been. Lame White Man, the Southern Cheyenne chief, came on his horse and called us to come back and fight. In a few minutes the warriors were all around these soldiers. Then Lame White Man called out: "Come. We can kill all of them."

All around, the Indians began jumping up, running forward, dodging down, jumping up again, down again, all the time going toward the soldiers. Right away, all of the white men went crazy. Instead of shooting us, they turned their guns upon themselves. Almost before we could get to them, every one of them was dead. They killed themselves.

The Indians took the guns of these soldiers and used them for shooting at the soldiers on the high ridge. The shots quit coming from the soldiers. Warriors who had crept close to them began to call out that all of the white men were dead. All of the Indians then jumped up and rushed forward. All of the boys and old men on their horses came tearing into the crowd. The air was full of dust and smoke. Everybody was greatly excited. It looked like thousands of dogs might look if all of them were mixed together in a fight.

A strange incident happened: It appeared that all of the white men were dead. But there was one of them who raised himself to a support on his left elbow. He turned and looked over his left shoulder, and then I got a good view of him. His expression was wild, as if his mind was all tangled up and he was wondering what was going on here. In his right hand he held his six-shooter. Many of the Indians near him were scared by what seemed to have been a return from death to life. But a Sioux warrior jumped forward, grabbed the six-shooter, and wrenched it from the soldier's grasp. The gun was turned upon the white man, and he was shot through the head. Other Indians struck him or stabbed him. I think he must have been the last man killed in this great battle where not one of the enemy got away.

Noisy Walking was badly wounded. He was my same age, and we often had been companions since our small boyhood. White Bull, an important medicine man, was his father. I asked the young man, "How are you?" He replied, "Good." But he did not look well. He had been hit by three different bullets, one of them having passed through his body. He had also some stab wounds in his side. Word had been sent to his relatives in the camp.

Sitting Bull (Hunkpapa): I tell no lies about dead men. These men who came with Long Hair [Custer] were as good men as ever fought. When they rode up, their horses were tired and they were tired. When they got off from their horses, they could not stand firmly on their feet. They swayed to and fro—so my young men have told me—like the limbs of cypresses in a great wind. Some of them staggered under the weight of their guns. But they began to fight at once; but by this time, as I have said, our camps were aroused, and there were plenty of warriors to meet them. They fired with needle guns. We replied with magazine guns—repeating rifles. Our young men rained lead across the river and drove the white braves back.

Black Elk (Oglala): I watched the big dust whirling on the hill across the river, and horses were coming out of it with empty saddles. We knew there would be no soldiers left. There were many other boys about my age and younger up there with their mothers and sisters, and they asked me to go over to the battle with them. So we got on our ponies and rode over across the Greasy Grass [Little Bighorn River area] to the mouth of a gulch that led up through the bluff to where the fighting was. We rode around shooting arrows into the soldiers.

I saw something bright hanging on this soldier's belt, and I pulled it out. It was round and bright and yellow and very beautiful and I put it on for a necklace. At first it ticked inside, and then it did not anymore. I wore it around my neck a long time before I found out what it was and how to make it tick again.

Then the women all came over and we went to the top of the hill. Gray horses were lying dead there, and some of them were on top of dead soldiers, and dead soldiers were on top of them. After a while I got tired looking around. I could smell nothing but blood, and I got sick of it. So I went back home with some others. I was not sorry at all. I was a happy boy. Those white soldiers had come to kill our mothers and fathers and us, and it was our country.

Wooden Leg: After sundown I visited Noisy Walking. He was lying on a ground bed of buffalo robes under a willow dome shelter. His father, White

Bull, was with him. His mother sat just outside the entrance. I asked my friend, "How are you?" He replied, "Good, only I want water." I did not know what else to say, but I wanted him to know that I was his friend and willing to do whatever I could for him. I sat down upon the ground beside him. After a little while I said, "You were brave." Nothing else was said for several minutes. He was weak. His hands trembled at every move he made. Finally he said to his father, "I wish I could have some water—just a little of it."

"No. Water will kill you."

White Bull almost choked as he said this to his son. But he was a good medicine man, and he knew what was best. As I sat there looking at Noisy Walking, I knew he was going to die. My heart was heavy. But I could not do him any good, so I excused myself and went away.

Low Dog (Hunkpapa): The next day we fought [Major Marcus] Reno and his forces again and killed many of them. Then the chiefs said these men had been punished enough, and that we ought to be merciful and let them go. Then we heard that another force was coming up the river; this was General [Alfred] Terry's command. The chiefs and wise men counseled that we had fought enough and that we should not fight unless attacked. So we took our women and children and went away.

Antelope Woman: I may have seen Custer at the time of the battle or after he was killed. I do not know. At the time I did not know he was there. All of our old warriors say the same—none of them knew of his being there till they were told of it at the soldier fort or at the agencies or heard it from Indians coming from the agencies. But I learned something more about him later from our people in Oklahoma. Two Southern Cheyenne women who had known him in the south had seen Custer lying dead on the battlefield after the fight ended. They pushed the point of a bone sewing awl [Indian knitting needle] through his ears. They did this to improve his hearing in the spirit world. He must not have listened very well in this life, or he would have heard what our chiefs said about broken promises.

Source: Viola, Herman J. *It Is a Good Day to Die: Indian Eyewitnesses Tell the Story of the Battle of the Little Big Horn.* New York: Crown, 1998, pp. 21-23, 27-29, 33, 40, 48-49, 57-60, 63-64, 67, 68, 71.

White Officials Call for Dismantling of the "Tribal Organization"

In the 1880s lawmakers and bureaucrats within the U.S. government became convinced that the best way to solve the nation's "Indian problem" was to 1) break up the tribal organizations that had long governed American Indian societies and 2) encourage Indian assimilation into white society by dividing communally-held reservation lands into smaller plots of individually owned private property. This land conversion strategy, known as allotment, became the centerpiece of the 1887 Dawes Act.

The following is an excerpt from a report written by Commissioner of Indian Affairs Merrill E. Gates in 1885. His remarks provide a good overview of the attitudes held by supporters of allotment policies.

Has our Government in its dealings with the Indians hitherto adopted a course of legislation and administration, well adapted to build up their manhood and make them intelligent, self-supporting citizens?

They are the wards of the Government. Is not a guardian's first duty so to educate and care for his wards as to make them able to care for themselves? It looks like intended fraud if a guardian persists in such management of his wards and such use of their funds intrusted to him as in the light of experience clearly unfits them and will always keep them unfit for the management of their own affairs and their own property. When a guardian has in his hands funds which belong to his wards, funds which have been expressly set apart for the education of those wards, funds which from time to time he has publicly professed himself to be about to use for that particular end, yet still retains the money from year to year while his wards suffer sadly in the utter lack of proper educational facilities, we call his conduct disgraceful—an outrage and a crying iniquity. Yet our Commissioner of Indian Affairs again and again calls attention to the fact that the Government has funds, now amounting to more than $4,000,000, which are by treaty due to Indians for educational purposes alone. Who can doubt that a comprehensive plan looking to the industrial and the general education of all Indians should be undertaken at once? ...

But it is not merely in neglecting to provide direct means for their education that we have been remiss in our duty to the Indians. The money and care which our Government has given to the Indians in most cases has not been wisely directed to strengthening their manhood, elevating their morals, and fitting them for intelligent citizenship. We have massed them upon reserva-

183

tions, fenced off from all intercourse with the better whites. We have given them no law to protect them against crimes from within the tribe—almost none to protect them against aggression from without. And above all else we have utterly neglected to teach them the value of honest labor. Nay, by rations dealt out whether needed or not, we have interfered to suspend the efficient teachings by which God leads men to love and honor labor. We have taken from them the compelling inspiration that grows out of His law, "if a man will not work, neither shall he eat!" Why, if a race inured to toil were cut off from all intercourse with the outside world, and left to roam at large over a vast territory, regularly fed by Government supplies, how many generations would pass before that race would revert to barbarism?

We have held them at arm's length, cut them off from the teaching power of good example, and given them rations and food to hold them in habits of abject laziness. A civilization like ours would soon win upon the Indians and bring them rapidly into greater harmony with all its ideas if as a nation in our dealings with them we had shown a true spirit of humanity, civilization, and Christianity. But such a spirit cannot be discerned in the history of our legislation for the Indians or our treaties with them. We have never recognized the obligation that rests upon us as a dominant, civilized people, the strong Government, to legislate carefully, honorably, disinterestedly, for these people.... How can we organize, enforce, and sustain institutions and habits among the Indians which shall civilize and Christianize them? The fine old legend, *noblesse oblige* [a belief that people of great power and superior breeding have an obligation to behave kindly toward the less fortunate], we have forgotten in our broken treaties and our shamefully deficient legislation....

We must as rapidly as possible break up the tribal organization and give them law, with the family and land in severalty as its central idea. We must not only give them law, we must force law upon them. We must not only offer them education, we must force education upon them. Education will come to them by complying with the forms and the requirements of the law....

While we profess to desire their civilization, we adopt in the Indian reservation the plan which of all possible plans seems most carefully designed to preserve the degrading customs and the low moral standards of heathen barbarism. Take a barbaric tribe, place them upon a vast tract of land from which you carefully exclude all civilized men, separate them by hundreds of miles from organized civil society and the example of reputable white settlers, and having thus insulated them in empty space, double insulate them from Christian civilization by surrounding them with sticky layers of the vilest, most designingly wicked men our century knows, the whiskey-selling whites and the debased half-breeds who infest the fringes of our reservations, men who have the vices of the barbarian plus the worst vices of the reckless frontiersman and the city criminal, and then endeavor to incite the electrifying, life-giving currents of civilized life to flow through this doubly insulated mass. If an Indian now and then gets glimpses of something better and seeks to leave this seething mass of in-and-in breeding degradation, to live in a civilized community, give him no protection by law and no hope of citizenship. If he has won his way as many have done through the highest institutions of learning, with honor, tell him that he may see many of our largest cities ruled by rings of men, many of whom are foreigners by birth, ignorant, worthless, yet naturalized citizens, but that he must not hope to vote or to hold office.

If he says "I will be content to accumulate property, then," tell him "you may do so; but any one who chooses may withhold your wages, refuse to pay you money he has borrowed, plunder you as he will, and our law gives you no redress." Thus we drive the honest and ambitious Indian, as we do the criminals, back to the tribe and the reservation; and cutting them off from all hopes of bettering themselves while we feed their laziness on Government rations, we complain that they are not more ambitious and industrious.

Christian missionaries plunge into these reservations, struggle with the mass of evil there, and feeling that bright children can be best educated in the atmosphere of civilization, they send to Eastern institutions these Indian children plucked like fire-stained brands from the reservations. They are brought to our industrial training schools. The lesson taught by the comparison of their photographs when they come and when they go is wonderful.

The years of contact with ideas and with civilized men and Christian women so transform them that their faces shine with a wholly new light, for they have indeed "communed with God." They came children; they return young men and young women; yet they look younger in the face than when they came to us. The prematurely aged look of hopeless heathenism has given way to that dew of eternal youth which marks the difference between the savage and the man who lives in the thoughts of an eternal future....

Break up the reservation. Its usefulness is past. Treat it as we treat the fever-infected hospital when life has so often yielded to disease within its walls that we see clearly the place is in league with the powers of death, and the fiat goes forth, "though this was planned as a blessing it has proved to be a curse; away with it! burn it!"

Guard the rights of the Indian, but for his own good break up his reservations. Let in the light of civilization. Plant in alternate sections or townships white farmers, who will teach him by example. Reserve all the lands he needs for the Indian. Give land by trust-deed in severalty to each family.

Among the parts of the reservation to be so assigned to Indians in severalty retain alternate ranges or townships for white settlers. Let only men of such character as a suitable commission would approve be allowed to file on these lands. Let especial advantages in price of land, and in some cases let a small salary be offered, to induce worthy farmers thus to settle among the Indians as object-teachers of civilization. Let the parts of the reservations not needed be sold by the Government for the benefit of the Indians, and the money thus realized by used to secure this wise intermingling of the right kind of civilized men with the Indians....

Source: Gates, Merrill E. *Seventeenth Annual Report of the Board of Indian Commissioners.* Washington, DC: Government Printing Office, 1885. Reprinted in Prucha, Francis Paul, ed. *Americanizing the American Indians: Writings by the "Friends of the Indian," 1880-1900.* Lincoln: University of Nebraska Press, 1978, pp. 45-54.

A Lakota Indian Recalls the Ghost Dance

In 1889 a Paiute Indian named Wovoka announced that he had received a prophetic vision of a future world in which the whites were swept away and Indians once again experienced prosperity and happiness. This future world could be ushered in, said Wovoka, if Indian nations performed a ritual "Ghost Dance."

As word of Wovoka's vision spread, the "Ghost Dance" movement spread like wildfire among the tribes of the Great Plains. Many white observers viewed this development as cause for alarm, but as the following testimony from one Ghost Dance participant indicates, the movement was more desperate than dangerous.

It was over fifty years ago. A big new government school had been put up at Pine Ridge, and we were kept there, boys and girls *together*—an unheard-of thing. We wore *Wasicu* [white] clothes, which neither fitted nor felt right on us. In fact, we looked terrible in them, but we had to wear them or be punished.

The rumor got about: "The dead are to return. The buffalo are to return. The [Sioux] people will get back their own way of life. The white people will soon go away, and that will mean happier times for us once more!"

That part about the dead returning was what appealed to me. To think I should see my dear mother, grandmother, brothers and sisters again! But, boylike, I soon forgot about it, until one night when I was rudely awakened in the dormitory. "Get up, put on your clothes and slip downstairs, we are running away," a boy was hissing into my ear.

Soon fifty of us, little boys about eight to ten, started out across country over hills and valleys, running all night. I know now that we ran almost thirty miles. There on the Porcupine Creek thousands of … people were in camp, all hurrying about very purposefully. In a long sweat lodge with openings at both ends, people were being purified in great companies for the holy dance, men by themselves and women by themselves, of course.

A woman quickly spied us and came weeping toward us. "These also shall take part," she was saying of us. So a man called out, "You runaway boys, come here." They stripped our ugly clothes from us and sent us inside. When we were well purified, they sent us out at the other end and placed sacred shirts on us. They were of white muslin with a crow, a fish, stars, and other symbols painted on. I never learned what they meant. Everyone wore one magpie and one eagle feather in his hair, but in our case there was nothing to tie them to. The school had promptly ruined us by shaving off our long hair till our scalps showed lighter than our faces!

The people, wearing the sacred shirts and feathers, now formed a ring. We were in it. All joined hands. Everyone was respectful and quiet, expecting something wonderful to happen. It was not a glad time, though. All walked cautiously and in awe, feeling their dead were close at hand.

The leaders beat time and sang as the people danced, going round to the left in a sidewise step. They danced without rest, on and on, and they got out of breath but still they kept going as long as possible. Occasionally someone thoroughly exhausted and dizzy fell unconscious into the center and lay there "dead." Quickly those on each side of him closed the gap and went right on. After a while, many lay about in that condition. They were now "dead" and seeing their dear ones. As each one came to, she, or he, slowly sat up and looked about, bewildered, and then began wailing inconsolably.

One of the leaders, a medicine man, asked a young girl, "My kinswoman, why do you weep?" Then she told him tearfully what she had just seen, and he in turn proclaimed it to the people. Then all wailed with her. It was very dismal....

The visions varied at the start, but they ended the same way, like a chorus describing a great encampment of all ... who had ever died, where all were related and therefore understood each other, where the buffalo came eagerly to feed them, and there was no sorrow but only joy, where relatives thronged out with happy laughter to greet the newcomer. That was the best of all!

Waking to the drab and wretched present after such a glowing vision, it was little wonder that they wailed as if their poor hearts would break in two with disillusionment. But at least they had seen! The people went on and on and could not stop, day or night, hoping perhaps to get a vision of their own dead, or at least to hear of the visions of others. They preferred that to rest or food or sleep. And I suppose the authorities did think they were crazy—but they weren't. They were only terribly unhappy.

Source: Deloria, Ella. "The Reservation Picture." From *Speaking of Indians*, 1944. Reprint. Lincoln: University of Nebraska Press, 1998, pp. 80-83.

A BIA Assessment of the Causes of Lakota Discontent

In the aftermath of the Ghost Dance movement and the Wounded Knee Massacre of 1890, Commissioner of Indian Affairs Thomas Jefferson Morgan submitted an extremely critical report that blamed government policies for much of the Indian unrest in the West. Morgan, who served as the head of the Bureau of Indian Affairs from 1889 to 1893, charged that shortsighted and foolish Indian policies had made an "outbreak" of native defiance almost inevitable. Following is an excerpt from his report.

"Causes of the Outbreak"

In stating the events which led to this outbreak among the Sioux, the endeavor too often has been merely to find some opportunity for locating blame. The causes are complex, and many are obscure and remote. Among them may be named the following:

First. A feeling of unrest and apprehension in the mind of the Indians has naturally grown out of the rapid advance in civilization and the great changes which this advance has necessitated in their habits and mode of life.

Second. Prior to the agreement of 1876 buffalo and deer were the main support of the Sioux. Food, tents, bedding were the direct outcome of hunting, and, with furs and pelts as articles of barter or exchange, it was easy for the Sioux to procure whatever constituted for them the necessaries, the comforts, or even the luxuries of life. Within eight years from the agreement of 1876 the buffalo had gone, and the Sioux had left to them alkali land and government rations. It is hard to overestimate the magnitude of the calamity, as they viewed it, which happened to these people by the sudden disappearance of the buffalo and the large diminution in the numbers of deer and other wild animals. Suddenly, almost without warning, they were expected at once and without previous training to settle down to the pursuits of agriculture in a land largely unfitted for such use. The freedom of the chase was to be exchanged for the idleness of the camp. The boundless range was to be abandoned for the circumscribed reservation, and abundance of plenty to be supplanted by limited and decreasing government subsistence and supplies. Under these circumstances it is not in human nature not to be discontented and restless, even turbulent and violent.

Third. During a long series of years, treaties, agreements, cessions of land and privileges, and removals of bands and agencies have kept many of the Sioux, particularly those at Pine Ridge and Rosebud, in an unsettled condition, especially as some of the promises made them were fulfilled tardily or not at all....

Fourth. The very large reduction of the great Sioux reservation, brought about by the Sioux commission through the consent of the large majority of the adult males, was bitterly opposed by a large, influential minority. For various reasons, they regarded the cession as unwise, and did all in their power to prevent its consummation, and afterwards were constant in their expressions of dissatisfaction and in their endeavors to awaken a like feeling in the minds of those who signed the agreement.

Fifth. There was diminution and partial failure of the crops for 1889, by reason of their neglect by the Indians, who were congregated in large numbers at the council with the Sioux commission, and a further diminution of ordinary crops by the drought of 1890. Also, in 1888, the disease of black leg appeared among the cattle of the Indians.

Sixth. At this time, by delayed and reduced appropriations, the Sioux rations were temporarily cut down. Rations were not diminished to such an extent as to bring the Indians to starvation or even extreme suffering, as has been often reported; but short rations came just after the Sioux commission had negotiated the agreement for the cession of lands, and, as a condition of securing the signatures of the majority, had assured the Indians that their rations would be continued unchanged....

[Morgan then quotes from an 1889 Sioux commission report that explicitly warned against reducing government rations for Indians.]

"Such diminution certainly should not be allowed, as the government is bound in good faith to carry into effect the former treaties where not directly and positively affected by the act, and if under the provisions of the treaty itself the ration is at any time reduced, the commissioners recommend that the Indians should be notified before spring opens, so that crops may be cultivated. It is desirable that the recent reduction made should be restored, as it is now impossible to convince the Indians that it was not due to the fact that the government, having obtained their lands, had less concern in looking after their material interests...."

Seventh. Other promises made by the Sioux commission and the agreement were not promptly fulfilled; among them were increase of appropriations for education, for which this office had asked an appropriation of $150,000; the payment of $200,000 in compensation for ponies taken from

190

the Sioux in 1876 and 1877; and the reimbursement of the Crow Creek Indians for a reduction made in their per capita allowance of land, as compared with the amount allowed other Sioux, which called for an appropriation of $187,039. The fulfillment of all these promises except the last named was contained in the act of January 19, 1891.

Eighth. In 1888 and 1889 epidemics of la grippe, measles, and whooping cough, followed by many deaths, added to the gloom and misfortune which seemed to surround the Indians.

Ninth. The wording of the agreement changed the boundary line between the Rosebud and Pine Ridge diminished reservations and necessitated a removal of a portion of the Rosebud Indians from the lands which, by the agreement, were included in the Pine Ridge reservation to lands offered them in lieu thereof upon the diminished Rosebud reserve. This, although involving no great hardship to any considerable number, added to the discontent.

Tenth. Some of the Indians were greatly opposed to the census which Congress ordered should be taken. The census at Rosebud, as reported by Special Agent Lea and confirmed by a special census taken by Agent Wright, revealed the somewhat startling fact that rations had been issued to Indians very largely in excess of the number actually present, and this diminution of numbers as shown by the census necessitated a diminution of the rations, which was based, of course, upon the census.

Eleventh. The Messiah craze, which fostered the belief that "ghost shirts" would be invulnerable to bullets, and that the supremacy of the Indian race was assured, added to discontent the fervor of fanaticism and brought those who accepted the new faith into the attitude of sullen defiance, but defensive rather than aggressive.

Twelfth. The sudden appearance of military upon their reservation gave rise to the wildest rumors among the Indians of danger and disaster, which were eagerly circulated by the disaffected Indians and corroborated by exaggerated accounts in the newspapers, and these and other influences connected with and inseparable from military movements frightened many Indians away from their agencies into the bad lands and largely intensified whatever spirit of opposition to the government existed.

Source: *Sixteenth Annual Report of the Commissioner of Indian Affairs to the Secretary of the Interior.* Vol.1. Washington, DC: Government Printing Office, 1891, pp. 132–35.

Black Elk Recounts the Massacre at Wounded Knee

Black Elk (c. 1863-1950) was an Oglala Lakota medicine man who witnessed—or participated in—many of the most famous events of the nineteenth century Indian Wars on the Great Plains, including the Battle of Little Bighorn and the Wounded Knee Massacre. In 1932 he collaborated with John G. Neihardt to publish Black Elk Speaks, *an account of his early life that also spent a great deal of time explaining the spiritual beliefs of the Lakota people. This work remains one of the best-known works of American Indian literature in U.S. history.*

The following excerpt from Black Elk Speaks *is an account of the December 29, 1890, massacre of more than 250 Indian men, women, and children at Wounded Knee. Some of the details of Black Elk's account do not match exactly with those of other survivors and witnesses, which also differ in some details from one another. But historians generally agree with the broad outlines of Black Elk's account.*

That evening before it happened, I went in to Pine Ridge and heard these things, and while I was there, soldiers started for where the Big Foots were. These made about five hundred soldiers that were there next morning. When I saw them starting I felt that something terrible was going to happen. That night I could hardly sleep at all. I walked around most of the night.

In the morning I went out after my horses, and while I was out I heard shooting off toward the east, and I knew from the sound that it must be wagon-guns (cannon) going off. The sounds went right through my body, and I felt that something terrible would happen.

When I reached camp with the horses, a man rode up to me and said: "Hey-hey-hey! The people that are coming are fired on! I know it!"

I saddled up my buckskin and put on my sacred shirt. It was one I had made to be worn by no one but myself. It had a spotted eagle outstretched on the back of it, and the daybreak star was on the left shoulder, because when facing south that shoulder is toward the east. Across the breast, from the left shoulder to the right hip, was the flaming rainbow, and there was another rainbow around the neck, like a necklace, with a star at the bottom. At each shoulder, elbow, and wrist was an eagle feather; and over the whole shirt were red streaks of lightning. You will see that this was from my great vision, and you will know how it protected me that day.

I painted my face all red, and in my hair I put one eagle feather for the One Above.

It did not take me long to get ready, for I could still hear the shooting over there.

I started out alone on the old road that ran across the hills to Wounded Knee. I had no gun. I carried only the sacred bow of the west that I had seen in my great vision. I had gone only a little way when a band of young men came galloping after me. The first two who came up were Loves War and Iron Wasichu. I asked what they were going to do, and they said they were just going to see where the shooting was. Then others were coming up, and some older men.

We rode fast, and there were about twenty of us now. The shooting was getting louder. A [man on] horseback from over there came galloping very fast toward us, and he said: "Hey-hey-hey! They have murdered him!" Then he whipped his horse and rode away faster toward Pine Ridge.

In a little while we had come to the top of the ridge where, looking to the east, you can see for the first time the monument and the burying ground on the little hill where the church is. That is where the terrible thing started. Just south of the burying ground on the little hill a deep dry gulch runs about east and west, very crooked, and it rises westward to nearly the top of the ridge where we were. It had no name, but the Wasichus [whites] sometimes call it Battle Creek now. We stopped on the ridge not far from the head of the dry gulch. Wagon guns were still going off over there on the little hill, and they were going off again where they hit along the gulch. There was much shooting down yonder, and there were many cries, and we could see cavalrymen scattered over the hills ahead of us. Cavalrymen were riding along the gulch and shooting into it, where the women and children were running away and trying to hide in the gullies and the stunted pines.

A little way ahead of us, just below the head of the dry gulch, there were some women and children who were huddled under a clay bank, and some cavalrymen were there pointing guns at them.

We stopped back behind the ridge, and I said to the others: "Take courage. These are our relatives. We will try to get them back." Then we all sang a song which went like this:

"A thunder being nation I am, I have said.
A thunder being nation I am, I have said.

You shall live.
You shall live.
You shall live.
You shall live."

Then I rode over the ridge and the others after me, and we were crying: "Take courage! It is time to fight!" The soldiers who were guarding our relatives shot at us and then ran away fast, and some more cavalrymen on the other side of the gulch did too. We got our relatives and sent them across the bridge to the northwest where they would be safe.

I had no gun, and when we were charging, I just held the sacred bow out in front of me with my right hand. The bullets did not hit us at all.

We found a little baby lying all alone near the head of the gulch. I could not pick her up just then, but I got her later and some of my people adopted her. I just wrapped her up tighter in a shawl that was around her and left her there. It was a safe place, and I had other work to do.

The soldiers had run eastward over the hills where there were some more soldiers, and they were off their horses and lying down. I told the others to stay back, and I charged upon them holding the sacred bow out toward them with my right hand. They all shot at me, and I could hear bullets all around me, but I ran my horse right close to them, and then swung around. Some soldiers across the gulch began shooting at me too, but I got back to the others and was not hurt at all.

By now many other Lakotas, who had heard the shooting, were coming up from Pine Ridge, and we all charged on the soldiers. They ran eastward toward where the trouble began. We followed down along the dry gulch, and what we saw was terrible. Dead and wounded women and children and little babies were scattered all along there where they had been trying to run away. The soldiers had followed along the gulch, as they ran, and murdered them in there. Sometimes they were in heaps because they had huddled together, and some were scattered all along. Sometimes bunches of them had been killed and torn to pieces where the wagon guns hit them. I saw a little baby trying to suck its mother, but she was bloody and dead.

There were two little boys at one place in this gulch. They had guns and they had been killing soldiers all by themselves. We could see the soldiers they had killed. The boys were all alone there and they were not hurt. These were very brave little boys.

194

When we drove the soldiers back, they dug themselves in, and we were not enough people to drive them out from there. In the evening they marched off up Wounded Knee Creek, and then we saw all that they had done there.

Men and women and children were heaped and scattered all over the flat at the bottom of the little hill where the soldiers had their wagon-guns, and westward up the dry gulch all the way to the high ridge, the dead women and children and babies were scattered.

When I saw this I wished that I had died too, but I was not sorry for the women and children. It was better for them to be happy in the other world, and I wanted to be there too. But before I went there I wanted to have revenge. I thought there might be a day, and we should have revenge.

After the soldiers marched away, I heard from my friend, Dog Chief, how the trouble started, and he was right there by Yellow Bird when it happened. This is the way it was:

In the morning the soldiers began to take all the guns away from the Big Foots, who were camped in the flat below the little hill where the monument and burying ground are now. The people had stacked most of their guns, and even their knives, by the tepee where Big Foot was lying sick. Soldiers were on the little hill and all around, and there were soldiers across the dry gulch to the south and over east along Wounded Knee Creek too. The people were nearly surrounded, and the wagon-guns were pointing at them.

Some had not yet given up their guns, and so the soldiers were searching all the tepees, throwing things around and poking into everything. There was a man called Yellow Bird, and he and another man were standing in front of the tepee where Big Foot was lying sick. They had white sheets around and over them, with eyeholes to look through, and they had guns under these. An officer came to search them. He took the other man's gun, and then started to take Yellow Bird's. But Yellow Bird would not let go. He wrestled with the officer, and while they were wrestling, the gun went off and killed the officer. Wasichus and some others have said he meant to do this, but Dog Chief was standing right there, and he told me it was not so. As soon as the gun went off, Dog Chief told me, an officer shot and killed Big Foot who was lying sick inside the tepee.

Then suddenly nobody knew what was happening, except that the soldiers were all shooting and the wagon-guns began going off right in among the people.

Many were shot down right there. The women and children ran into the gulch and up west, dropping all the time, for the soldiers shot them as they ran. There were only about a hundred warriors and there were nearly five hundred soldiers. The warriors rushed to where they had piled their guns and knives. They fought soldiers with only their hands until they got their guns.

Dog Chief saw Yellow Bird run into a tepee with his gun, and from there he killed soldiers until the tepee caught fire. Then he died full of bullets.

It was a good winter day when all this happened. The sun was shining. But after the soldiers marched away from their dirty work, a heavy snow began to fall. The wind came up in the night. There was a big blizzard, and it grew very cold. The snow drifted deep in the crooked gulch, and it was one long grave of butchered women and children and babies, who had never done any harm and were only trying to run away.

Source: Neihardt, John G. *Black Elk Speaks: Being the Life Story of a Holy Man of the Oglala Sioux.* 1932. Reprint. Albany: State University of New York Press, 2008, pp. 207-12.

Looking for Survivors at Wounded Knee

Charles A. Eastman (1858-1939) was a prominent writer, physician, and reformer of mixed white and Santee Dakota descent who worked throughout his life to improve the lives of his fellow American Indians. Eastman's first job after graduating from medical school in 1890 was as the physician at the Pine Ridge Indian reservation in South Dakota. He thus became an eyewitness to the turmoil that enveloped Pine Ridge in the second half of 1890, including the Ghost Dance movement and the massive governmental repression efforts that culminated with the December 29, 1890, Wounded Knee Massacre. Eastman did not see the actual massacre, but he led the search party for survivors. His account of that grim task, which he wrote about in his autobiography From the Deep Woods to Civilization *(1916), is excerpted below.*

At dusk, the Seventh Cavalry returned with their twenty-five dead and I believe thirty-four wounded, most of them by their own comrades, who had encircled the Indians, while few of the latter had guns. A majority of the thirty or more Indian wounded were women and children, including babies in arms. As there were not tents enough for all, Mr. Cook offered us the mission chapel, in which the Christmas tree still stood, for a temporary hospital. We tore out the pews and covered the floor with hay and quilts. There we laid the poor creatures side by side in rows, and the night was devoted to caring for them as best we could. Many were frightfully torn by pieces of shells, and the suffering was terrible. General Brooke placed me in charge and I had to do nearly all the work, for although the army surgeons were more than ready to help as soon as their own men had been cared for, the tortured Indians would scarcely allow a man in uniform to touch them. Mrs. Cook, Miss Goodale, and several of Mr. Cook's Indian helpers acted as volunteer nurses. In spite of all our efforts, we lost the greater part of them, but a few recovered, including several children who had lost all their relatives and who were adopted into kind Christian families.

On the day following the Wounded Knee massacre there was a blizzard, in the midst of which I was ordered out with several Indian police, to look for a policeman who was reported to have been wounded and left some two miles from the agency. We did not find him. This was the only time during the whole affair that I carried a weapon; a friend lent me a revolver which I put in my overcoat pocket, and it was lost on the ride. On the third day it cleared, and the ground was covered with an inch or two of fresh snow. We had feared that some of the Indian wounded might have been left on the field, and a number of us volunteered to go and see. I was placed in charge of the expedition of about a hundred civilians, ten or fifteen of whom were white men. We were supplied with wagons in which to convey any whom we might find still alive. Of course a photographer and several reporters were of the party.

Fully three miles from the scene of the massacre we found the body of a woman completely covered with a blanket of snow, and from this point on we found them scattered along as they had been relentlessly hunted down and slaughtered while fleeing for their lives. Some of our people discovered relatives or friends among the dead, and there was much wailing and mourning. When we reached the spot where the Indian camp had stood, among the fragments of burned tents and other belongings we saw the frozen bodies lying close together or piled one upon another. I counted eighty bodies of men who had been in the council and who were almost as helpless as the women and babes when the deadly fire began, for nearly all their guns had been taken from them. A reckless and desperate young Indian fired the first shot when the search for weapons was well under way, and immediately the troops opened fire from all sides, killing not only unarmed men, women, and children, but their own comrades who stood opposite them, for the camp was entirely surrounded.

It took all of my nerve to keep my composure in the face of this spectacle, and of the excitement and grief of my Indian companions, nearly every one of whom was crying aloud or singing his death song. The white men became very nervous, but I set them to examining and uncovering every body to see if one were living. Although they had been lying untended in the snow and cold for two days and nights, a number had survived. Among them I found a baby of about a year old warmly wrapped and entirely unhurt. I brought her in, and she was afterward adopted and educated by an army officer. One man who was severely wounded begged me to fill his pipe. When we brought him into the chapel he was welcomed by his wife and daughters with cries of joy, but he died a day or two later.

Under a wagon I discovered an old woman, totally blind and entirely helpless. A few had managed to crawl away to some place of shelter, and we found in a log store near by several who were badly hurt and others who had died after reaching there. After we had dispatched several wagon loads to the agency, we observed groups of warriors watching us from adjacent buttes; probably friends of the victims who had come there for the same purpose as ourselves. A majority of our party, fearing an attack, insisted that some one ride back to the agency for an escort of soldiers, and as mine was the best horse, it fell to me to go. I covered the eighteen miles in quick time and was not interfered with in any way, although if the Indians had meant mischief they could easily have picked me off from any of the ravines and gulches.

All this was a severe ordeal for one who had so lately put all his faith in the Christian love and lofty ideals of the white man....

Source: Eastman, Charles Alexander. *From the Deep Woods to Civilization: Chapters in the Autobiography of an Indian.* 1916. Lincoln: University of Nebraska Press, 1977, pp. 109-14.

Life at an Indian Boarding School

During the late nineteenth century the U.S. government opened numerous boarding schools for American Indian children. These schools were designed to strip the "Indian" elements of language, culture, and religion out of their lives and indoctrinate them in the practices and traditions of the dominant white society. Some Indian families and communities willingly participated in these programs; they were known to school administrators and government officials as "friendlies." Other Indians who wanted to preserve their cultural traditions and ways of life, however, angrily opposed sending their children to these boarding schools. The children of these natives, known as "hostiles," were sometimes forcibly removed from their families.

The following account of life at an Indian boarding school was written by Helen Sekaquaptewa, a Hopi Indian who, at age eight, was forcibly shipped off from her family's tribal village to a distant boarding school called Keams Canyon. Sekaquaptewa was seized by government authorities after her family and other traditionalists in the village lost a power struggle with "friendlies" and "progressives" who favored adaptation to white ways.

Very early one morning toward the end of October, 1906, we awoke to find our camp surrounded by troops who had come during the night from Keams Canyon. Superintendent Lemmon called the men together, ordering the women and children to remain in their separate family groups. He told the men it was a mistake to follow Yokeoma blindly; that the government had reached the limit of its patience; that the children would have to go to school. Yokeoma angrily defied them and refused to yield. He was taken to a house and put under guard.

All children of school age were lined up to be registered and taken away to school. Eighty-two children, including myself, were listed. It was late in the afternoon when the registration was completed. We were now loaded into wagons hired from and driven by our enemies, the Friendlies. There were not enough wagons, so the bigger boys had to walk. We were taken to the schoolhouse in New Oraibi, with military escort. We slept on the floor of the dining room that night.

The next morning three more wagons were hired, covered wagons drawn by four horses. All were loaded in, boys and girls in separate wagons. We just

Credit: "To School in Kearns Canyon," from *Me and Mine: The Life Story of Helen Sekaquaptewa* by Helen Sekaquaptewa as told to Louise Udall. © 1969 The Arizona Board of Regents. Reprinted by permission of the University of Arizona Press.

sat on the floor of the wagon, and still with military escort, started for Keams Canyon. In each wagon the older boys or girls looked after the little ones. I was one of the little ones. One little boy was about five years old. They let him live in the dormitory with the big girls so they could mother him. Everyone called him "Baby," and he was still called "Baby" when he was a grown man.

It was after dark when we reached the Keams Canyon boarding school and were unloaded and taken into the big dormitory, lighted with electricity. I had never seen so much light at night. I was all mixed up and thought it was daytime because it was so light. Pretty soon they gave us hardtack and syrup to eat. There were not enough beds, so they put mattresses on the floor. When I was lying down I looked up and saw where the light came from just before the matron turned out the lights.

For the next few days we were all curious about our new surroundings. We thought it was wonderful and didn't think much about home, but after a while, when we got used to the school, we got real homesick. Three little girls slept in a double bed. Evenings we would gather in a corner and cry softly so the matron would not hear and scold us or spank us. I would try to be a comforter, but in a little while I would be crying too. I can still hear the plaintive little voices saying, "I want to go home. I want my mother." We didn't understand a word of English and didn't know what to say or do.

Our native clothing was taken away from us and kept in boxes until our people came to take them. We were issued the regular school clothes. Each girl had two every-day dresses, three petticoats, two pairs of underwear, two pairs of stockings, one pair of shoes, one Sunday dress, and two white muslin aprons to be worn over the dresses, except on Sunday. The dresses were of striped bed ticking, with gathered skirts and long sleeves.

Some of the Friendly girls and those from other villages used to call us Hostiles and tease us until we would cry. At night when the doors were closed and locked and little girls were supposed to be in bed for the night, our tormentors would take our native clothes from the boxes and put them on and dance around making fun of us.

Boys and girls marched to the dining room from their separate dormitories. Usually the bigger boys got there first. Meals were served on twelve long tables, family style. Older boys and girls set the tables, and one of the older ones sat at the head of the table and served the food. There were Navajos there, even though it was a school for Hopis. It seemed a Navajo was always at

201

the head and the Navajos would have their plates heaping full, while little Hopi girls just got a teaspoonful of everything. I was always hungry and wanted to cry because I didn't get enough food. They didn't give second helpings, and I thought I would just starve. You can't go to sleep when you are hungry.

In the center of the table was a big plate of bread. The big boys would grab it as they went in. By the time little boys and girls got in, there was no bread. Sometimes the big boys would even take bread away from the little ones. There was a matron who was supposed to watch, but she didn't seem to notice these things.

For breakfast we had oatmeal mush, without milk or sugar, and plain bread. The Navajos didn't like the mush, so they took the bread and we had the mush. At noon it was beef, potatoes, and gravy, with prunes or bread pudding for dessert. At night we had the leftovers, sometimes with beans. Another dish often served was salt bacon gravy over bread; bacon was fried in small pieces, flour was added and browned in the grease, water was added, and the mixture was boiled until it was thickened into gravy. Without the bread there wasn't much nourishment. Sometimes we little ones were hunger driven to ask the boys to give us just one slice of bread to go with our gravy, but they would never do it, so we just drank the gravy. Day after day, the food had a sameness. How we longed for some food cooked by our mothers—the kind and quantity we were used to eating.

On the few occasions when the girls did beat the boys to the dining room, we marched right in and did as they did. We took all the bread and piled it on our stools and covered it with our aprons, while we stood waiting until everyone was in place and the blessing on the food was said. Then we would pick up our bread and sit on the stools. Later on they changed the system, and instead of seating the boys on one side of the table and the girls on the other, girls of one age were put at tables by themselves, and the same for the boys. I fared better then.

When you were sick the matron put you to bed in the dormitory. She was sympathetic and tried to comfort you. She brought your meals on a tray, and there was enough food. The trouble was when you were sick you didn't feel like eating.

It seemed like everything was against us at first.

We were a group of homesick, lonesome, little girls, huddled together on the schoolgrounds early one morning, when we wondered what was making the approaching clinking sound. Running to the high, woven wire fence around the playground, we saw a long line of men walking down the road. They were some of the seventy or so fathers from Hotevilla who had been arrested for resisting the government and had been sentenced to ninety days of hard labor; the Superintendent was using them to improve and build a dug-way into the canyon, thereby shortening the route by several miles. Supplies for the military post and the school were hauled along this road, and the traders who came by team and wagon from Holbrook also used it. What a thrill as one little girl after another recognized her father and pressed against the fence, calling out to him.

The construction gang walked four miles out to the job every morning. They were fastened together in twos with ball and chain. If one didn't keep step with his partner he might fall down, but they would only laugh about it. They were not ashamed of their condition because they knew in their hearts they had done no wrong; they had only protested having their lives interfered with. An officer with a stick would see to it that they did not stop to talk to their little girls. After that, each morning we ran out to see if our fathers went by. We would cry if we saw them and cry if we didn't. I recognized my father in the chain gang only once. He was put on kitchen duty, and I saw him there once before he was sent to prison at Fort Huachuca.

Following is a letter from the wife of one of the prisoners at Keams Canyon. It is dated December 28, 1906, and addressed to the Agency Superintendent.

> *My husband raised corn at Oraibi this year, but he did not gather it because soldiers took him away. Horses and cattle ate up the corn. I have no beans, only the food they give me from the village. These women want to go to school and be with their husbands and have food. Even if the husbands return here at once it will not change the condition of poverty. A year must pass, another grow-ing season, before we can grow crops.*

Investigation showed that they had lost their crops and did need food, and some were taken to Keams Canyon.

Being a little girl and away at Keams Canyon, I hardly realized until later the very sad plight of my mother, along with the other exiles back at Hotevil-la; there were seven old men and a handful of younger ones who had promised to cooperate, twenty-three children under school age, and sixty-three women—aged ones, middle-aged ones bereft of their children, and young mothers with little babies, all longing and crying for their old homes and fields and for their men folk and their children who had been taken away. Few had the strength to gather and chop wood and to bring in the water. Their corn baskets were empty. They were so hungry! Sometimes the younger women would organize a rabbit hunt. The best time for this is when snow is on the ground. They wrapped their feet in whatever was available; a piece of sheepskin with the wool inside is good if tied on securely. They had no guns, just rocks and sticks and maybe a dog. If your dog caught it, it was your rabbit. Somehow they managed to survive the winter, while I had three meals each day and a comfortable bed and a warm building to shelter me.

The months passed by, and then it was the last day of school that first year at Keams Canyon. Parents in wagons, on horseback, and burros converged on the campgrounds around the school from all directions. They had come to take their children home for the summer. There were parents from Hotevilla, but they would not promise to bring us back to school in September, so I was left to spend the summer at the school along with other boys and girls of Hostile parentage.

During the summer we fared better in the dining room because there were only about twenty girls and six boys and no Navajos. The big girls who worked in the kitchen and dining room favored us. In the cellar behind the kitchen there were many sacks of potatoes. Sometimes one of the older girls on kitchen duty would slip a raw potato to us little girls. They tasted good and sweet. I have tasted raw potato many times, but have never found any that tasted as sweet.

Come September, 1907, all the other children were brought back to school by their parents, and were back in the regular routine again. One October afternoon, our eyes followed a few government wagons as they wended their way down the dug-way into the canyon and stopped at the campgrounds, and lo! the cargo unloaded itself—men, the prisoners being returned from Fort Huachuca. They had come by train to Holbrook, and then by team and wagon on out to Keams Canyon. We watched as the men filed by on their way to the dining room to be fed, and what a thrill, I recognized my own father. He was dressed in an old military uniform and looked fine and young and straight to me, and I was proud of him.

We talked together for a little while that night and again in the morning. My father's Hopi name is Talashongnewa, but he was given the name of Sam at Huachuca, and from then was known as Sam Talashongnewa. He didn't feel mean toward the soldier guards. He said they treated the Hopis well and were loved by them, and that many of them had tears in their eyes when they said "good-by" to their Indian prisoners. But the prisoners came back still Hostile. My father's attitude had not changed, and it was many years before he could even begin to tolerate any part of the white man's culture. The prisoners were released to walk the forty miles on home to Hotevilla; it probably seemed a short forty miles to them.

As soon as they could, which was a year after we were taken away to Keams Canyon, some of the mothers came to visit their children. They came in a burro caravan of eight to ten. If one did not own a burro she would borrow or hire one on which she packed blankets and food for herself and as much as she could load on of piki, parched corn, dried peaches, and the like to give to her children. Mothers who couldn't make the trip would send bundles to their children. These travelers got everything ready the night before so they could start early in the morning. It was a long day's journey. The women walked most of the way, each driving her burro before her. When a woman got very tired she would stop the burro near a stump or rock and climb on and ride for a while.

Arriving at the school late, they found shelter in the rock rooms built by the big boys and slept in their own blankets and ate their own food during their stay. Meat was not expensive, and the school had lots of meat. If the cook was good natured, he would give a Hopi mother a bone with a little meat on it, which she could boil with her corn.

My mother did not come the first time—she came two times during the four years I was at Keams. I had a good godmother, a very nice one. She came every time and brought me food and even some bone dolls to play with. We thought we were sitting on top of the world to have our mothers with us for a little while and to have some food they had cooked over the campfire. After school they were permitted to come over and visit for a little while, bringing with them some parched corn or some piki. They usually stayed three days.

We learned by sad experience to have our housemother lock up our precious bundle of piki or parched corn, otherwise it would be pilfered. The matrons were usually older women who were pretty good to us. On the first visit, the mothers took home the native clothing that we were wearing at the time we were—shall we say—kidnapped.

Source: Sekaquaptewa, Helen. *Me and Mine: The Life Story of Helen Sekaquaptewa.* As told to Louise Udall. Tucson: University of Arizona Press, 1969, pp. 91-102.

Indian Activists Issue the Alcatraz Proclamation

In November 1969 a group of American Indian activists seized control of Alcatraz prison, an abandoned federal facility located on Alcatraz Island in San Francisco Bay. Early in their eighteen-month occupation, the activists issued a proclamation, reprinted below, in which they explained their reasons for taking the island. Their grand plans to remake the island into a center of American Indian study never came to fruition. By June 1971 all of the activists had left the island, either voluntarily or under the direction of federal authorities. But the occupation is still credited by historians as an important milestone in the drive to expand and strengthen Native American rights in the United States.

THE ALCATRAZ PROCLAMATION to the Great White Father and His People

Fellow citizens, we are asking you to join with us in our attempt to better the lives of all Indian people.

We are on Alcatraz Island to make known to the world that we have a right to use our land for our own benefit.

In a proclamation of November 20, 1969, we told the government of the United States that we are here "to create a meaningful use for our Great Spirit's Land."

We, the native Americans, reclaim the land known as Alcatraz Island in the name of all American Indians by right of discovery.

We wish to be fair and honorable in our dealings with the Caucasian inhabitants of this land, and hereby offer the following treaty:

We will purchase said Alcatraz Island for twenty-four dollars in glass beads and red cloth, a precedent set by the white man's purchase of a similar island about 300 years ago. We know that $24 in trade goods for these 16 acres is more than was paid when Manhattan Island was sold, but we know that land values have risen over the years. Our offer of $1.24 per acre is greater than the $0.47 per acre the white men are now paying the California Indians for their lands.

We will give to the inhabitants of this island a portion of the land for their own to be held in trust ... by the Bureau of Caucasian Affairs ... in per-

---

Credit: Copyright © 1997 Red Ink. Reprinted by permission.

petuity—for as long as the sun shall rise and the rivers go down to the sea. We will further guide the inhabitants in the proper way of living. We will offer them our religion, our education, our life-ways in order to help them achieve our level of civilization and thus raise them and all their white brothers up from their savage and unhappy state. We offer this treaty in good faith and wish to be fair and honorable in our dealings with all white men.

We feel that this so-called Alcatraz Island is more than suitable for an Indian reservation, as determined by the white man's own standards. By this, we mean that this place resembles most Indian reservations in that:

- It is isolated from modern facilities, and without adequate means of transportation.
- It has no fresh running water.
- It has inadequate sanitation facilities.
- There are no oil or mineral rights.
- There is no industry and so unemployment is very great.
- There are no health-care facilities.
- The soil is rocky and non-productive, and the land does not support game.
- There are no educational facilities.
- The population has always exceeded the land base.
- The population has always been held as prisoners and kept dependent upon others.

Further, it would be fitting and symbolic that ships from all over the world, entering the Golden Gate, would first see Indian land, and thus be reminded of the true history of this nation. This tiny island would be a symbol of the great lands once ruled by free and noble Indians.

What use will we make of this land?

Since the San Francisco Indian Center burned down, there is no place for Indians to assemble and carry on tribal life here in the white man's city. Therefore, we plan to develop on this island several Indian institutions:

A Center for Native American Studies will be developed which will educate them to the skills and knowledge relevant to improve the lives and spirits of all Indian peoples. Attached to this center will be traveling universities, managed by Indians,

which will go to the Indian Reservations, learning those necessary and relevant materials now about.

An American Indian Spiritual Center, which will practice our
ancient tribal religious and sacred healing ceremonies. Our
cultural arts will be featured and our young people trained in
music, dance, and healing rituals.

An Indian Center of Ecology, which will train and support our
young people in scientific research and practice to restore our
lands and waters to their pure and natural state. We will work
to de-pollute the air and waters of the Bay Area. We will seek
to restore fish and animal life to the area and to revitalize sea-
life which has been threatened by the white man's ways. We
will set up facilities to desalt sea water for human benefit.

A Great Indian Training School will be developed to teach our
people how to make a living in the world, improve our standard of living, and to end hunger and unemployment among all
our people. This training school will include a center for Indian
arts and crafts, and an Indian restaurant serving native foods,
which will restore Indian culinary arts. This center will display
Indian arts and offer Indian foods to the public, so that all may
know of the beauty and spirit of the traditional Indian ways.

Some of the present buildings will be taken over to develop an American
Indian Museum which will depict our native food and other cultural contributions we have given to the world. Another part of the museum will present
some of the things the white man has given to the Indians in return for the
land and life he took: disease, alcohol, poverty, and cultural decimation (as
symbolized by old tin cans, barbed wire, rubber tires, plastic containers, etc.).
Part of the museum will remain a dungeon to symbolize both those Indian
captives who were incarcerated for challenging white authority and those
who were imprisoned on reservations. The museum will show the noble and
tragic events of Indian history, including the broken treaties, the documentary of the Trail of Tears, the Massacre of Wounded Knee, as well as the victory over Yellow-Hair Custer and his army.

In the name of all Indians, therefore, we reclaim this island for our Indian nations, for all these reasons. We feel this claim is just and proper, and that

this land should rightfully be granted to us for as long as the rivers run and the sun shall shine.

We hold the rock!

Source: "Proclamation to the Great White Father and to All His People, 1969." Reprinted in *This Country Was Ours: A Documentary History of the American Indian.* New York: Harper & Row, 1972, pp. 228-29.

One Indian's Perspective on Modern Society and Traditional Ways

American Indians living in contemporary American society often speak of the challenges they face to preserve and carry on the traditional heritage of their tribespeople, yet still prosper in the wider "white" world. Finding a healthy balance between the demands of these very different worlds can be very difficult, as the following commentary attests. This column was written by an anonymous Cherokee writer for Red Ink, *a journal of American Indian studies published by the University of Arizona. The writer, who uses the pen name Watt Scraper, adopts a lighthearted and conversational tone throughout. Beneath the humor, however, the writer makes it clear that his primary allegiance is to his native culture.*

Now listen. When I look around nowadays I get the feelin' that the government is a-tryin' to do us in again. Or maybe it's just the white men's way of talkin' outin' both sides of they mouths at once'd. I'll show what I mean.

I got a Granddaughter goes to school with the white boys and girls in a city. Every once'd and awhile she comes to visit me and tell me about her schoolin'. She says that all the white peoples tell her that she needs to get educated so's she can get a job in the big city. Now she don't like that much, but she knows that she can't get no job around here, except maybe for pluckin' chickens in Arkansas. Now pluckin' chickens in Arkansas might be good for some peoples, and I don't want to tear them down for somethin' they like to do. But I'd just as soon not have my Granddaughter, who's real smart, going into Arkansas to ring a chicken's neck.

Sometimes it gets hard knowin' what to do. I guess it's real hard for some of the young Indin boys and girls. They want to know about who they is. They want to know who they come from. They want to know about traditions and the stories and the ceremonies that keep us in with the spirits. We want them to know about all them things and still not have to go off to Arkansas. They're good Grandchildrens. On the other hand, they gotta go out and make a buck. Can't just live like we used to, 'cause they got laws about huntin', and fishin', and the like.

Now I think that the white mens got us boxed in. The young Indins is a-feelin' bad. Us old folks can't come up with answers for 'em, but a lot of 'em look up to us anyways. We got a duty as old peoples to tell 'em straight out how the bird gets plucked.

Now it appears to me that our young peoples are a-goin' upstream with one foot in an Indin canoe and the other in a speedboat. Ones a-goin' real fast and the other is a-goin' pretty slow. Now what that does is make you go 'round in a circle without gettin' upstream. The Old Peoples used to say that everythin' goes in a circle and that's good. You always know where you're a-going. There's power in a circle. You see the strength. It's even. It's balanced. It's kind of like everythin's been put into one complete whole thing.

But I think white mens like us circlin' around in mid-stream. They say, "It's good that you peoples is getting' in the speedboat, 'cause that means you're a-makin' progress." At the same time, they's sayin' that, "It's a good you peoples is stayin' in the canoe, 'cause you're keepin' your traditions alive." But I think they're just happy we ain't gettin' upstream.

I guess we got to decide if we want to get upstream or not. I think gettin' upstream means freedom. We once'd had that. Had our land, our ways, our own schools, our own ceremonies. Made our own way in the world. Had our own laws, which was good laws. We could do things on our own that we thought was best for us. It appears to me that if we get upstream we'd be on even ground with the white peoples again. 'Cause I don't think we can make 'em go back to where ever they come from no more, maybe we could get 'em to make deals with us again. The only way to do that is to be equal with 'em.

Now that might sound like I'm sayin' we should all jump into the speed-boat. We could sure get upstream quicker. I reckon that's what a lot of the Indins is doin' with the gamblin' halls. Now I don't mind gamblin' and I sure don't mind takin' the white mens' money, but travelin' that fast in a gas-powered boat might not be too good either. We'd miss the beauty of the shore and the forest beyond that. We wouldn't be able to see the things that live in the river. The speedboat would foul up the water to boot. We couldn't even dip our hand in the stream to cool ourselves for fear it might be took off. Besides that, without usin' our muscles to paddle upstream how we gonna make ourselves stronger?

Toward the other side, if we all pile into the canoe it might just tip over. It's slow-goin' and everybody has to use the same muscle a-paddlin', just to keep us goin' straight. But if we was in the canoe, we wouldn't foul the water and we could look at the beauty around us. Not only that but usin' our muscles to paddle against a hard current is goin' to make them muscles grow and get real strong. When we finally get upstream to even ground we'd be much stronger than if we took the speedboat to get there.

211

I guess maybe I'll stick with the canoe.

Source: Scraper, Watt. "Unegadihi Speaks." In *Red Ink: A Native American Student Publication,* vol. 5, no. 2, Spring 1997. Reprinted in Nabokov, Peter. *Native American Testimony.* 1978. Revised edition. New York: Penguin, 1999, pp. 462-64.

American Indians Take Stock on the Bicentennial of the Lewis and Clark Expedition

One of the major historical milestones in the United States' settlement of the west was the Lewis and Clark Expedition. This exploration of previously unknown territories of the western frontier began in 1803, and by the time it concluded in 1806, Meriwether Lewis and William Clark—with the help of Indian tribes along the way—had mapped out more than 8,000 miles of American wilderness and filled numerous journals with their impressions of the native peoples and natural resources of the west.

White Americans have long praised the exploits of Lewis and Clark, but American Indians have far more complex feelings about their expedition. On the one hand, they take pride in their contributions to the success of their so-called Voyage of Discovery. But they also view Lewis and Clark as men who helped usher in the great waves of white settlement that pushed Indians off the lands of their ancestors. In 2003 historian Timothy Egan visited Indian communities in the Great Plains to gauge their response to bicentennial celebrations of the launching of Lewis and Clark's famed expedition.

Indian Country is a place where people gather in late June to celebrate the day Custer was whipped at Little Big Horn, where cars sometimes run only in reverse and casinos run all night, and where a Nez Percé guide who led Lewis and Clark over the Bitterroot Mountains is remembered by his native name, which means "Furnishes White Men With Brains."

But on the map—be it the road atlas handed out by the state or the statistical one issued by the Census Bureau—the homelands of the first Americans seem to possess little life or magic. Across vast stretches of the northern plains, Indian lands are blank patches, nations within a nation, landlocked islands foreign to most other Americans.

Certainly, the scars of memory are layered as thick as the dam water that buries so many old Indian villages and sacred sites here. Generations after the scourges of smallpox, war and forced resettlement, much of what a traveler finds in Indian Country is emptiness.

213

Still, those looking to find some link across 200 years, to the people whose nations Lewis and Clark passed through, need only peek into daily life on the reservations along the trail from St. Louis to the Pacific.

Here in New Town [North Dakota], home of the Mandan, Hidatsa and Arikara, Amy Mossett has just planted her garden, using seed corn that is the antithesis of genetically engineered agriculture; it is the same sweet corn given members of the American expedition to help them through the winter of 1804-05, at their fort just down river. At that time, the Indian urban complex 1,600 miles from the mouth of the Missouri River had more people (about 4,000) than St. Louis or Washington.

"Indians have the strongest sense of place of anyone in the world," said Ms. Mossett, a Mandan-Hidatsa who is a scholar on Sacagawea, the young Lemhi Shoshone woman who saved Lewis and Clark from disaster at two points when the expedition was at low ebb. "Look at me: why would I choose to live in little New Town, North Dakota, when I could live anywhere? It's because we've been a part of the Missouri River for a thousand years."

New Town, by its name, raises the question of what happened to Old Town. And this is where the Mandans, who did perhaps more than any other tribe to help Lewis and Clark, turn bitter.

It was one thing for the tribe to lose 90 percent of its members to small-pox, a disease that did more than the United States Cavalry to wipe out American Indians. But in the mid-20th century, just as the population was rebounding, the federal government built the Garrison Dam. It choked off the Missouri River here and buried 155,000 acres of prime Indian farmland under a reservoir, dividing a tight-knit reservation into five districts. Many tribal members wound up in this community, on higher ground.

"Some gratitude, huh?" said Frederick Baker, the Mandan-Hidatsa archivist at the tribal museum here. "One guy I know had his house moved as he was eating dinner. But, hey, we want people to understand our people are alive. Everywhere else in North Dakota, schools are closing and towns are dying. We're growing. We're alive!"

The Corps of Volunteers for North Western Discovery, as Lewis called the expedition, passed through roughly 50 Indian nations in their journey of nearly 8,000 miles. Some of those tribes were forcibly removed to Oklahoma. Others—including the Chinook, who lived at the mouth of the Columbia River on the Pacific Coast—are today without a homeland, even a tiny reservation.

The indignities are piled like bleached buffalo bones. Some of the friendliest tribes were later treated the worst. The Nez Percé, who saved the corps from starvation in Idaho, were chased from their treaty-promised homeland and rounded up near the Canadian border in 1877. The Lemhi Shoshone were erased from the land they had lived on for hundreds of years, and lumped with other tribes in the desert of southern Idaho.

But now as then, big pieces of the trail, particularly in the Dakotas, run through solid Indian Country. These lands hold the bones of Sitting Bull, the great Sioux chief, and of Sacagawea. They contain towns full of heartbreak, where suicide is the No. 1 killer. They also hold prairie grass untouched by the plow, and bison herds roaming free, giving the tribes something to connect pop-culture-jaded teens on the reservation of 2003 to the warriors whose spirit so impressed travelers in 1803.

This year, even the Blackfeet of Montana, the only nation to lose people in mortal conflict with Lewis and Clark, and the aggressive Teton Sioux of the Plains, have the bicentennial.

It is time, the Indians say, to tell their own story of Lewis and Clark, an epic about Indians bailing out whites, showing them where to go, what to eat, whom to avoid along the way, and how to get back home in one piece.

"One reason we're opening our doors to people is because there are so many dumb images of what Indians are like," said Denelle High Elk of the Cheyenne River Sioux Reservation in South Dakota. "I was in Monticello in January, for the kickoff of the bicentennial, and the cab driver said to me, 'Oh, you're Indian. You people still live in tepees, don't you?'"

Forgotten by History

President Thomas Jefferson knew he was sending an expedition through lands populated by people who did not care a whit for lines drawn on maps in Paris or Virginia. But Jefferson, an Enlightenment-age man, had conflicted views of the native people. He thought some Indians could be "civilized" back East, while others had to be removed to the far Western plains, the continental equivalent of Mars.

"Jefferson appears both as the scholarly admirer of Indian character, archaeology and language, and the planner of cultural genocide, the architect of the removal policy, the surveyor of the Trail of Tears," wrote the historian

Anthony F. C. Wallace, in his book, "Jefferson and the Indians: the Tragic Fate of the First Americans."

Lewis and Clark had trouble finding Indians at first. The swift plague of smallpox had come before them, and in some places it left a deathly resonance.

On Aug. 12, 1804, the corps passed the empty village of Tonwantonga, where the once powerful Omahas had lived. Today Nebraska's largest city is named for this tribe, which has a tiny toehold in the state.

Further north lived the Otoe, who joined the Missouri Tribe about 200 years ago. They were the first Indians to have a council with Lewis and Clark.

Today the Otoe and the Missouri have vanished from the trail. They can [be] found in distant Oklahoma, where about 1,300 members live near Red Rock. They feel forgotten by history, some members said, left out of the bicentennial.

But in rummaging through the belongings of a well-traveled tribe, the Otoe found something recently that has electrified historians—two documents written by Meriwether Lewis, which are not in his journal, describing Indians on the middle Missouri.

"My grandmother kept these in her trunk," said Rhoda Dent, treasurer of the tribe. "After she died, my cousin found them. It was just phenomenal for us to read them, even though Lewis refers to native people as children."

The documents are now in the Oklahoma Museum of History, and curators there say they believe they are authentic.

The Otoe would like to reconnect to their old homeland. "We were the first to greet Lewis and Clark, and look what happened to us," Ms. Dent said.

Upriver, the expedition met different reactions among the large nations that roamed the Dakota prairie. Among the Yankton Sioux, the men dined at a tidy village on a meal of stewed dog meat—"good & well-flavored," as one expedition member described it.

William Clark described the Yankton Sioux this way: "Stout bold looking people (the young men hand Sum) and well made. The Warriors are Very much deckerated with porcupin quils & feathers, large legins & mockersons, all with Buffalow roabes of Different colours."

The late historian Stephen Ambrose called such descriptions "pathbreaking ethnology." But the next encounter, with the Teton Sioux, appears to have been a textbook case of diplomatic blundering.

The corps showed off its air gun and a magnifying glass, while offering medals and tobacco. The Teton Sioux, unimpressed, wanted something in return for letting these people pass through their lands. At one point guns were drawn, arrows aimed, and the small cannon mounted to the corps' keelboat ready to fire. The standoff ended peacefully after three days, but with both sides steamed.

Clark never forgot nor forgave. "They are the vilest miscreants of the savage race and must ever remain the pirates of the Missouri," he wrote of the Teton Sioux.

Living Between 2 Worlds

The Sioux fought for their lands to the end, helping to defeat Custer, only to be slaughtered at Wounded Knee in 1890. Today the bands of the Great Sioux Nation, as they call themselves, are spread throughout South Dakota, while Jefferson's granite visage is carved near an Indian sacred site in the Badlands.

They have shown the same fierce spirit in taking hold of the Lewis and Clark bicentennial in their state, despite opposition from some Sioux elders, and some initial snubs from other tribes. The Sioux have organized an intertribal tourism council, and set up a Native American Scenic Byway—"a journey through the lands of the least known and most misunderstood nations in America," as the Indians say in a brochure for the road and its highlights.

"We were entrepreneurs back then," said Daphne Richards Cook, who lives on the Lower Brule Sioux Reservation in South Dakota. "And we're entrepreneurs now."

The reservations are breathtaking, the prairie grass high and green, the towns bursting with one quirky story after another. They are the biggest population centers for hundreds of miles, with 12,000 Indians living on the Cheyenne River Reservation, 11,000 on the Standing Rock, and 4,300 total on the smaller Crow Creek and Lower Brule reservations. One out of every 12 people in South Dakota, population 756,600, is Indian.

"I call Indian Country the last of the real frontier," said Wanda Wells Crowe of the Crow Creek Sioux. "Take a look — it's not your typical America."

The Sioux say they walk a fine line between two worlds. "A lot of Indians don't want people here," Ms. Crowe said. "And in truth, I sometimes wonder myself why I'm doing this, trying to promote Lewis and Clark as a way to tell our story." Perhaps the greatest cross-cultural mingling on the expedition happened in what is now North Dakota, where the corps wintered just across the river from Mandan and Hidatsa villages. Lewis and Clark spent more time in the area than anywhere else.

What the natives who descended from those tribes want people to know is that they already had an advanced society when Lewis and Clark arrived. It was a sophisticated agricultural society, with clans and large earth lodges run by women. The Indians shared food, building tips and wives with the new-comers.

"Jefferson wanted to make Indians into farmer and traders," Ms. Mossett said between bites of a fajita salad at a restaurant here in New Town. "But we were already doing all of that. The difference is, we were doing it without slave labor."

Of course, the Mandan and Hidatsa captured other Indians in raids, and later adopted them into their culture. That is how Sacagawea came to live with the Mandan and Hidatsa. She joined the corps in the winter, just after giving birth to a boy she would carry across the West and back.

"In some ways, the Hidatsa thought these guys were a joke," said Mr. Baker, the museum archivist. "We saw them as a trading opportunity, but also felt sorry for them. And we joked about their crummy trade items."

Farther along the trail, the Nez Percé also pitied the corps. At one point, the explorers might have been killed just after crossing the Continental Divide, but a Nez Percé woman intervened.

"The expedition owed more to Indian women than either captain ever acknowledged," Mr. Ambrose wrote in "Undaunted Courage," his best-selling account of the voyage. Mr. Ambrose also noted the bitter irony that when the Nez Percé were driven out of their homeland in 1877, among the stragglers were a handful of old men who had been children when Lewis and Clark visited.

The Nez Percé, alone among American Indian tribes, selectively bred horses, and say they produced the appaloosa. On this bicentennial, the tribe is reviving its horse-breeding registry and language as part of a Lewis and Clark Rediscovery Project.

A sign on the Weippe Prairie, in Idaho, reads: "Lewis and Clark Route, First Contact Between Two Cultures."

218

Like the Sioux, the Nez Percé, with 3,296 tribal members today, suffered the indignity of not even being called by their real name. Sioux is a Chippewa word, shortened by the French, which means little snake, or enemy. Nez Percé is also a French misnomer. Tribal members say they did not pierce their noses.

At the very least, the Nez Percé, like other Indians along the route from the flatlands to the ocean, hope the Lewis and Clark bicentennial will dispel certain myths.

With the kind of humor found often in Indian Country, the tribe is taking to the revisionist task. After discussing efforts to restore salmon in rivers stapled with government dams, the Nez Percé report on their Web site that "we also frequent restaurants and eat modern foods."

Source: Egan, Timothy. "2 Centuries Later, a Moment for Indians to Retell Their Past." *New York Times*, June 15, 2003. Available online at http://www.nytimes.com/2003/06/15/national/15LEWI.html.

IMPORTANT PEOPLE, PLACES, AND TERMS

Accommodationists
Native American groups that tried to cling to their ancestral lands by adopting white farming practices, political systems, religious beliefs, and other aspects of European culture.

Allotment
A U.S. government program that divided Indian reservation lands into small plots that were distributed to the head of every family; it was designed to encourage Indian assimilation into mainstream white society, but it spurred further losses of land, resources, and community cohesion within tribes.

Assimilation
The adoption of European-style religious, cultural, and political practices by Native American groups.

Big Foot (also known as Sitanka) (c. 1820-1890)
Chief of the Miniconjou Lakota band that was massacred by U.S. Cavalry troops at Wounded Knee Creek in 1890.

Bozeman Trail
A pathway connecting the Oregon Trail to gold deposits in Wyoming and Montana that passed through Lakota hunting grounds.

Collier, John (1884-1968)
Social reformer and advocate who served as head of the Bureau of Indian Affairs from 1933-1945.

Crazy Horse (c. 1841-1877)
Oglala Lakota warrior who played a key role in numerous battles against U.S. Army troops, including the Battle of Little Bighorn.

221

Custer, George Armstrong (1839-1876)
U.S. Cavalry officer who played a prominent role in the Indian Wars and was killed in the Battle of Little Bighorn.

Forsyth, James W. (1835-1906)
Commanding officer of the U.S. Seventh Cavalry troops that killed between 250 and 300 Lakota men, women, and children in the Wounded Knee Massacre of 1890.

Fort Laramie Treaty of 1868
An agreement in which the U.S. government granted the Lakota people a permanent reservation of 60 million acres west of the Missouri River in South Dakota, hunting access to a large area of unceded Indian territory, and the promise of food rations, annuity payments, and education services.

French and Indian War (1754-1763)
A conflict between England and France and their respective Indian allies for control of the Ohio Country, a frontier region that stretched from the Great Lakes to the Gulf of Mexico and from the Appalachian Mountains to the Mississippi River.

Ghost Dance
A religious movement that swept through the Indian tribes of the West in 1890; it promised followers that if they performed a ritual dance, everything in the world would return to the way it was before the arrival of white people.

Indian Removal
A policy of the U.S. government, officially sanctioned by Congress under the Indian Removal Act of 1830, that involved transplanting entire Indian nations to reservations west of the Mississippi River.

Jackson, Andrew (1767-1845)
A Southern planter, war hero, and U.S. president (1829-1837) who promoted and carried out Indian removal policies.

King Philip's War (1675-1676)
A bloody clash that pitted white New Englanders against area Indian tribes in 1675-76.

Lakota (also known as Teton Sioux)

A Native American people comprising seven subgroups or bands: Hunkpapa, Miniconjou, Oglala, Sihi Sapa (also known as Blackfeet), Brulé (Sicangu), Sans Arc (Itazipco), and Two Kettle (Oohenopa).

Little Bighorn, Battle of

The famous June 25, 1876, clash in which Lakota warriors led by Crazy Horse and Sitting Bull wiped out George Armstrong Custer and 260 U.S. Cavalry soldiers under his command.

Manifest Destiny

A belief that God specially favored the United States and wanted it to have dominion over the entire continent of North America, from the Atlantic to the Pacific.

New France

The section of North America claimed by France from the 1600s through the early 1800s, stretching from the Appalachian Mountains west to the Mississippi River, and from the Great Lakes region south to the Gulf of Mexico.

New Spain

The parts of the Americas ruled by Spain from the 1500s through the early 1800s, including the Caribbean, Mexico, Central America, the American Southwest, and modern-day California.

New World

A term applied to North America when the first explorers, traders, and colonists began arriving in the late 1400s and early 1500s.

Ohio Country

A region of the United States encompassing modern-day Ohio, Illinois, Indiana, Michigan, and Wisconsin.

Oregon Trail

The pathway across the Great Plains, sometimes called the Holy Road, that pioneers in wagon trains used to get to the Rocky Mountains and points further west.

Pan-Indian Movement

The view that local problems affecting specific Indian tribes were part of the wider struggle that concerned *all* American Indians.

Pontiac's Rebellion (1763-1765)

An effort by several allied Great Lakes Indian tribes to force British soldiers and settlers out of their ancestral territory.

Powhatan (Wahunsonacock)

The leader of a powerful alliance of Algonquin tribes, known to historians as the Powhatan Confederacy.

Red Cloud (c. 1822-1909)

Lakota chief whose campaign of military resistance to white encroachment helped convince U.S. government officials to negotiate the Fort Laramie Treaty of 1868.

Red Cloud's War (1865-68)

A coordinated series of attacks, directed by the Lakota chief Red Cloud, intended to disrupt the building of forts along the Bozeman Trail; it was the most cohesive and successful military action ever waged by an Indian nation against the United States.

Removal

See Indian Removal

Ross, John (1790-1866)

Cherokee chief who led the resistance to the U.S. government's Indian removal policies.

Sioux

A term used by white people in reference to American Indians from three related groups: the Dakota or Santee Sioux of Minnesota; the Nakota or Yankton Sioux of eastern South Dakota; and the Lakota or Teton Sioux of western South Dakota and eastern Montana and Wyoming.

Sitting Bull (1831-1890)

Hunkpapa Lakota chief, holy man, and resistance leader whose death at the height of the Ghost Dance controversy started a chain of events leading to the Wounded Knee massacre.

Tecumseh (1768-1813)

Shawnee chief who united thousands of warriors from various Midwestern tribes in a military campaign against white encroachment known as Tecumseh's War (1805-1813).

Termination

A U.S. government policy enacted in the 1950s that ended all federal support for Indian nations, wiped out all of the government's treaty obligations to the tribes, and made all Indians subject to state and federal taxes and laws.

Trail of Tears

The 1838 forced relocation of the Cherokee Nation to Oklahoma, during which an estimated 4,000 tribal members died of disease, exposure, exhaustion, or starvation.

Wampanoag

An Indian tribe that helped save the English pilgrims of Plymouth, Massachusetts, from starvation and joined them in the first Thanksgiving celebration.

Wounded Knee Massacre

The tragic incident of December 29, 1890, in which U.S. Cavalry troops killed between 250 and 300 Lakota men, women, and children near Wounded Knee Creek in South Dakota.

Wovoka (c. 1856-1932)

Paiute prophet who created the Ghost Dance religion.

CHRONOLOGY

1500s
> European explorers and traders begin arriving in the New World, which is inhabited by between two and ten million Native Americans. *See p. 5.*

1607
> Jamestown, the first permanent English settlement in North America, is founded in modern-day Virginia. *See p. 10.*

1609
> French explorer Samuel de Champlain introduces firearms to the New World. *See p. 16.*

1620
> English pilgrims establish the second permanent English colony in North America in Plymouth, Massachusetts. *See p. 11.*

1621
> The Plymouth pilgrims and local Wampanoag Indians celebrate a successful harvest with a feast that becomes known as the first Thanksgiving. *See p. 11.*

1622
> A major assault by Algonquin Indians on English settlements and tobacco plantations claims the lives of more than a quarter of the colonial population. *See p. 10.*

1640s
> British military actions, combined with the ravages of European diseases, destroy the last remnants of the once-powerful Algonquin tribes. *See p. 11.*

1675-76
> King Philip's War, a bloody clash between white New Englanders and area Indian tribes, reduces the Wampanoag and Narragansett tribes to a few hundred members. *See p. 12.*

1680
> Pueblo tribes in Mexico, California, and the Southwest stage a stunning revolt and overthrow Spanish rule. *See p. 8.*

1692
> Spain regains control of its territories in the Southwest. *See p. 8.*

1700

More than 100,000 European settlers live in the Virginia, Maryland, and South and North Carolina colonies. *See p. 11.*

The Lakota Indians begin migrating from the western Great Lakes to the northern Great Plains. *See p. 37.*

1744

British colonial powers pressure leaders of the Iroquois Confederacy to sign the Treaty of Lancaster, which allows English settlers to enter the "Ohio Country." *See p. 18.*

1754

A long-simmering conflict between England and France for control of the eastern half of the modern-day United States erupts into the French and Indian War. *See p. 17.*

1763

The French and Indian War ends with the signing of the Treaty of Paris, in which France relinquishes virtually all of its land in North America east of the Mississippi River to England. *See p. 18.*

Several allied Indian tribes make a bid, known as Pontiac's Rebellion, to overtake British forts and outposts around the Great Lakes. *See p. 19.*

The British crown issues a proclamation designating the lands between the Appalachian Mountains and the Mississippi River as a permanent Indian Territory, but colonists eager to claim frontier lands ignore it. *See p. 19.*

1776

The American colonies begin their fight for independence from British rule. *See p. 20.*

1779

During the Revolutionary War, American forces under the command of future president George Washington burn 40 Iroquois towns to the ground. *See p. 20.*

1783

The Revolutionary War ends in victory for the newly independent United States. *See p. 20.*

1785

Indian tribes in the Ohio Country unite to resist American settlers in the Northwest Indian War. *See p. 20.*

1787

The Northwest Ordinance opens the entire Northwest Territory/Ohio Country to white settlement and specifies how various parts of the region can become states. *See p. 23.*

1795

The Northwest Indian War ends in the Treaty of Greenville, in which tribal leaders formally relinquish their claims on the Ohio Country to the U.S. government. *See p. 21.*

1803

The United States executes the Louisiana Purchase, by which it gains control over more than 800,000 square miles of former French territory west of the Mississippi River. *See p. 24.*

The Lewis and Clark expedition begins its three-year journey deep into the heart of the modern-day northwestern United States.

1805

Warriors from various Midwestern tribes unite under the leadership of Shawnee chief Tecumseh to resist white encroachment. *See p. 24.*

1812

The War of 1812 between the United States and Great Britain begins. *See p. 25.*

1813

Tecumseh is killed in battle in Canada. *See p. 25.*

1816

The U.S. government begins enforcing Indian removal policies in the South; over the next 35 years more than 100,000 American Indians from 28 tribes are deported from their ancestral homelands to territories west of the Mississippi River. *See p. 29.*

1819

Spain sells its colony in Florida to the United States. *See p. 24.*

1828

Andrew Jackson is elected President of the United States. *See p. 30.*

John Ross is elected principal chief of the Cherokee Nation. *See p. 30.*

1830

The U.S. Congress passes the Indian Removal Act, which gives Jackson sweeping authority to relocate all Indian tribes in the eastern United States to new territory west of the Mississippi River. *See p. 30.*

1832

In *Worcester v. Georgia,* the U.S. Supreme Court rules that the Cherokee people comprise a sovereign nation, are not subject to state authority, and can only be removed to Oklahoma with their approval. *See p. 30.*

The Black Hawk War in the upper Midwest claims the lives of hundreds of women, children, and elderly members of the Sauk and Fox tribes. *See p. 25.*

1835

In December, a minority faction of Cherokee tribal members sign the Treaty of New Echota, which enables the U.S. government to forcibly relocate the Cherokee Nation to Oklahoma. *See p. 30.*

1838

On May 26, federal troops begin rounding up the Cherokee and marching them 1,000 miles to Oklahoma-a journey that becomes known as the Trail of Tears. *See p. 31.*

1846

The United States acquires the Oregon Country from England. *See p. 24.*

1848

The United States emerges victorious from the Mexican-American War and gains control over California and the Southwest. *See p. 24.*

1851

On September 17, U.S. negotiators announce the signing of a major new treaty with northern Plains Indian tribes at Fort Laramie in present-day Wyoming. *See p. 40.*

1862

Angered by the U.S. government's failure to deliver on treaty obligations, Dakota (also known as Santee Sioux) Indians under the direction of a chief named Little Crow kill hundreds of white settlers in Minnesota. *See p. 41.*

1863

In an effort to defuse rising tensions with the Plains Indians, the administration of President Abraham Lincoln meets with a delegation of Indian chieftains in Washington, D.C. *See p. 41.*

1864

On November 29, a civilian cavalry regiment under the command of John M. Chivington attacks peaceful encampment of Cheyenne and Arapaho Indians in Colorado, killing an estimated 200 people, in what becomes known as the Sand Creek Massacre. *See p. 42.*

1866

On December 21, Lakota warriors under the direction of Red Cloud kill eighty U.S. Army soldiers under the command of William J. Fetterman near Fort Phil Kearny in Nebraska; the Fetterman Massacre is the deadliest confrontation in the two-year conflict known as Red Cloud's War. *See p. 43.*

1868

In January, the Indian Peace Commission releases a report that condemns living conditions on Indian reservations, blames most incidents of Indian violence in the West on white treaty breaking, and recommends setting aside vast areas of land for Great Plains tribes. *See p. 45.*

The Fort Laramie Treaty creates the Great Sioux Reservation, encompassing an area of 60 million acres—or about 93,000 square miles—west of the Missouri River in South Dakota. *See p. 48.*

1874

On July 2, U.S. Cavalry officer George Armstrong Custer leads a large expedition into the Black Hills of South Dakota and discovers gold. *See p. 50.*

1875

A U.S. government commission headed by Senator William Boyd Allison of Iowa offers Lakota leaders $6 million to purchase reservation lands in the Black Hills. *See p. 52.*

When Lakota leaders refuse to sell the Black Hills, Bureau of Indian Affairs officials order all Lakota to report to the Great Sioux Reservation by January 31, 1876, or be subject to attack by the U.S. Army. *See p. 52.*

1876

On June 17, Lakota warriors led by Crazy Horse turn back U.S. Army forces under the command of General George Crook in the Battle of the Rosebud. *See p. 128.*

On June 25, Lakota warriors led by Crazy Horse and Sitting Bull defeat U.S. Cavalry troops under the command of George Armstrong Custer in the Battle of Little Bighorn. *See p. 53.*

Under the Indian Appropriation Act of 1876, the U.S. government threatens to cut off all federal funding for food rations unless the Lakota hand over the Black Hills. *See p. 55.*

Lakota leaders give up the Black Hills, reducing the size of the Great Sioux Reservation from 60 million to 21.7 million acres. *See p. 55.*

1877

Pursued by U.S. Army forces, Sitting Bull leads his followers across the border into Canada. *See p. 55.*

In May, Crazy Horse surrenders and settles on the Pine Ridge Reservation. *See p. 54.*

On September 5, Crazy Horse dies of a stab wound inflicted under mysterious circumstances. *See p. 54.*

1879

Richard Pratt opens the first Indian boarding school, the U.S. Training and Industrial School in Carlisle, Pennsylvania. *See p. 80.*

1881

Sitting Bull returns from Canada and settles on the Standing Rock Reservation. *See p. 59.*

1885

Sitting Bull tours with William "Buffalo Bill" Cody's traveling Wild West Show. *See p. 149.*

1887

In February, the U.S. Congress unanimously passes the General Allotment Act, also known as the Dawes Act, which allows the federal government to divide Indian reservation lands into small plots and distribute them to individual owners. *See p. 57.*

1889

On January 1, the Paiute prophet Wovoka experiences the mystical vision that leads him to create the Ghost Dance religion. *See p. 63.*

A commission headed by General George Crook collects enough Lakota signatures to approve an allotment program which distributes small plots of reservation land to the head of each Lakota family and sells the remaining "surplus" land to white settlers and business interests. *See p. 57.*

Allotment divides the Great Sioux Reservation into six smaller reservations and shrinks the overall area of Lakota lands from 21.7 million to 12.7 million acres. *See p. 58.*

Lakota leaders send a delegation to visit Wovoka and learn about the Ghost Dance. *See p. 64.*

1890

The Ghost Dance movement sweeps through the Indian nations of the West. *See p. 63.*

In October, inexperienced federal agent Daniel F. Royer takes charge of the Pine Ridge Reservation and requests military troops to prevent an Indian uprising. *See p. 66.*

On November 17, the U.S. Army responds to rising concerns about the Ghost Dance movement by sending troops to South Dakota. *See p. 68.*

On December 15, Sitting Bull is killed during a struggle with tribal police officers sent by Standing Rock agent James McLaughlin to arrest him. *See p. 70.*

Thousands of Lakota react to the death of Sitting Bull by fleeing their reservations. *See p. 70.*

On December 29, U.S. Cavalry troops under the command of James W. Forsyth kill between 250 and 300 Lakota men, women, and children in what becomes known as the Wounded Knee Massacre. *See p. 72.*

1891

On January 3, U.S. Cavalry soldiers return to the scene of the Wounded Knee Massacre and bury 153 dead Lakota in a mass grave. *See p. 74.*

1900

Disease, starvation, warfare, and other hardships reduce the total population of native peoples in the United States to 250,000. *See p. 79.*

1906

The Burke Act, which gives the Bureau of Indian Affairs the authority to approve proposed sales of allotted land by "competent" Indians, leads to widespread loss of reservation lands. *See p. 86.*

1910

Nearly 500 Indian boarding schools and day schools are in operation across the United States. *See p. 80.*

1917

Between 10,000 and 16,000 Native American men serve in the military after the United States enters World War I. *See p. 88.*

1924

The impressive wartime performance of Native American servicemen helps convince Congress to award U.S. citizenship to all Native Americans. *See p. 89.*

Native American writer and activist Gertrude S. Bonnin publishes her exposé *Oklahoma's Poor Rich Indians: An Orgy of Graft and Exploitation of the Five Civilized Tribes-Legalized Robbery. See p. 85.*

1926

Secretary of the Interior Hubert Work commissions a major study of American Indian tribes and federal Indian policies. *See p. 88.*

1928

The Meriam Report criticizes virtually every federal Indian policy and recommends a complete overhaul of the Bureau of Indian Affairs. *See p. 89.*

1933

President Franklin D. Roosevelt selects social reformer John Collier to head the Bureau of Indian Affairs. *See p. 90.*

1934

The landmark Indian Reorganization Act (IRA), or Wheeler-Howard Act, increases the self-governing powers of Indian tribes, restores Indian religious and cultural freedoms, and returns large expanses of unsold "surplus" reservation lands to the tribes. *See p. 90.*

1941

More than 25,000 Indians serve in the U.S. armed forces during World War II, including the Navajo "code talkers" who help defeat Japanese forces in the Pacific. *See p. 92.*

1944

The National Congress of American Indians (NCAI) is founded.

1948

Sculptor Korczak Ziolkowski begins carving a memorial to Crazy Horse on the face of Thunderhead Mountain in the Black Hills of South Dakota. *See p. 129.*

1950

President Harry S. Truman names Dillon S. Myer, a strong supporter of ending all federal support for Indian nations, as his commissioner of Indian affairs. *See p. 94.*

1953

The U.S. Congress enacts the policy of "termination," or ending federal government support programs for Indians, with a series of bills aimed at specific tribes. *See p. 94.*

1961

The National Indian Youth Council (NIYC) is established by a group of young, urbanized, and college-educated Indians. *See p. 99.*

1968

The radical protest group American Indian Movement (AIM) is founded. *See p. 99.*

1969

Native American author Vine Deloria Jr.'s publishes *Custer Died for Your Sins: An Indian Manifesto.* *See p. 101.*

American Indian Movement activists occupy Alcatraz Island in San Francisco Bay to draw attention to problems affecting Native American communities. *See p. 102.*

1970

The nonprofit Native American Rights Fund (NARF) is founded to provide legal services to Indian tribes, communities, and individuals across the country.

1971

On June 11, FBI agents, federal marshals, and other forces take over Alcatraz Island and remove the last protesters. *See p. 102.*

1972

Native American activists stage a protest called the Trail of Broken Treaties, in which they travel in a caravan from the West Coast to Washington, D.C., to demand new programs to help distressed Indian communities and fulfillment of various treaty rights. *See p. 103.*

1973

On February 27, about 200 AIM activists and local Lakota seize control of the village of Wounded Knee and are quickly surrounded by heavily armed U.S. troops. *See p. 106.*

The siege at Wounded Knee ends quietly on May 8, when the U.S. government and AIM leaders reach a settlement after 71 days. *See p. 106.*

1979

Seminole Indians in southern Florida open a for-profit bingo hall on their reservation, marking the beginning of Indian casino gambling operations. *See p. 113.*

1985

Wilma Mankiller becomes the first female chief of the Cherokee Nation. *See p. 111.*

1987

Northern Cheyenne lawmaker Ben Nighthorse Campbell of Colorado is elected to the U.S. House of Representatives (1987-1993) and later serves in the U.S. Senate (1993-2005). *See p. 111.*

The U.S. Supreme Court clears the path for Indian casino gambling with its ruling in *California v. Cabazon Band of Mission Indians,* which says that states have no right to restrict gambling on Indian reservations if they allow it elsewhere. *See p. 113.*

2005

Nearly 400 casinos and gambling rooms on Indian lands generate total annual revenues of $22.6 billion—more than the combined total generated by the U.S. gambling capitals of Las Vegas, Nevada, and Atlantic City, New Jersey. *See p. 114.*

2009

In December, the U.S. government announces a $3.4 billion settlement in *Cobell v. Salazar,* a longstanding class-action lawsuit over royalty payments owed to American Indians for land held in trust under the General Allotment Act (Dawes Act) of 1887. *See p. 108.*

SOURCES FOR FURTHER STUDY

Brown, Dee. *Bury My Heart at Wounded Knee: The Illustrated Edition: An Indian History of the American West*. New York: Sterling Innovation, 2009. This version of Dee Brown's 1970 classic work of popular history is enhanced with hundreds of photographs, maps, and other images, as well as essays, book excerpts, and other contributions from major historians and American Indian leaders and writers.

Deloria, Vine, Jr. *Custer Died for Your Sins: An Indian Manifesto*. New York: Macmillan, 1969. Frequently described as the most influential and important book ever written by an American Indian, this entertaining but passionate work challenged white audiences to confront the historic mistreatment of native peoples of America, while simultaneously urging Indian readers to embrace their history and culture.

Josephy, Alvin M., Jr. *500 Nations: An Illustrated History of North American Indians*. New York: Knopf, 1994. This coffee table-sized book supplements numerous beautiful and historically significant illustrations and photographs with a historical overview of American Indian history by one of the nation's leading experts on the subject.

Riley, Patricia, ed. *Growing Up Native American*. New York: William Morrow, 1993. This collection gathers the personal recollections of twenty-two American Indians who grew up in the United States in the nineteenth and twentieth centuries.

Rozema, Vicki, ed. *Voices from the Trail of Tears*. Winston-Salem, NC: John F. Blair, 2003. This work combines excerpts from journals, letters, military records, and other primary sources to trace the heartbreaking and deadly journey undertaken by the Cherokee nation in the 1830s from their longtime homeland in the Southeast to the Oklahoma Territory.

Viola, Herman J. *Trail to Wounded Knee: Last Stand of the Plains Indians, 1860-1890*. Washington, DC: National Geographic Society, 2003. This work by an imminent Indian historian traces the events that led up to the Massacre at Wounded Knee. It includes many high-quality photographs, maps, and other illustrations.

"We Shall Remain." *American Experience,* 2009. Available online at http://www.pbs.org /wgbh/amex/weshallremain/. This multimedia website is the companion to a five-part series on American Indian history that was broadcast on PBS in 2009. Visitors to the website can watch all five episodes, which cover major events like the Trail of Tears, the Battle of Little Bighorn, and the Wounded Knee Massacre. The site also includes a variety of supplementary features.

BIBLIOGRAPHY

Books

Armstrong, Virginia I., ed. *I Have Spoken: American History Through the Voices of the Indians.* Athens: Ohio University Press, 1971.

Ballantine, Betty, and Ian Ballantine, eds. *The Native Americans: An Illustrated History.* Atlanta: Turner Publishing, 1993.

Brown, Dee. *Bury My Heart at Wounded Knee: The Illustrated Edition: An Indian History of the American West.* New York: Sterling Innovation, 2009.

Deloria, Vine, Jr., ed. *American Indian Policy in the Twentieth Century.* Norman: University of Oklahoma Press, 1985.

Di Silvestro, Roger L. *In the Shadow of Wounded Knee: The Untold Final Story of the Indian Wars.* New York: Walker, 2005.

Eastman, Charles A. *From the Deep Woods to Civilization: Chapters in the Autobiography of an Indian.* New York: Little, Brown, 1916.

Evans, Sterling. *American Indians in American History: A Companion Reader.* Westport, CT: Praeger, 2002.

Geist, Valerius. *Buffalo Nation: History and Legend of the North American Bison.* Stillwater, MN: Voyageur Press, 1998.

Iverson, Peter. *"We Are Still Here": American Indians in the Twentieth Century.* Wheeling, IL: Harlan Davidson, 1998.

Jennings, Francis. *The Invasion of America: Indians, Colonialism, and the Cant of Conquest.* New York: Norton, 1976.

Josephy, Alvin M., Jr. *500 Nations: An Illustrated History of North American Indians.* New York: Knopf, 1994.

Josephy, Alvin M., Jr. *Now That the Buffalo's Gone: A Study of Today's American Indian.* Norman: University of Oklahoma Press, 1982.

Landau, Elaine. *Cornerstones of Freedom: The Wounded Knee Massacre.* New York: Children's Press, 2004.

McMurtry, Larry. *Crazy Horse: A Life.* New York: Lipper/Penguin, 1992.

Mooney, James. *The Ghost Dance Religion and the Sioux Outbreak of 1890.* Lincoln: University of Nebraska Press, 1991.

Nabokov, Peter. *Native American Testimony: A Chronicle of Indian-White Relations from Prophecy to the Present, 1492-2000.* 1978. Revised ed. New York: Penguin Books, 1999.

Nichols, Roger L. *American Indians in U.S. History.* Norman: University of Oklahoma Press, 2003.

O'Neill, Laurie A. *Wounded Knee and the Death of a Dream.* Brookfield, CT: Millbrook Press, 1993.

Page, Jake. *In the Hands of the Great Spirit: The 20,000 Year History of American Indians.* New York: Free Press, 2003.

Perdue, Theda, and Michael D. Green. *The Cherokee Nation and the Trail of Tears.* New York: Penguin, 2008.

Rozema, Vicki, ed. *Voices from the Trail of Tears.* Winston-Salem, NC: John F. Blair, 2003.

Sturgis, Amy H. *The Trail of Tears and Indian Removal.* Westport, CT: Greenwood Press, 2007.

Utley, Robert M. *The Indian Frontier of the American West, 1846-1890.* Albuquerque: University of New Mexico Press, 1984.

Utley, Robert M. *Last Days of the Sioux Nation.* New Haven, CT: Yale University Press, 1963.

Viola, Herman J. *Trail to Wounded Knee: Last Stand of the Plains Indians, 1860-1890.* Washington, DC: National Geographic Society, 2003.

Wilkinson, Charles F. *Blood Struggle: The Rise of Modern Indian Nations.* New York: W.W. Norton, 2005.

Online

"Alcatraz Is Not an Island." 2005. *PBS* companion website to the television documentary produced by Independent Television Service (ITVS) and KQED. Available online at http://www.pbs.org/itvs/alcatrazisnotanisland/activism.html.

"Behind the Scenes: Still Wounded." *New York Times "Lens Blog,"* October 20, 2009. Available online at http://lens.blogs.nytimes.com/2009/10/20/behind-22/?scp=2&sq=Native%20American%20Wounded%20Knee&st=cse.

"New Perspectives on the West." *PBS* website, 1996. Available online at http://www.pbs.org/weta/thewest/program/.

"The Pendulum Swings of Indian Policy." *America.gov,* June 1, 2009. Available online at http://www.america.gov/st/peopleplace-english/2009/June/20090612143011mlenuhret0.8493159.html.

"We Shall Remain." *American Experience,* 2009. Available online at http://www.pbs.org/wgbh/amex/weshallremain/.

PHOTO AND ILLUSTRATION CREDITS

INDEX

Congressional Medal of Honor, 76

Corps of Volunteers of Western Discovery.
See Lewis and Clark Expedition

Crazy Horse, 121, 125 (ill.)
    and Battle of Little Bighorn, 133, 141,
      177, 54, 55
    and Fetterman Massacre, 44, 139-40
    as leader of non-treaty Lakota, 50, 52
    biography, 125-29
    death of, 54

Crazy Horse Memorial, 129

Creek, 26, 134, 143

Crockett, Davy, 143

Crook, George, 57-58, 58 (ill.), 127-28, 129,
    148

Crow Creek Reservation, 217

Curtis Act, 85

Curtis, Charles, 111

Custer, Boston, 54

Custer, Elizabeth "Libbie" Bacon, 131

Custer, George Armstrong, 76, 122, 130
    (ill.), 208, 213, 217
    and Battle of Little Bighorn, 53-55, 128,
      141, 149, 177-79, 181, 182
    and Black Hills expedition, 50, 141, 148
    biography, 130-33

Custer, Tom, 54

Custer Died for Your Sins: An Indian Manifesto
    (Deloria Jr.), 100, 101

D

Dakota, 41, 216

Dawes, Henry L., 83

Dawes Act. *See* General Allotment Act of
    1887

Delaware, 18

Deloria Jr., Vine, 100, 101

Democratic Party, 136

Democratic Republicans. *See* Democratic
    Party

diseases, impact on American Indians, 6, 12,
    20, 40, 86-88, 170-71, 191, 214, 216

Dog Chief, 195, 196

E

Eastern Band of Cherokee Indians, 33

Eastman, Charles A., 197-99

Eastman, Elaine Goodale, 58-59

Egan, Timothy, 213-19

Elementary and Secondary Education Act of
    1965, 110

Emerson, Ralph Waldo, 26-27

England, colonization of North America, 6,
    10-12

F

Fetterman Massacre, 43-44, 126, 140

Fetterman, William J., 43-44, 126, 139, 140

Five Civilized Tribes, 85, 91

Florida, 8, 24

Forsyth, James W., 71, 71 (ill.), 72, 76, 123,
    154

Fort Laramie Treaty of 1851, 40

Fort Laramie Treaty of 1868, 46-50, 52, 55-
    56, 121-22, 126-27, 132, 140, 148
    negotiations of, 172-76

Fort Phil Kearny, 126, 139

Four-Wheel Warpony, 117 (ill.)

Fox, 18

France
    colonization of North America, 6, 8-10
    relations with American Indian tribes, 18

French and Indian War, 17-20

From the Deep Woods to Civilization
    (Eastman), 197-99

G

Garrison Dam and Reservoir Project, 94, 214

Gates, Merrill E., 183-86

General Allotment Act of 1887, 57, 83, 85,
    108, 183